THE
WARRIOR'S
CODE

Jackie Tyrrell

THE
WARRIOR'S
CODE

Jackie Tyrrell

With Christy O'Connor

Trinity Mirror Sport Media

To Mam and Dad.
Love and thanks

Trinity Mirror Sport Media ⑤

Written with Christy O'Connor.

With thanks to Eoin Conroy and Gill Hess Ltd.

First published in Great Britain and Ireland in 2017 by
Trinity Mirror Sport Media, PO Box 48, Old Hall Street, Liverpool, L69 3EB.

www.tmsportmedia.com
@SportMediaTM

Trinity Mirror Sport Media is a part of Trinity Mirror plc.
One Canada Square, Canary Wharf, London, E15 5AP.

1

Hardback ISBN: 978-1-910335-72-7.
eBook ISBN: 978-1-911613-03-9.

Photographic acknowledgements:
Jackie Tyrrell personal collection, Inpho Photography, Sportsfile.

Design and typesetting by Trinity Mirror Sport Media.
Editing and production: Roy Gilfoyle.
Design: Rick Cooke and Colin Sumpter.

Printed and bound by CPI Group (UK) Ltd,
Croydon, CR0 4YY.

Contents

Acknowledgements

I WOULD like to express my sincerest thanks to so many people who have played such an important part in my life. The natural starting point is my family. My dad, Dermot, my mam, Mary, my sisters, Emer and Sarah, my brother, Mark, nephew, Luke, David, brother-in-law, Deo and Granny Mini have all played an important part in my development. Words alone could never express my appreciation to them.

Since coming into my life, my fiancée, Clare, has always been there for me and her patience, support and love means so much. Clare's parents, Paul and Kay, and family have also been a tremendous support over the past few years.

Brian Cody has been a constant presence throughout my career, from teaching me in 4th, 5th and 6th classes in primary school, and coaching me to schools' finals right up to winning All-Irelands with Kilkenny. Brian has been a massive part of my journey and I will always be grateful to him. I also want to thank all of Brian's management teams.

I am grateful to the Kilkenny medical and backroom teams, the Kilkenny County Board and the Supporters Club. I would also like to acknowledge the contribution made to my career by St. Patrick's De La Salle and St Kieran's College.

To James Stephens GAA club, I will be eternally grateful for how the club shaped my life, both as a hurler and person; of how all the great people there nurtured and developed my love of the game. I have always been a proud 'Village' man, and I look forward to many more great years with the club.

I consider myself lucky to have met Br. Damien Brennan who agreed to accompany me on a journey to develop a code to achieve my very best. He challenged me to embrace my talents in order to bring my best to every situation, and achieve things I would have never thought possible.

My employer, Glanbia, have accommodated me in every way possible over the years, for which I am very grateful.

Sincere thanks to Christy O'Connor for writing my story. Christy's professionalism, patience and understanding was second to none at all times.

Thanks to Eoin Conroy of Titan Marketing, and Paul Dove at Trinity Mirror Sport Media, both of whom planted the seed in my mind to write a book and encouraged me to be courageous enough to put pen to paper. I would also like to thank Roy Gilfoyle at Trinity Mirror. Thanks also to Simon and Declan at publishing agents Gill Hess.

Hurling has been such a huge part of my life and I am so

Acknowledgements

grateful to hurling people everywhere, those from Kilkenny and all over the country, who have encouraged and supported me in so many different ways at various times during my career.

And finally, to the magnificent Kilkenny panels that I was privileged to be a part of, and which gave me such happiness and fulfilment. The memories we made, and have, will last forever.

We had the time of our lives.

Jackie Tyrrell, August 2017

'If you don't go after what you want, you'll never have it. If you don't ask, the answer is always no. If you don't step forward, you're always in the same place.'

chapters
I-V

The Beginning
Of The End

'I accept all that will happen over the next three days with an open mind. I may be disappointed or delighted but every challenge, success, achievement is a blessing. I learn from yesterday. I live for today and look forward to tomorrow. The challenge of the next three days is to make the most of them, to enjoy the happy moments, to challenge the challenges. Anyone can give up. It's always the easiest thing to do. Not me. I hold it together when those who don't matter, or who don't care, let it fall apart.

I see these precious days as an opportunity to savour, to remember with gratitude, and to live my life to the fullest. I am defined not by my success, or by my perceived failures, but how I respond to both. I have the power and courage to overcome whatever challenges come my way between now and Sunday. So I will meet it head on and be all that I can be and, thus, be the person I am.

Medals, All-Stars and honours won't define me or my legacy. They will support it but my journey from where I came from to where I am right now is what will define me. If I am to leave, I believe I will leave the Kilkenny jersey I earned and craved all my life in a much better state than I got it. That makes me smile.

Sunday is another day in a great sporting life that I created for myself. My emotions are very high right now but that lets me know that I loved, cared and devoted myself to my own cause. That makes me so happy. When others walked, I stayed the course. I refused to be defeated. I never give up.'

– Diary entry, Friday September 2nd, 2016

I WAS warming up on the sideline when Kevin Kelly scooped home Kilkenny's first goal on 42 minutes. The great shriek of elation and thunder rose up from the belly of the Hogan Stand behind me. It looked and felt like a landmark score. We were two points ahead. This is Kilkenny's territory. The third quarter is normally where we kill teams. And it just felt like we'd wounded Tipperary with a deep laceration.

It wasn't deep enough. Tipp got up. They came right back at us. They hit the next three points. John 'Bubbles' O'Dwyer pushed Tipp four points in front when he hit Tipp's first goal on 48 minutes. 'Bubbles' took advantage of Paul Murphy losing his hurley but the goal had been coming.

We've owned the third quarter of matches for so long now that we almost expect, by instinct, to start trampling over fellas. It wasn't happening. Tipp were wiping Kilkenny fellas from the soles of their boots.

We were in trouble everywhere but our full-back line was getting destroyed. As Rob Lennon and I stayed warming up,

I had a word in his ear. 'Don't go too hard here now,' I said. 'We'll both probably be going in here in a few minutes. And when we get in there, we need to be ready for these boys.'

I had stayed stretching. I looked straight down the line at Brian Cody. I sensed from his body language that I wouldn't be coming on. 'I'm going back up to the subs bench,' I said to Rob.

I sat back and watched the misery continue to unfold. Tipperary were doing a number on us; score after score after score. Every fibre of my being was railing against what was unfolding before me. I wanted to be in there. I felt I needed to be in there.

Shortly afterwards, Derek Lyng called Lester Ryan down. A few minutes later, he beckoned for Rob. My heart sank into my boots. The Tipp inferno was burning the Kilkenny house down and Brian Cody clearly felt I had nothing in me to douse the fire.

My blood was boiling. I couldn't believe what I was seeing. We lay down. Kilkenny didn't lay a hand on a Tipp player. We didn't even break a hurley. We didn't even pick up a yellow card. I'm not advocating anarchy. I wasn't going to go in swinging my hurley like a scythe as if I was the Grim Reaper in a bad mood. But I know that I wouldn't have let Tipperary men waltz around me like this was a dance.

If I had been brought on, the first thing I'd have done was let 'Bubbles' or John McGrath know that I hadn't gone away. If a yellow card was going, I'd have gladly taken it. At least I might have got the Kilkenny crowd revved up.

I may not be the player I was but I don't think some of those Tipperary forwards would have fancied seeing me around the place either. I took a lot of stick for cutting Seamus Callanan in two early on in the 2009 All-Ireland final but it had to be done. I had to lay down the law. Kilkenny had to lay down the law. Callanan is a different animal now. He was doing what he liked to us in the 2016 All-Ireland final. I'm not saying I'd have got a handle on him but seeing me nearby may have triggered memories of that hit seven years earlier. Maybe it wouldn't but I'm pretty sure it's still in the back of his mind.

Callanan continued to do what he liked. It was like a casual training match for him. 'Bubbles' and John McGrath were only toying with our defence. Almost every time the ball went into the Tipp full-forward line, they registered a score. And we just stood back and took it.

This was wrong. All wrong. It felt wrong from early in that third quarter. At one stage, Shane Prendergast fouled John McGrath. It was a foul. There was some banter between Shane and McGrath but Shane was smiling with him. Shane is a good fella but the image actually sickened my stomach. 'We're getting rolled over by these boys,' I said to myself. 'And here is our captain laughing with them. What the hell is going on here?'

Shane is a gentleman. He was a good captain but it wasn't happening for him. I could read his body language because I've been in that position before myself. He may have wanted out of there, I don't really know, but I desperately wanted to be in the middle of it all.

The more it went on though, I wasn't sure if I even wanted to be part of this humiliation. It might sound selfish, especially when we have always built our identity in Kilkenny on spirit and fighting the cause to the last together. But I couldn't correlate that philosophy to how I was feeling. My head was all over the shop. I wasn't in a good place mentally.

I asked myself a very simple question. 'What happens if Brian says to me with five minutes to go, 'Jackie, get warmed up, you're going in'. My mind was racing. Would I have gone in? I don't know. Probably not. It probably would have been the ultimate sense of betrayal in Brian's eyes but, in that moment, that's just how I felt. This was a massacre. What was I going to do – go in looking for survivors?

It never happened anyway. When the final whistle went, Tipp were nine points ahead. It would have been more only for a couple of brilliant saves by Eoin Murphy. It was an annihilation. It felt like a massacre. I shook hands with Padraic Maher and Noel McGrath. As the blue and good ribands from the shower of Tipp confetti began gathering in my boots, I headed for the dressing room.

I was the first one there. I wanted to be the first one back into the room. The place was deserted. I took off my Kilkenny jersey. I looked at it for a handful of seconds. I wondered if I would ever see it again. In that moment, I didn't think I would.

I stood motionless under the showers, almost oblivious to the water hammering against my body. I was devastated for Kilkenny. The manner of the defeat contradicted everything we stood for. Most of all though, I felt lost.

I went straight up to the players' lounge.

I met my girlfriend, Clare. She was with Richie Hogan's girlfriend, Anne, and Cillian Buckley's girlfriend, Niamh. I didn't care. I lay my head down on the table and started crying.

The next couple of hours were a blur. I didn't want to be there. I had a few beers in me and was desperately trying to keep my emotions in check. I nearly lost it again when Michael Ryan, the Tipperary manager, approached me. I congratulated him. He told me that he had always admired me and how I played the game.

I really appreciated the comment but it almost set me off again. On the bus journey back to the City West hotel, a close friend, from our club-team James Stephens, rang.

'How are ya?'

'Not great, to be honest.'

'I wouldn't blame you. I'd never forgive Cody for what he has done to you.'

He was hurt for me. He was probably a little sauced up from liquor too but that thought did go through my head when we got back to the hotel. We went upstairs and got changed into our suits. Before the meal I was chatting to Kieran O'Connor of Glanbia when I saw Brian approaching.

'Can I have a word with you?' he asked.

'Yeah Brian.'

He started talking. 'I just want to let you know the reason we didn't bring you on. I know the lads inside (in the full-back line) were in trouble but I felt the problems were further out the field. I don't think bringing you on would have made much difference.'

I didn't tell him what I really thought. 'Look it Brian, you don't have to explain yourself to me.'

'Oh, I'm not explaining anything,' he replied. 'I just said I'd say it to you out of respect. Although I will admit that the full-back line was being cleaned.'

'Sure that says it all Brian, doesn't it?'

He just looked at me. Nothing else needed to be said.

The rest of the evening was very difficult. The banquet was torture. We have probably become selfish because we're not used to defeat but this felt more than just a loss. To me, it felt like the end. There's never an easy way to go but this felt like the worst ending possible.

I couldn't escape the turmoil. Everywhere I turned, it was like listening to a broken record, with the same recurring soundtrack.

'You should have been brought on, Jackie.'

'We missed your physicality in the full-back line.'

'Tipp went to town on us.'

It was all just pure hollow bullshit to me by that stage. I took no solace or comfort from endorsements long after the battle had finished. Listening to it only made me angrier. I wanted to get as far away from it all as possible.

I was lucky I had a way out. Clare was bridesmaid for her best friend Joanna who was getting married in Marbella on the Friday. That flight couldn't come quickly enough.

I was convinced we would win. I thought it might be my last All-Ireland and I had planned to soak up every last drop of satisfaction associated with those golden victories. Clare was heading out to Spain early in the week but I debated about holding off until the Thursday morning.

At least now, I could go earlier and just forget about everything.

'I am awake before Clare. I lie in bed with a headache and run everything over in my mind. Is it over? Yes it is. Where do I go from here? Why the fuck didn't Cody trust me? In his after-meal speech he singled me and Feno (Michael Fennelly) out for praise but I felt it was somewhat false.

It sounded like pure tokenism, which had no depth to it.

I had breakfast with my family in a back room, away from other people in the hotel. It was nice to have that time. We talked about everything but hurling. I texted Fog (Conor Fogarty), Joycey (Kieran Joyce) and Pádraig (Walsh) to go for a drink so we met up and headed to Jacobs in Saggart. Some lads were quiet. Others were in good form. I was in good form. I wanted to really enjoy it all. We got the bus home. We arrived in Kilkenny to a big crowd. I began to feel the emotion as people cheered for us. My heart got heavy. I got a great reception as I walked on the stage. As soon as I did though, I slipped off to the side as I began to cry. Nobody saw me. As Brian spoke, I slipped off to the dressing room (in Nowlan Park) and sat where I have sat since the first time back in 2003. I cried with a smile. I could hear the lads coming back so I straightened up. It was really nice to have that time alone in that dressing room.

I met Clare in Langton's, had a meal and laughed. Later in the night, I was drinking red wine with Fogarty when the Coldplay song 'Rule the World' came on. I started crying again. Earlier in the evening, a girl asked me for a photograph and I obliged. She asked me if I was retiring. I said I wasn't sure but that I was thinking about it. She started to cry. It was sad but nice that I had such a positive influence on the girl. A nice moment.'

– Diary entry, Monday September 5th, 2016

Where do I go from here? Is it all over? Probably. Still, I'm not too sure. Will Brian want me back? I honestly don't know. He may want me around for my leadership role within the squad but he won't want me near the place if he doesn't think I can contribute on the pitch.

Can I? I think I can. I've never been in better shape. My body fat levels have never been lower. I'm still hurling well. Not bringing me on in an All-Ireland final when our full-back line was being cleaned may have been Brian's way of telling me I'm finished at this level. But I don't think I am. I still believe I'm one of the best six defenders in Kilkenny at present.

We played Johnstown in the club championship between the Leinster final and All-Ireland semi-final and I felt I was one of the best players on the pitch. It may have only been a club match against one of the slightly weaker teams in the championship but, after all these years, I still know how to gauge my body, and the limits to which I can push it.

Ten days out from the final, I marked Kevin Kelly in a training game. Our trainer Mick Dempsey planted himself in our corner. I knew he was there to monitor Kevin closely but I saw it as a golden opportunity to muscle my way into his, and Brian's, thinking. I cleaned Kevin out.

I got no feedback. You rarely do with Brian. He just kept telling me to keep going. To be ready. I've been fucking ready since January. I've put my heart and soul into this. Brian knows the effort I've put in all year.

At times, that lack of feedback and encouragement is crippling. At least when Derek Lyng, our selector, talks to you, there is real depth and meaning to the discussion, to the information he offers you.

I have that connection with Derek from being a former team-mate. I don't have that with Brian but you still hope for some meagre form of direction when you're so desperate to play. And especially when you're playing Tipperary.

I always felt I played well against Tipp. I wasn't great in the 2014 drawn All-Ireland final but I felt I had 'Bubbles' in my pocket for the replay. That was two years ago. I'm 34 now. I have overcome a number of injuries but I still believed I was showing enough to put me into the frame. 'Surely,' I asked myself, 'the management will see some role for me in a game like this against Tipp?'

What's my role now? Have I anything to offer going forward? It's all irrelevant unless Brian thinks I do. When I met him in November 2015, I asked Brian what my future prospects were for 2016. Brian will never offer anyone any guarantees but he said he saw a role for me. I'll meet him again now in November 2016. I'm not sure what he has in mind for me but I think I have something worth fighting for.

I still have that fight in me. Maybe he needs to ask himself the very same question. When we were getting rolled over by Tipperary, where was the fight in Cody? Why didn't he show the same passion that was visible against Waterford in the All-Ireland semi-final replay? He has been such an icon for us that we often take our lead from him, from the intensity of his body language on the sideline. The lack of fight from us on the pitch was almost mirrored by Brian's meekness on the line.

We all need to ask ourselves hard questions. We may have been on the road too long. Injuries piled up. Tipp had every reason to be hungrier than us. But we never used those excuses or reasons in the past. And the hardest part of all was how we just stood there and took it. That wasn't good enough. We may not have won but at least have a fucking go at them anyway.

There have been so many times throughout 2016 when I wanted to vent my frustration from deep within the pit of my stomach. I didn't. I just kept my counsel. I spoke before the replayed All-Ireland semi-final against Waterford but I didn't feel entitled to be more vocal when I had so little involvement throughout the season.

When Kilkenny won the 2015 All-Ireland final, I addressed the lads at half-time, purely out of frustration at what I was seeing in front of me from the sideline. We weren't playing with the intensity or physicality that we needed to bring. We did in the second half.

I got far more attention afterwards for what I said than anything I did. I didn't intend it to happen that way but it did. I have always wanted to do my talking on the pitch but is that half-time speech 12 months ago going to be my legacy now?

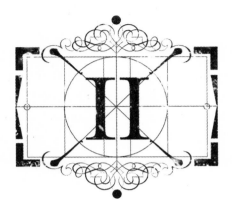

Never Enough

'Good session done this morning. Started the year as I mean to go on. And I mean business.'

— Diary entry, Friday January 1st, 2016

I ARRIVED at James Stephens' old pitch in Larchfield just after 9am. I was fresh and well rested because I was asleep just after midnight. I rang in the New Year with Clare but as 2015 segued into 2016, I was already resetting my body-clock and mind to prepare for what I hoped a new season would bring.

It was cold and frosty. Air temperatures were close to zero. A blanket of frost had coated the ground like icing sugar so I stamped my feet along both 20-metre lines, my footprints acting as markers for the starting and finishing points for a set of runs designed to punish my muscles and unleash torture on my mind.

I was fully ready for the pain. I wanted it. I needed to feel that burn, almost as a reminder of the hurt of missing out on the 2015 All-Ireland final, as another mental note of never wanting to miss out on that kind of action again.

I won my ninth All-Ireland medal that day but I played no part in the match. That admission may sound vulgar to so many players who would kill for just one All-Ireland medal but that is who I am. That's the kind of wild ambition and selfishness which has made us who we are in Kilkenny. Henry Shefflin is the only GAA player in history with ten All-Ireland medals. And I desperately want to join him.

The rest of the Kilkenny squad are in Thailand since the end of December celebrating that success on our team holiday. Clare couldn't get time off from work in January so the two of us went on the same break in November. It suited me down to the ground because it granted me the time to do some extra work during those two weeks. I was in the gym in Nowlan Park one afternoon over Christmas when I spotted an image on Snapchat of the boys drinking and going mad on a boat. My muscles were screaming for respite with how hard I was pushing myself but the picture provided the rocket fuel for me to drive myself even harder. 'I'll be ready for these boys when they come back,' I said to myself. 'I'll just blow them out of the water when the hard running begins in a couple of weeks.'

This is the start of it now for me. I didn't have anyone there to push or encourage me. That didn't matter. The stopwatch on my phone was my timer, which wasn't ideal, but I wasn't worried about split-seconds for now. At this stage, it's about getting the legs pumping, the lungs opened up and storing some juice in the tank for the long-haul journey ahead.

I was sluggish. By now, I know my usual times for those runs

Kilkenny do between both 20-metre lines. My January time is normally 18 seconds. By February, I'd usually be clocking 17. Sixteen seconds is my ultimate target for the summer but I'm almost four seconds off that time now. My average recording over the series of sprints was 19.5. My lungs were screaming for oxygen. The lactic acid was piercing my muscles but I still felt great. Energised. Alive.

I haven't felt that way since the 2015 Leinster final but even that day carried as asterisk. I was taken off against Galway. I was bull-thick and mad keen to prove myself again before the All-Ireland semi-final against Waterford.

Three weeks out from the match, I was marking Mark Kelly in a training game. It was a typical Nowlan Park match, raw and sparky. I was already on edge so I was like a powderkeg waiting to explode. I did when Mark hit me a sneaky slap on the hand.

I turned around and pulled head high on him. It was probably the worst stroke I ever pulled on anyone. It was mean and dangerous. Brian Cody went bananas.

I had pulled plenty of loose strokes in training over the years and Brian would have just signalled his disapproval by calling my name with the tone of an exclamation mark. 'Jaaackie!'

This time, he stopped the game and cut me in two.

'Don't ever fucking do that again,' he roared.

I was so thick that I never turned around. I just kept walking. 'Jackie, get back here.'

I faced towards Brian. 'If you ever do that again, I'll fire you out that gate and you won't be back.'

Brian normally never loses the rag in a match to that extent but he was still in my ear after training. 'You can't be carrying on like that,' he said. 'You're no good to anyone on the sideline. Because that's where you'll be if you pull like that again.'

I was still trying to justify my actions, for which I had no defence. 'Brian, you didn't see the stroke Mark pulled beforehand.'

'I don't care,' said Brian. 'I'll have a word with Mark. I know you're probably a little frustrated that you're not going as well as you'd like but you'll be playing the next day against Waterford. And I need you to be ready.'

That endorsement and faith was what I needed to hear. I began to channel my anger and frustration more positively over the following couple of sessions. I hit a good groove of form.

A week later, I was marking Chris Bolger in another training game in Nowlan Park. A ball was going over my head when I stopped it with one hand, breaking it down in front of me. Chris was coming behind me so I began moving forward at pace. Suddenly, I heard a crack.

I handpassed the ball off and immediately hit the ground in pain. When I tried to get up, I couldn't put my weight on my foot. By the time I arrived at the A&E in St Luke's Hospital afterwards, the pain had gone to another level. I struggled to make the 200-metre walk from the car to the front door.

A nurse from Waterford, who knows my sister, took my details. 'Hopefully, it will be a break,' she said jokingly. 'We could do without facing you in two weeks' time.'

I wasn't laughing because I knew that was a strong possibility. An x-ray confirmed as much shortly afterwards. I could see the break myself on the screen. 'I'm sorry my friend,' an Indian doctor said to me. 'There is a stress fracture in your foot.'

The poor nurse was almost frantic with her apologies but nothing was going in. I couldn't believe this was happening. As the nurse began rolling on the plaster of Paris, I was questioning the doctor's opinion. All I was thinking about was Waterford.

'Are you sure you need to put on this thing? Is there not another way to help speed up the recovery?'

Brother Damien Brennan, a very close friend, called over to my house that evening. Straight away, he sought to turn my train of thought around. 'You either go at this 100%, with 2016 in mind, and go again. We get you back that way. Or else this is it – it's all over.'

There was no decision to be made. I wanted to do everything I could to get back now.

I knew the risk involved from a similar injury that Henry had in 2013, which carried into 2014. He had pins inserted into his foot. The pins broke. A screw could just as easily break under pressure, especially if you pushed your body hard. Infection was always a risk. At that stage though, the Waterford game wasn't even in my sightline. The 2016 season was irrelevant. Kilkenny men make their name in September and that's where my focus turned to.

On the Monday, I went to see Dr Alan Laing in Aut Even Hospital in Kilkenny. He looked at the x-rays and gave it to me straight. If I wasn't a sportsman, he'd have encased my foot in a boot for six weeks. That wasn't an option. Dr Laing knew it but I told him anyway. The only alternative was to operate and insert a screw. That meant missing the Waterford game but returning for an All-Ireland final was a possibility.

The operation involved Dr Laing drilling down through the

back of my foot, through the middle of the bone, in through the crack, where he inserted the screw to pull the bone back together. The screw also acts as a brace to help the broken bone knit back together.

I had the operation in the Beacon Hospital in Dublin two days later. I was supposed to stay the night but I was so keen to get ahead of the schedule that I got Clare to drive me back home to Kilkenny at 11pm.

I was already like a man possessed. I rang work and asked for a month off. I had a sick cert but I wanted to be upfront with my boss; I wasn't going to be lying in bed for four weeks; I was going to be out and about, working like a maniac every day to make it back for the All-Ireland final.

For most of the first week, I didn't move from the couch. I couldn't put any weight on my leg but Brother Damien started working on my foot, massaging the muscles around the bone, getting the blood flowing to that area.

We planned everything in minute detail. I had been prescribed a dose of antibiotics and anti-inflammatories but we were able to gradually reduce that intake through Brother Damien working so hard on the muscles to reduce the swelling and accelerate the recovery time.

The schedule was slow and tedious but it was relentless. I poured six hours into every day, every single day; massage, stretch, walk around, up on the table again to try and get more of the swelling down. And then go again.

When he wasn't working on my foot, Brother Damien was trying to keep me as sharp and strong as possible for someone in my condition. He would throw balls at me to catch. He had me bench-pressing tables. I focussed hard on a core programme. A lot of the training was as primitive as what Rocky Balboa did before he fought Ivan Drago in Rocky IV but I was building up my mind as much as my body for the massive challenge I faced.

I tried everything. To encourage bone-growth, I paid €1,500 for a bone stimulator machine, a device which applied low-intensity pulled ultrasounds and electrical stimulation to the fracture. Any time I went back to Dr Laing for a check-up, you could see the gap in the bone getting closer and closer together. It just wasn't knitting at the pace I needed it to.

I didn't care. When I finally got out of the boot two weeks before the All-Ireland final, I went straight into a Nike Air Max runner, which had a sole as big as a mattress. As soon as I started walking without a limp, I began slow jogging. Ten days before the All-Ireland final, I squeezed my foot into a football boot and started upping the pace.

I did all my fitness and mental preparation in Callan with Brother Damien but as soon as I was able to jog, I went straight into Kilkenny training in Nowlan Park. It wasn't to train, just to show up and show the players and management what stage I was at in my recovery process.

I would have worked in Callan with Damien that afternoon. I would be sore but I'd be so wound up that pain was irrelevant. I'd jog up and down the sideline for five minutes to show Brian and the players that I hadn't gone away, that I was still an option. As soon as I had finished, I'd tog in and head straight back out to Damien to massage the pain out of the muscles I had punished so hard.

Getting back to fitness required everything I had but I became so obsessive in that pursuit that it took over my whole life. I wasn't an easy person to live with for those five weeks. I was cranky with Clare. I didn't want my family around me. I was narky and bitchy with everyone because my only focus was getting out to Brother Damien and accumulating another one or two per cent along the road to recovery to get me where I needed and wanted to go.

I knew my foot could break at any moment but I didn't care. Henry's foot had broken in similar circumstances, when he had far more time to recuperate, but I suppressed every fear and negative outcome through total positivity. In my own mind, I had convinced myself that the bone wouldn't crack. I knew if I was careful and I stuck to the plan that it wouldn't.

I had pushed myself as hard as possible but no matter how hard you try and firewall your system, the doubts will still find a way into your mind. The calf muscle on my right leg was like a matchstick compared to my left. To banish the doubts, I went looking for pain. When we went on a training camp to Fota Island in Cork two weeks before the match, I nearly killed myself on a spinning bike. I pushed myself so hard, I thought my heart was going to come out through my ribcage.

At that stage, I thought it was too late but Brother Damien kept me going. I was still out in Callan with him twice every day. When I went back to Dr Laing a week before the final, the risk was still there but he told me what I wanted to hear. 'At this stage,' he said, 'you're either going for it or you're not.'

I was ready to drop the pedal. On the Monday before the game, the crowd were allowed in to Nowlan Park to watch us train. We were only doing drills but I could feel my foot tightening after about 20 minutes. It was getting sore but I just gritted my teeth and got through it.

I upped the pace again on Wednesday. I was feeling better

already. Stronger. Brian said to me that they would do a fitness test on Friday to see where I was really at. I was ready for it.

We did the fitness test in Nowlan Park at 6.15pm. The test lasted 35 minutes. Mick Dempsey didn't spare me; twisting, turning, short sprints, 100-metre sprints, bounding, jumping.

When the lads were coming onto the pitch at 6.50, I was walking off drenched in sweat. I went in and showered and was sitting on a bench waiting for everyone else to come back in. It was a short session so before everyone went upstairs to hear the team announcement, Brian called me out. He brought me into a room along with the other three members of management, and the team doctor, Dr Tadhg Crowley.

'Look Jackie,' said Brian, 'we're not going to start you at the weekend. You're moving well but we just don't feel you are ready yet.'

I think Brian had his decision already made before the test but he said that Tadhg felt I hadn't enough power in my foot during one of the jumping exercises.

I lowered my head. I looked away, avoiding eye contact with anyone. I didn't say anything. I just got up and headed straight for the door.

'You're disappointed, Jackie,' said Cody.

'Of course I'm disappointed. I'm not happy. I know I can play. I feel ready to play. You're basing your judgement on a technicality over my jumping. I never had the greatest jump.

'I feel I should be playing but your decision is made so there's no point in me saying any more.'

Brian raised his voice and spoke with more authority. 'We need everyone pulling together for Sunday.'

'Of course I'll be ready. You don't have to doubt me.'

As I was about to walk out the door, Brian checked me again. 'The most important thing for Sunday is to get Joey Holden up the steps of the Hogan Stand to collect that cup.'

'Look,' I replied, 'you know I'll be doing everything in my power to try and make that happen.'

I was bull thick. I appreciated management would be taking a risk by starting me but I still felt that I had got myself ready to play and to perform. It may sound selfish of me to have wanted to take that risk, to put the team at risk, but, in my own mind at that moment, I felt ready for anything. I've no doubt that the foot would have started to swell and get sore after about 45 minutes but if I lasted that long, I'd have chewed nails to get myself through the 70 minutes. I'd have taken a cortisone injection, or swallowed a cocktail of painkillers but I'd have mentally driven myself over the line.

To me, Shane Prendergast was unproven. He had played in the All-Ireland semi-final but Waterford set up with a two-man full-forward line that day. That didn't mean Shane got a handy spin but Galway were going to present a whole different challenge. I felt you should go with your tried and tested corner-back ahead of a rookie that wasn't fully battle-hardened against these top forwards.

Maybe I took it for granted but I always believed that if I got back, and was running a week before the All-Ireland final, that Brian would start me. That had dominated my whole thought process. Once I got myself back, I hadn't expected any other outcome other than to be handed that number four jersey.

When I thought back afterwards about that fitness test, I felt they were nearly trying to get me to break down, almost to make the decision easier for them. It was the doctor's call but in my head, declaring me unfit on the basis that I could jump a foot further on my right than I could on my left was a bullshit technicality. 'Is this what yere measuring me on now?' I thought. 'What about the big-day experience, the physicality, the absolute ruthlessness I will bring to the battle?'

My mind was racing. I wasn't even going to go to Langton's for food but as I began to rationalise the decision, I just parked it. Brother Damien said that the biggest challenge was just to get back. That was an achievement in itself. The normal recovery time for that kind of injury is 12 weeks. I was back in six.

I could hear Damien's voice in my head so I almost began to celebrate what I actually had achieved. 'Fuck it, I am back. I proved to myself that I could make it back. I will be needed on Sunday. And when I am called upon, I'll be ready for it.'

If Ireland are playing a rugby or soccer match now, and if they are struggling at half-time, I'll always get a text message, or a notification on Twitter, with the same line: 'They need a Jackie Tyrrell speech now to get the boys going.'

I don't think what I said to the lads at half-time in that 2015 All-Ireland final was that inspirational. If anything, I think it was more that the lads acknowledged my frustration, of how I would have given anything to have the chance that they had, but weren't taking.

The dressing room in that moment was completely silent. Dead. Normally, two or three fellas would be talking but nobody was. Lads seemed to have gone into themselves. I was standing by the water-cooler. Then I took two steps forward.

'We talked the talk but we're not walking the walk. We said we were going to dictate, that we were going to bring the fight to Galway. Well, you know what lads, we've done fuck all. Galway have brought the fight. They've brought the war. And we're just standing back and letting them roll all over us.

'I've seen so many examples of it. Galway lads are fucking us out of the way all over the field. AND IT'S NOT FUCKING GOOD ENOUGH FOR KILKENNY.

'If we're not very careful, this game will be over five minutes into the second half. Picture it. Just fucking picture it; Andy Smith – who is no friend of ours – could be going up those steps and taking our cup. Picture that. Just fucking picture it. ARE WE GOING TO FUCKING ALLOW THAT TO HAPPEN?'

I was like a lunatic by that stage. I was eyeballing lads, especially the fellas who hadn't stepped up, and who desperately needed to. If guys responded to my words, it was probably an acknowledgement of the effort I had put in to getting back. The hurt and sense of want, the manic desire to be out there crashing into Galway fellas was smeared all over my face.

Kilkenny won. History proved Brian was right in the decision he made but I still struggled to accept it afterwards. That may sound selfish of me but I am selfish. I want to play. I felt I was able to play. My mindset was so strong at that time that I've no doubt that I would have done the job if I had been given the jersey.

The injury may have restricted me physically but, if anything, it had made me mentally even stronger. The Leinster final had been a wake-up call. When Davy Glennon was taken off me after not having touched the ball, I got comfortable in myself. Jason Flynn came on and scored a goal. I made a mess of another ball. When I clinically assessed my performance afterwards, I had been ropey.

I dissected everything afterwards. We hammered Wexford in that 2015 Leinster semi-final by 24 points. They posed us no threat on the day. Paul Morris didn't score off me. When Brian took me off with ten minutes remaining, he was clearly just running the bench. Yet it was only the second time he had ever substituted me.

I don't think he was losing faith in me. I felt he was giving Shane Prendergast a run because Brian wanted to strengthen our depth in defence. Maybe he was thinking, 'We need to mind this fella. Maybe he doesn't have 70 minutes in him any more.'

If Brian felt I wasn't physically fit enough to play in the All-Ireland final, he could argue he was definitely proven right when I didn't play for James Stephens against Ballyhale Shamrocks in the club championship the following week. I wasn't because I had emptied myself so much, mentally and physically, that I had nothing left in me after those six relentless weeks of trying to get myself right.

I went back to Dr Laing for another x-ray and he said I should weigh up the risk. I knew if I broke the bone again that it would torpedo me for at least three months, which would have impacted on my 2016 season. It killed me to make the call but I decided not to chance it. I continued to train hard over the following months but it was only on December 13th, 2015, that I got the final all-clear on the injury. And then, I really ramped up the pace and intensity.

During the first 12 days of January 2016, I trained every day. I mixed it up; running, gym, bike sessions, the ball-alley, spinning sessions. I was out in Callan with Brother Damien every second day. By the time the lads arrived back from their holiday on January 12th, I was ready for them.

I knew Brian would give them a few days off before going hard again so I took a break myself to be fresh for training. I was visualising myself on that first night back in Dunmore, of how fit and strong I wanted to be, and of the image I wanted to project to everyone else. 'I'm going nowhere here, lads.'

I wasn't. On that first night back, I was jumping out of my skin. When we began the long running in groups of four, I made my way to the top of the pack with the thoroughbred greyhounds. I had always positioned myself in the top two groups, more as a statement of intent to the younger lads than any great endorsement of my own athletic prowess. Cillian Buckley and Conor Fogarty are the real running machines in our squad and I wanted to test myself against that kind of pace-setting. I was just about to take up station beside the two lads when our trainer Mick Dempsey approached me.

'It's your first night back, Jackie; maybe you should go into the back group.'

A part of me could see Mick's point. It took a little pressure off me having, in my own mind, to try and lead out some guys over ten years younger than me. Maybe Mick had planned it. It could have been an instinctive call too but it still pissed me off.

I didn't have any rust caking on my limbs. I had no cobwebs to blow off. I was the strongest runner in our group. It only steeled my resolve even more.

'That's the last night that's going to happen,' I said to myself. 'Even if I have to die a death in the top groups, I'll be up there. I'll never be back here in this last group again.'

And I promise, I won't be.

The Sacred Cloth

'When I was small, nine or ten years old, all I wanted to do
was play hurling for Kilkenny. I actually prayed at night
and promised God that I could help Kilkenny win All-
Irelands if he helped me become good enough to play for
them. I now motivate myself by believing that in some small
way, I have kept that promise. As a boy, and a man, I have
had to work very hard, probably a lot harder than some of
my peers, to be a good club and inter-county player. There
were plenty of times when I didn't know if it would happen
but I kept believing the time would come and it did. I still
love going into battle, fighting against the odds. There were
times when I seemed to have lost, or it seemed to others that
I had lost, but I never gave up. To have given up, to have
listened to those who said I was not good enough would
have meant losing. My motivation now is that if you knock
me down, make me look poor or average, I will get up again
and again and come back stronger. Nobody can make me

feel inferior without my consent. No-one can or will stop me from achieving my best. I am a dreamer and in years to come, I hope my children, and maybe even my critics, will see what I was about, and what I tried to achieve.'

– Diary entry, Tuesday January 26th, 2016.

WHEN we were young, my brother, two sisters and I all said the same prayer in our house every night before we went to bed.

'There are four corners on my bed
There are four angels overhead
Matthew, Mark, Luke and John
God bless this bed that we lay on.'

My uncle, my mother's brother, is a priest, Father Jackie Robinson. There was always a strong devotion to God in our house but as I got older, I got bored with the repetition of those words to those four saints. What did I really, really want in life? To win All-Irelands with Kilkenny. So that is what I prayed for.

The Kilkenny jersey was always sacred to me. When I first made the Kilkenny U-14s, and the dream finally started to materialise, I almost felt spiritual, like a young priest about to wear the sacred cloth for the first time. 'Will I actually get to wear it today?' I asked myself. It was only a substitute jersey but I was so happy to have that black and amber garment on.

I played with the Kilkenny minors for two years but they weren't particularly happy experiences. I won a Leinster title in 1999 but Galway's David Forde destroyed me in the All-Ireland semi-final, taking me for five points from play. The following year, Offaly defeated us in the Leinster semi-final. I was brutal at centre-back. That was a shit-hot team. It contained future multiple All-Ireland winners – JJ Delaney, Tommy Walsh, Aidan Fogarty, David Herity – but nobody had any expectation for us after that night. We were the black sheep of Kilkenny for a time because we were the first Kilkenny team to lose a minor championship match in Leinster in 11 seasons.

I made the Kilkenny U-21 team in 2002. We were leading Wexford by two points deep into injury time of the Leinster semi-final when Rory Jacob skinned me for a goal. We lost by one point. The game was on in Nowlan Park. I knew what was being said. That it was my fault. It was.

A few days later, I heard how Paul Kinsella, a member of the county board, had reacted. 'If I ever see Jackie Tyrrell in a Kilkenny jersey again,' he reportedly said, 'I'll go out on the pitch and physically remove him myself.'

Paul taught me in school in St Patrick's. I am good friends with him now but when I heard what Paul had said, I wasn't that hurt or angry. My main feeling was: 'He is probably right.'

At the time, I was only deluding myself. I was always desperate to play for the Kilkenny seniors some day. But I never fully believed that I could.

That summer of 2002, I was working with the Kilkenny corporation, picking up rubbish and sweeping the streets. I was teamed up with Tommy Walsh. For us, the job spec translated into ducking and diving and hiding for most of the day.

We were working around Coote's Lane one day, which is around the corner from St Patrick's School, where Brian Cody used to teach. Brian spotted us and ambled over for a chat.

It was a week before the Wexford match. 'I hear ye are both going very well,' said Brian.

We were nodding away, with the big thick heads on us, not knowing where to look. 'Ah yeah Brian, we're going alright.'

'Keep it going,' he said.

'We will, Brian.'

I don't know whether it was the ringing endorsement from Cody or what, but Tommy and I got this notion to go supernova by dying our heads white. The plan was simple; we would say nothing, play the match and remove the helmets halfway through to announce our rock-star status.

We bought this tub of bleach up town and got Brian Dowling to wash it in for us. Dowling may have thought he was Vidal Sassoon but he made a balls of it. The sun was splitting the rocks that week, which diluted the colour of our manes even more. We looked like two right apes.

As we'd decided, we took the helmets off in the second half. It made no difference to Tommy, who was unbelievable. He hurled the world of ball. And there was me in the corner, letting Rory Jacob waltz around me like a bollard.

I could picture what was being said about me above in the stands. 'Look at that fucking eejit Tyrrell below. He must think he's Ronan Keating. Well, Keating would do a better job than him on the pitch.'

Tommy was called into the senior panel that weekend. I was left thinking that I had blown what little chance I ever had of making that grade. Whatever about the defending, you can imagine what Brian was thinking about the bleached hair.

I was inside in Langton's that night with the white hair matching a white New Zealand rugby top, standing out like a spare prick. I hadn't even the cop on to not go out that night. I should have been at home hiding for a month.

Drink numbed the shame because I was embarrassed. It rekindled memories of the same feeling after Galway had beaten us in 1999. I had just started to drink at that time. I necked so many large ales that night in Pegasus' in Kilkenny that I was off my head drunk. I didn't have a mobile phone but I wanted to ring home. My mother gave me one of these old call-cards so I dialled home from a phone box. I was so drunk I couldn't even speak. The only word I said was 'Sorry'.

After that U-21 defeat to Wexford, I was embarrassed going back to club training. Deep down, I knew what lads in the club were thinking. 'Decent club hurler but he just doesn't have it for inter-county level. And he never will.'

My confidence was on the floor. Pat Critchley, the former Laois dual player, was our senior manager in James Stephens that year. He was a lovely man. Passionate but quiet and softly spoken. The week before we played O'Loughlin Gaels in the county senior semi-final, Pat named me centre-back.

'We're placing our trust in you now, Jackie,' he said to me. 'You're the future of this club.'

Peter Barry and Philly Larkin had just won All-Ireland senior medals with Kilkenny. They went on to win All-Stars later that winter. And here was Critchley now putting me in as the defensive pivot at number six.

All I was thinking was, 'Pat, are you stone mad?'

Pat was challenging me in the right way but I hadn't the mental strength or confidence to meet that challenge head on. I tormented myself with worry beforehand. I knew I would be marking Colin Furlong, a big strong fella from Wexford who had transferred to O'Loughlin's. Furlong bullied me all afternoon. I didn't hit a ball.

I remember thinking, 'Nah, this isn't for me at all'.

That sacred Kilkenny senior jersey never seemed further away. When the club U-21 championship kicked off shortly afterwards, part of me had no interest in playing. I nearly wanted to forget about hurling but a couple of decent performances helped rinse the toxins of that summer out of my system. When we won that U-21 championship, someone said to me, 'You're going to captain the Kilkenny U-21s next year.'

I almost went into shock. I couldn't even play well for Kilkenny, never mind captain the county. At the end of a bad season, this came out of nowhere. I wanted it so badly. I craved it. But I was just so afraid of it.

I knew the captaincy would be between me and Eoin McCormack but I was confident of being given the honour because I had already played on the team. I was delighted when I was but I wasn't looking forward to the opportunity. I had so many doubts. I wondered if I would have that unwanted distinction of being a non-playing captain. That would have been a complete nightmare.

A solid Fitzgibbon Cup campaign with CIT in 2003 couldn't have come at a better time. John Meyler was the manager and he showed huge faith in me. He gave me momentum and confidence when I needed it most. Our run to the final – CIT's first – was also restorative for my own inner belief. I was marking good players. I pitched up on Setanta O hAilpin in the Fitzgibbon final against Waterford IT. I spent most of the match pulling and dragging out of Setanta but I got away with it. WIT had a brilliant team and were hot favourites but it took a miraculous save from goalkeeper Damien Young to get them over the line and deny us a famous win.

My club form picked up that spring. I was training away with the Kilkenny U-21s. Coming into the summer, my father said he heard a rumour that myself and Ken Coogan were going to be called into the senior panel. I shrugged it off as a daft rumour because I couldn't see it coming.

I was in college preparing for exams at the start of May when my phone rang.

'Jackie, Brian Cody here. We'd like to invite you into the panel.'

I was shocked. I never thought it was going to happen. The call came just a few days after Kilkenny had beaten Tipperary in an epic league final in Croke Park. I remember watching that match and marvelling at the pace and intensity. To me, it looked like a standard I was incapable of reaching.

The first thing I did was go into a shop and buy an apple. It was almost a reflex response to what had just happened, as if eating fruit was going to give me more power. I went home and started pucking a ball off the wall. I was so pumped up that I broke a window.

When I first went into the setup, it was a major culture shock. I was miles off the pace. Martin 'Gorta' Comerford and Noel Hickey would be lacing the shit out of each other. Michael Kavanagh was always chasing DJ Carey around like a hare. I was in the other corner, operating at a different pace and on a far lower level.

I never made any impact in training. I never felt I was moving up the roster in the panel. I was number 26 on match days and lucky to even be there. I was just happy to be involved, hoping I might snaffle an All-Ireland medal and jet off to some fancy destination on the team holiday. At the end of that season, I got both; my first senior medal and a trip to Australia. I was sharing a room with Tommy Walsh for three weeks. Bingo.

I also had an All-Ireland U-21 medal by then. That final was played seven days after the senior final but I got hammered drunk that night. Martin Fogarty was our manager and he was policing the hotel to see who was drinking. Martin doesn't drink himself but he was issuing a warning to the U-21 players on the panel.

'I don't mind ye having a few pints,' he said. 'But none of those small blue yokes.'

It made no difference to me. I was sinking shots all evening. I drank hard again on the Monday. I took it handy on the Tuesday. We trained in Thurles on the Wednesday. I was back in Cork on Thursday because I was moving into a new house. I couldn't help myself – I ended up going out on the beer with the lads that night as well.

I had a nice fill of drink in the Bishopstown Bar, about eight or nine pints. I ended up in a nightclub in the city, 'Rafters'. I washed down a burger and a stack of chips afterwards with a half-gallon of Coca-Cola.

When I woke up the following day, I had a head cold, probably from lack of sleep and dehydration. My head was spinning. It was no preparation or example for a captain to be setting less than three days out from an All-Ireland final but it was just my mindset at the time. I wasn't thinking, 'I shouldn't be doing this'. I was thinking, 'Why shouldn't I go out with the lads for a few drinks?'

I didn't feel that bad. It could have been worse. There was an offer on in one of the local off-licences so the boys had loaded the fridge with cans of 'Dutch Gold', a low-cost brew that would blow the head off you. I couldn't resist the temptation to down a few tins but I stopped before I got out of hand.

I spotted a photograph of myself recently, a headshot taken a week before that U-21 final for the match programme. I am barely recognisable. I'm not bloated with weight around my gut but I have about three chins on me. I had a head like Paul Gascoigne's old mate, Jimmy 'Five Bellies'.

I hadn't a clue about nutrition. In college, I just ate whatever I could get my hands on, whatever was cheap or was in the house at the time; pot noodles, breakfast rolls, big fry-ups, every kind of shit imaginable. My lunch most days was a white roll with cheese, a chocolate bar and a bag of crisps.

To me, a good, hard individual training session was going out for a 15 or 20-minute hard run. And then I'd undo all the good work by polishing off a plate of chips and sausages and beans.

We used to stay up in the house until 3 or 4am watching movies, eating crisps and drinking shite. If it wasn't alcohol, it was soft drinks loaded with bags of sugar. My lifestyle was scandalous for an inter-county hurler.

I knew it wasn't what it probably needed to be but I used to comfort myself with this concocted belief: 'Sure I'm only a young fella, I'll be grand. I can eat what I want, sure I've no weight on me.'

I used to put on weight easily. That trait is in the family genes but it was no surprise either. I wasn't doing any weights.

Strength and conditioning training meant nothing to me. Core work was something that geologists did.

Noreen Roche, our nutritionist, was working with Kilkenny at the time. She would monitor what we'd eat after training but I never went near her for advice. If I had, I'd have realised that I was poisoning my system, not refuelling it.

I always thought a healthy meal was pasta. I'd boil the spaghetti or fusilli or penne, strain it, and then empty a tub of cheap, microwaveable carbonara across the top of the dish. I was thinking to myself, 'Jaysus, I'm eating fair healthy here.'

That stuff was loaded with salt and sugar and cream, and laced with processed additives. I was lucky I was only 102kg at the time, and not 110kg. Yet I still thought that I was eating as healthily as a rabbit.

'I'd the pasta last night,' I'd say to the boys the following day. 'I'll be hopping off the ground like a kangaroo at training tonight.'

After the shit I'd plied into my system, I was probably stuck to the ground like a bloated frog. It was no wonder Rory Jacob and other lads were running around me as if I was a training cone on the pitch.

My mindset for an inter-county hurler was a joke. I drank like a fish. We used to have this tradition in college on a Wednesday where we would challenge each other to see who could drink 24 cans of Dutch Gold. Six of us would buy a slab of beer each and line up the 144 cans across the sitting room. The test was to see who could finish the 24 cans. We gave it a right good shot but nobody ever managed the feat. It was just as well; if you had, you'd probably have been carried off unconscious in an ambulance.

I was lucky that I was so close to Kieran 'Fraggie' Murphy from Cork. He was living at home at the time so he used to drive a lot. His mother, Betty, regularly fed me with proper dinners out in Riverstown. 'Fraggie' didn't drink so he used to ferry me around the place. I was so paralytic one night that I was vomiting blood into an empty lasagne dish.

I was still training hard with Kilkenny at the time but I didn't have the cop on to tailor my regime to suit inter-county hurling because I didn't think I was going anywhere. I was just along for the spin, delighted to be there, happy to stay on the panel for as long as I could until I was eventually found out.

Even though I had captained Kilkenny to an All-Ireland U-21 title, I had no real belief in myself. We had an unreal team; JJ Delaney, Tommy Walsh, Ken Coogan, David Herity, Conor Phelan, Willie O'Dwyer, Aidan Fogarty, Michael Rice, Brian Dowling. I was centre-back but I wasn't thinking that I was a key player in such an impressive outfit. I was still thinking that the boys were carrying me.

The bad days had scarred me that much. Every match I played, I was half setting myself up for a fall through my own self-fulfilling prophesy. I almost expected to fail. Then if I did, I'd remind myself, 'Sure, I knew that was going to happen anyway. Of course that was going to happen.'

It was a form of self-strangulation. I'd tie myself up with anxiety because I was afraid to chase the one thing in life that I wanted so badly. I didn't believe that I could ever fulfil that dream. I used to have this phobia, this recurring nightmare of being cleaned out on a big day in Croke Park.

Big days in Croke Park with Kilkenny had always been my dream. I was so afraid to chase after it that I was driving myself further and further away from actually living it. Instead of biding my time and allowing it to come to me, to follow the process of time and maturation and letting life take its course, the fear of it never happening used to drive me crazy.

The more you hear of it, the more you believe it.

'He's not good enough.'

'He has no pace.'

'He can't turn.'

'He would be cleaned out at that top level.'

'He'll only make a good club hurler.'

Part of that crippling mentality and mindset was inflated by more than just doubts and demons. And I wasn't giving myself the best chance to get the most out of myself through my loose lifestyle.

I finished my final exam at CIT in the summer of 2004 on a Thursday. Kilkenny were training on the Friday but I told Brian that I wasn't finished until the Monday. I stayed up studying the whole night before that Law exam, which I sat at 9am on the Thursday morning. By 11am, I was in the pub drinking large bottles of cider. I hadn't slept and had barely eaten. By 5 o'clock that evening, I was drunk out of my mind.

I got kicked out of one pub. I went into the Bishopstown Bar and managed to get turfed out of there too. Myself and a friend from Waterford, Ger, decided to head into the city centre for more action. We crossed over through the forecourt of a Texaco station to get to a bus stop. A taxi driver had just filled his tank and was making his way into the shop to pay for the petrol. Myself and Ger checked to see if the car was open. It was. The keys were in the ignition. We got this notion to steal the car.

I sat into the passenger seat. My mate sat into the driver seat. He turned the keys, pressed on the accelerator and took off like lightning.

We didn't get far because we went straight into rush hour traffic. We were stuck just 30 metres from the petrol station so panic set in. Ger broke the lights and shot off like Lewis Hamilton.

The adrenaline rush only lasted 30 or 40 seconds for me. I knew we had fucked up. Reality hit me like a sledgehammer.

'Ger, we've got to get rid of this thing or we'll be fucking locked up.'

A mile down the road, we pulled into this layby. I don't know how we didn't crash the car because we were both tanked out of our heads.

As we abandoned the car, I took off my shirt and started wiping the car down for fingerprints. It was a bright, sunny, early-summer evening. People coming from work were staring at me, half-naked, clearly cleaning the evidence like I was a gangland hit-man after pulling off a job.

We kept our heads down and ran about a quarter of a mile before coming across this quiet pub. There was nobody inside. We were delighted with ourselves. We were sure we'd got away with it.

Our plan was to stay drinking there until it got dark before getting another taxi into town to meet the lads.

An hour later, the door opened. When I turned around, two Guards were standing behind me. I nearly lost my life.

Ger started protesting our innocence. 'Nah, that wasn't us at all.'

I knew we were snookered. They probably had us nailed on

CCTV footage from the garage. I put my hand up and admitted our guilt straight away.

By the time we'd been put into the back of the Garda car, my body was shaking with panic. I was computing the cost to come down the line; the shame, the embarrassment of telling my family, the collateral cost of Cody finding out and probably firing me off the Kilkenny panel.

I only had one card in the pack. One of the Guards might have had a GAA background. He might have heard my name after the U-21 success. So I dealt the only card I could.

'Lookit lads, I play for Kilkenny. If I get nailed here, my hurling career could be over. Brian Cody might never touch me again.'

My pleas made no difference. We were driven straight to Togher Garda station. As we were being shepherded in the door, Joe Young was just coming out. Joe used to play hurling for Graigue-Ballycallan before transferring to Blackrock after being stationed in Cork.

'Jesus, Jackie, what are you doing here?'

'I fucked up, Joe,' I said. 'I'm in trouble.'

Joe went back inside. The other two Guards marched us in the door. They took our shoes and phones and fired us into a holding cell.

I crouched down and started bawling. It was hard enough as it was to try and make it with Kilkenny. And now I thought I had just torpedoed whatever slim chance I may have had of developing and growing on the panel.

We were left there for three hours. It felt like about 12. Eventually, we were released, but told to return to Bishopstown Garda station the following day to fill out a statement. We just had to hope then that the taxi driver wouldn't press charges. If he did, we would have to face them.

As soon as we walked out the door, we didn't need the soft air from a mild summer breeze to freshen us up because worry and anxiety had already sobered us.

I knew I wouldn't be able to sleep so I suggested going back on the lash. I drank a heap of cider to try and erase the terror ransacking my mind. It worked but as soon as I woke the following morning, the guilt and worry came at me in waves. After I got myself together, I met up with Ger and we presented ourselves at Bishopstown Garda station.

Ger had already been arrested before but I warned him not to say anything.

'Any previous convictions?' the Guard asked.

'No.'

We gave the statement, telling as much truth as we could; it was out of character, we were up studying all night, we hadn't eaten all day, our minds were warped from tiredness and drink. After the interview, I produced €50 and handed it to a Guard. He looked at me as if I was trying to buy him off with money for sweets but I said it was for the taxi driver to cover any possible loss of earnings while the car had been missing.

We were lucky. The taxi driver didn't press charges but he wanted some dollars for loss of earnings. We sent him on €400 a couple of weeks later. It was the best few euros I ever spent because the last thing I needed was to go to court and end up with a conviction.

I had planned to stay down in Cork and go on the beer for another two days but I couldn't handle the stress hanging over me. I got out of town and was back in Kilkenny that afternoon.

I was in bed early, shaking with worry and the after-effects of such a hard day and night's drinking. I couldn't sleep but I wasn't able to anyway with the constant stream of texts dropping on my phone from the lads in Cork.

'Jackie, can you call us a taxi?'

Bastards.

Relentless

'We play Waterford tomorrow. Kilkenny have announced a strong team – 12 of the 2015 All-Ireland winning side. I'm not named. I would love a game. I am disappointed but in all honesty I felt worse for Lester Ryan than I did for myself. He has been flying in training and is super-fit. I expected him to start. I did an upper-body and core session as I want my legs to be light if I am called upon tomorrow. I need to keep my mind clear anyway because there's a fundraiser on in the club tonight, a 'Strictly Come Dancing' event in the Lyrath Estate. I am a judge with Tomas Mulcahy, Michael Duignan, Tracy Millea and Marty Morrissey. I wasn't dancing but I wanted to make a statement to them all of how fit and powerful and young I look. I dress up in a three-piece plum suit and dicky-bow. I want to turn heads. I wanted to let everyone in that room know that I haven't gone away, that I am as hungry for road as ever before.'

– Diary entry, Saturday February 13th, 2016

I DIDN'T get to bed until 2am. I was promised I would be home by 11.30pm but the 'Strictly' event dragged on and I couldn't say no to my club. I felt and looked tired and sluggish after being up so late but I was still confident my mind and body would have responded if I was called upon. I wasn't.

The whole day was a balls. The dressing room was casual pre-match. I was in getting a rub when I could hear lads talking outside. It was very generic, fellas talking almost for the sake of talking. It is still early in the season but I remember thinking beforehand that we needed fire, leadership and direction. And we lacked all three.

We were beaten by 0-14 to 0-10. The pitch was terrible. Waterford are back training since October. We are only just back four weeks but that's only bullshit excuses. They drove 18 wides. They should have beaten us by 10 points-plus. Brian said to us on Friday night that although we were a fair bit behind other teams in our preparation, that we would not be outworked by Waterford. Well, we were. Brian said that we set the standards on work rate and intensity. Well, they set them today. We were second best all day.

I was completely pissed off. I didn't want that feeling to linger so I approached Lester Ryan in the hotel in Waterford afterwards. 'Are you going to do anything when we get back home?'

'I might do a bit of running,' he replied.

'If you are, let me know and I'll hook up with you.'

I had made up my mind to go running anyway but I checked in again with Lester as soon as we arrived back to the Newpark Hotel. Lester said that himself and Rob Lennon were going running in Bennettsbridge, Rob's home club.

It was after 8pm when I arrived in the 'Bridge. It was absolutely freezing. Rob had turned on the floodlights but the glare was struggling to cut through a dense blanket of freezing fog.

We did three sets of six 100-metre runs. We did the first set in 17 seconds. We clocked 18 seconds in the second set. Lester was still coming in at 18 during the third set, when myself and Rob were dying a death, straining every sinew in our bodies to push them over the line before going over the dreaded 20-seconds mark.

Eighteen 100-metre runs would normally drench your body in mats of sweat but my back and torso were as dry as a bone. I couldn't feel my hands from the cold. I was wearing the socks I had worn in Waterford, which were still soaking wet from the warm-up in Walsh Park, so my feet were like blocks of ice. Beads of sweat had gathered on my forehead, concealed underneath a woolly hat, but my body temperature wasn't much different from before I started running. The air was so frigid and stifling that we didn't even do a proper warm-down.

I got straight into the car afterwards. My mind was blank from oxygen debt but I was so distracted from the cold that I don't think I even said goodbye to the two lads. I went home and had a shower. I turned the temperature gauge up to the highest notch but standing under near-boiling water for ten minutes still couldn't warm my body.

When I sat down on the couch afterwards, I was shaking my head. 'What the hell did I do that for?'

I thought I would feel better afterwards but I didn't. That high you sometimes get from pushing yourself hard was completely absent. I just felt frustration. I was angry with myself. I had got straight off a bus, hopped into a car, jumped onto a field and started running 100s in the freezing cold, without even stretching properly. It was asking to pull a hamstring.

Normally, if I knew I wasn't playing, or if I wasn't in the panel of 26, I'd have gone to the gym Saturday and done a run on the Sunday. I always felt that gave me an edge but when I was on the bench, I prepared as normal. I was eating loads of white bread beforehand, storing up on carbohydrates for energy. When I didn't get any game-time, I felt lethargic and heavy. That's why I was so keen to go running – to burn it off.

I wanted to stay positive. Even though Kilkenny didn't win, I wanted to feel I got something from the day. Sometimes when you don't play, you can self-accumulate more positives than when you do. The two corner-backs that day didn't exactly set the place on fire. I knew I had more in me. I thought a hard running session would deposit more fuel in the tank but I just felt emptied afterwards.

I was pissed off with everything. Even having Rob Lennon out running with us irked me. He is another defender, another guy challenging me for my spot on the team. In the middle of the torture, I was thinking to myself, 'I wish Rob was at home lying down.' It was killing me that whatever edge I might get from the exercise, it would be negated by the similar edge it may have given Rob.

I didn't want him there. I wanted Lester, not just because he is a good friend, but, selfishly, for what I could get out of him. Lester is fitter and faster than me. I knew he would push me more than Rob could in the runs. Lester was always five yards ahead of me and I was breaking my back trying to catch him.

Subconsciously, that's why I asked Lester in the first place. He hadn't played either so maybe me asking about a running session planted a seed in his head to do something similar. There were other subs I could have asked but I didn't for a couple of reasons; they wouldn't have been as competitive or as fast as me, or they would have been in direct competition with me for a place on this team.

I have always loved training. I love pushing myself but the desire for that edge in Kilkenny is often overpowering. I don't want anybody else in my spot. I want to give myself every possible chance to make this team but to me, every day is also an opportunity to get faster, fitter, sharper and psychologically stronger.

Brian never says that openly but you know that's what he expects of you; it's what he expects of everyone. I am in my 14th year on the panel but there is no backing off here. There is no opportunity to back off. I wouldn't want that anyway but keeping the accelerator pressed to the floor is inspired as much by fear as necessity. You don't worry about trying to keep yourself fresh for the summer, about trying to preserve gas in your tank for another long-haul journey. If you drop your intensity at that stage, the train will just move on without you.

There is never a hint of holding back or dropping off. I never got that from Brian anyway. During the 2010 league, he rested some of his most trusted warriors; Henry was given an extended sabbatical after Ballyhale's All-Ireland club success; Michael Kavanagh also got an extended break after a similarly long Intermediate club campaign with St Lachtain's that spring; Eddie Brennan was given time off because he got married; Martin Comerford was also married that spring; Derek Lyng was allowed some time to recover from a hip operation.

We had just come off winning the four-in-a-row and Brian

didn't want to flog lads who had been on the treadmill for so long. We may have had a stronger panel at the time, which allowed for more leeway, and more experimentation, but we didn't win the league that year and Tipperary beat us in the All-Ireland final that September. Unless lads were injured or getting married, Brian was never as generous with sabbaticals or down-time again during the spring.

Lads don't want them anyway. I certainly never did. I always had this fear of a physical break being correlated to a mental weakness. A fear that if I took it easy in March that I wouldn't be ready for the championship. Or worse again, that I might not even have a place on the team.

Other counties may have had the luxury of allowing players to rest up so they would be right for the summer. I remember hearing these stories about Ken McGrath and Tony Browne arriving back with Waterford in March. They were unbelievable players who minded themselves but I never wanted that to happen to me.

Waterford and other counties could afford to take that approach because those teams couldn't do without those players in the first place. But anyone could be done without in Kilkenny. Even if I had that luxury, I don't think I'd have taken it anyway. I'd be afraid of not being ready. My mind would have been playing tricks with me. 'Sure how could I be ready when I took it easy for two weeks in March?' I have never known that way. I have only ever known 100 miles an hour.

Clare is always on at me to slow down; to take time to myself, as opposed to trying to fit in more training sessions in the one day. At one stage I had ten penalty points from chasing my ass around the country in order to fit in that extra gym or alley workout. I've always tried to pack so much into my day. I couldn't think of anything worse than taking it easy.

I would love to have gone travelling or globetrotting for a few months but hurling for Kilkenny suppressed that urge. Society has changed now. The mindset of inter-county players is vastly different to what it was. The world is a much smaller place and many players want to travel it rather than make the huge lifestyle choice that demands so much from them as inter-county players. The lure of an All-Ireland medal or big days out in Croke Park are no longer compelling for some players but you rarely hear of Kilkenny hurlers taking time off to go travelling. Some lads have over the winter but most lads wouldn't enjoy it. I know I wouldn't. Our only focus is on winning as many All-Irelands as we possibly can.

I'll enjoy the shit out of life when I'm finished hurling with Kilkenny. But that time isn't here yet.

It was a different and funny way to spend a Valentine's night. I had been away from home since 11 that morning. I could have been back an hour earlier than I was. I left a card and a rose on the table for Clare that morning but there was no point in planning a meal that evening. I know it. And so does Clare.

I am selfish. There are times during a hurling season when I won't see my family for ages. Part of that might be down to not wanting to see them. There were occasions when I was asking myself why I was even going to my parents' house. I don't want questions. I don't want to be asked about how I am going, how my foot is, how the team are shaping up in training. I would prefer to go into a coffee shop and read a paper on my own for an hour.

I am always on the clock. Most inter-county players are but I'm nearly paranoid about it. When we visit family and friends, Clare and I normally have a plan of action beforehand, especially if it's an evening visit. 'An hour, an hour-and-a-half max, and we will hit for home.'

I just want to be resting or going to bed early to store up on sleep. It's the same when we go to the cinema. Clare looks at the detail, the cast of actors, the reviews. I only check to see what time it starts, and more importantly, what time the movie finishes. If it's a three-hour classic that everyone is raving about, I have no interest in the movie if it starts after 8pm.

I don't like late nights. They put me on edge. The 'Strictly' event was bothering me too because I swore I would never get caught like that again.

In 2013, I agreed to do a charity leg shave in Carlow the night before we played Galway in the league. I was promised it would only take up an hour of my time but I didn't get back to Kilkenny until close to midnight and we were travelling to Galway early the following morning.

I was bull thick on the journey up. I played with my socks pulled up because I was embarrassed to show off my smooth thighs and calves. I was fucking brutal the same day. Niall Healy took me for a goal. I was coming out with a ball at another stage and handpassed it straight to a Galway fella who fired it back over the bar. I was lucky not to be taken off. My head was up my hole.

Ever since then, I have learned to put myself first. If I have to say no to people and it pisses them off, I don't care. If they're completely pissed off with me, even to the point of annoyance, I still don't care. All I want to do is give myself every chance to be successful with Kilkenny.

Nothing cuts across my routine but Clare fully understands me, and how I operate. Clare likes chocolate but she will eat it in the bedroom because she knows I don't want to see it around the kitchen. I said to her recently, 'If I ever have a weak day and I ask for chocolate, don't give it to me.'

I sound like an alcoholic craving a drink but that's the level of abstinence I try to apply to my lifestyle. There will be times when I'll see some chocolate lying around the bedroom, I'll break, eat it, and then the guilt will come at me in waves. As a form of punishment, I'll get down on the floor and start doing press-ups.

I do a core session every night before I go to bed anyway; press-ups, press-ups on the medicine ball, sit-ups, Russian twists. Every night. I'm so fixated on that routine that if I had a very late night, and I missed that workout, I'd double it the following night. A bar of chocolate might force me to treble it.

There are times when there aren't enough hours in the day for me to get what I want, and feel I need, to get done. There are days that I would do a 90-minute gym session, a swim workout, a ball-alley session, while I could have spent two hours with Brother Damien, all before 6pm. And even then, I struggle to switch off. I just always feel there is something else I can be doing. If I'm not training with Kilkenny, there is a window there to get my healthy shopping done that evening. I can start preparing my meals for tomorrow. I'll get my porridge ready for the morning.

At times, you can feel obsessive. A routine basket shop should take any normal person ten minutes. It could end up taking me double that time. I'd be there checking sodium levels and saturated fat levels on the back of food packets in supermarkets. I'd tell myself that the Tipp lads were doing the same thing in the supermarkets they were shopping in.

I would build in treat days once every two or three weeks. I always allowed myself a pizza and wedges for the Superbowl, a big bag of pick 'n' mix on Paddy's Day. It may sound extreme but when you get into the routine of that lifestyle…

Even when it was a chore, it never occurred to me not to do it. My attitude was that it was the very least you had to do to be able to survive at inter-county level. I relished the idea of doing all this so that when the summer came around, I was going into the championship with a hard, strong body to use as a weapon.

That relentless pursuit is also just another means of scratching around looking for that extra fraction. I need to search for it now more than ever because the last year is the first time in a decade that I have felt heat on my position. This is all new to me. I always played 85 to 90% of our league games. I always played well during the spring. If I had to sit out a match, I never felt threatened by whoever had my jersey for that 70 minutes. 'I'll have it back next week,' I'd remind myself. 'And nobody else will get near it again for the rest of the year.'

When Shane Prendergast got a starting jersey during my injury-enforced absence in 2015, I never saw Shane as a threat to take the jersey off me. I always felt better than him. Rob Lennon wasn't even on my radar until he arrived into the squad after Bennettsbridge won the All-Ireland club Intermediate title and he was being tried out at corner-back in some training sessions.

I felt if it came down to a choice between the three of us, I would win. Not only was I a better hurler and more experienced, I felt I could contribute more to the team. But now I'm wondering what Brian really thinks of me. Does he just see me as cover going forward?

Am I slipping? The running sessions over the last month in Dunmore have been torturous. It has been the toughest physical work I have done. Around the turn of the decade, I always classed myself among the top three fittest players in the squad. Up to 2015, I always believed I was in the top eight. Now, I know I am outside that bracket for the first time. I can feel it.

I am 34 now. Science is science. You cannot cod yourself. I have had injuries. Age is naturally going to slow you down but I had always convinced myself that age was as much a state of mind than physical shape.

I am still striving to be in that top eight. I still gravitate towards the machines in the running groups; Brian Kennedy, Lester, Conor Fogarty, Cillian Buckley. It is getting tougher to keep pace with those thoroughbreds but I'm not sure if that is more mental than physical. Because I have relied so much on Brother Damien, I've even noticed myself slightly off on the Tuesday sessions if I haven't been to see him that day.

Doing 20 100-metre sprints with those elite guys, with possession games interspersed between some of those runs, can be murderous. When we do sets of four 100s, you literally have 10 to 15 seconds to catch your breath before you go again. If you came in one second behind the guy who crossed the line before you, that meant one less second recovery time. And Cody standing in the middle watching everyone like a hawk.

It was pure hardship, but in a weird way, I love it. I don't like the pain but I'm not afraid to go after it as a means to getting what I want. The torture chamber is often a great place to be. It's almost like an addiction to being pushed so far outside your comfort zone that you actually get a buzz from suffering pain.

Over the years, as the runs got harder, you could always see guys gradually breaking down. Fellas would be bent over, their lungs burning, their legs on fire from lactic acid. Even when I was dying inside, I never showed any weakness. I never bent over to catch my breath. No weakness. Body language was everything. So was the satisfaction of not breaking.

There have been times over the last four weeks when I've wondered if I was going to break. I know I won't because I just won't allow myself to. I fucking hate those 100-metre sprints. The torture I endure during them is severe but that pain can often spread to the dread that often precedes it. The time spent thinking about the pain, listening to that little fucker on your shoulder saying, 'Jackie, don't annihilate yourself tonight. Nobody expects you to out-run the racehorses tonight.'

There were nights when I would subconsciously say to myself, 'I'll go into group three or four here now, the pace won't be as hectic as in group one or two.' And then I'd check myself immediately. 'I need to be up there. I need that pain.'

If anything, I feel I need to keep pushing myself even harder because I am still playing catch-up with everyone else after the foot injury. I feel like I am chasing the whole time but that has made me more driven than ever. If anything, it has made me even more obsessive. The pursuit now has become even more relentless, where every extra session, every extra run is another down-payment on greater glory to come.

The Master

C LARE and I will sometimes go for a walk around St Kieran's College. After passing through the gates under the arch, we veer left and follow a familiar path, strolling past the main part of the building, the front pitch and the old borders house quarters, before the path turns at a right angle. As you make your way down that gravel track, parallel to a stone wall and a line of trees, the bottom pitch is facing you.

I often tell Clare of the memories from that patch of ground. As young kids in Kieran's, we learned our trade there in that crucible before it later became a crucifixion site with Kilkenny. The road to September often started in that small corner of Kieran's. The pain was part of that process but All-Irelands always seemed so far away during those winter purgatories.

After doing a warm-up and some circuit training in the college hall, we would put on our boots and slowly make our way down to that field, computing in our brains the pain about to come.

Mick Dempsey would set down cones to mark out a series of six interval and stamina runs which we would normally repeat eight to ten times. It was hell. It always seemed to be raining. The ground slopes down to that field but there is a much steeper incline onto the main pitch, which made that corner field even wetter because the rain used to roll off the higher ground like a river.

It was often like running through a swamp. The place was dimly lit from street lamps from the housing estate beyond that stone wall but there was never any hiding place in the shadows. Brian always stood in the middle like a sentry. Martin Fogarty had a better overview because he normally took up station at the incline on the top pitch as Mick Dempsey and Noel Richardson ran us around like greyhounds.

The usual crew were always struggling at the back of the pack; PJ Ryan and Mick Kavanagh. Dempsey would often roar at the boys to push themselves up closer to the top of the group. I routinely tried to position myself high up in the pack. I was one of the fitter lads in the squad but it was still always torture on that soft patch of ground.

When we were young in Kieran's, loads of us had this ritual on a Friday lunchtime. We would make our way across that pitch, climb over the stone wall and cram into Rocco's chipper. For £1, you could get a bag of chips, a battered sausage and a bottle of Coca-Cola. When the pound changed over to the euro, the same deal still applied.

Rocco's is still there. During those winter nights at Kilkenny training, when you'd be deep in oxygen debt, when your muscles were screaming for respite, the wafting aroma of fried sausages and burgers would turn your stomach like a spin drier.

Guys used to despise the training on that pitch. 'Terrible Tuesday' we christened it. Richie Power used to dread it so much that he calculated the exact number of hours and minutes between sessions. 'Until the next time we are here,' Richie would often say as we were togging in, 'there is only…' He'd normally be told to shut the hell up. Lads didn't need to be reminded.

It was pure hardship but we still all suffered together, which frames those memories differently now. As you get older, you become more aware of time, of how it slips by quicker, especially in the twilight of an inter-county career. Yet instead of lamenting what has gone, and what little time may be left in a Kilkenny jersey, you also become more aware of how much a privilege every day still is in that jersey.

It always has been. One of the classrooms at the back of the college – our old technology room – peers right over that pitch, a steep incline above that gravel path. There were plenty of times when I stared blankly out onto that pitch during class, wondering would I even make a St Kieran's panel, never mind a Kilkenny minor team. Playing with Kilkenny for as long as I have transforms those memories of all that pain and suffering on that pitch into a deep appreciation of having had the opportunity for so long to spill my guts for the honour of us as Kilkenny people.

There is a picture in our sitting room at home of my uncle, Kevin Robinson, up on the shoulders of my father, Dermot, after the 1973 All-Ireland minor final. Kevin is hoisting the

Irish Press Cup after Kilkenny defeated Galway in the final. Just three years later, they became brothers-in-law when Dermot married Kevin's sister, Mary.

My father was a sub on that minor team. Kevin, or 'Scrapper' as he was known, was a better hurler. My father got a few runs in the league with Kilkenny but he was never good enough to make it. He was a solid hurler with O'Loughlin Gaels. My mam was also an O'Loughlin's woman, growing up in the shadow of Nowlan Park. After they got married, they bought a site and built a house three miles outside the town in Wallslough, which is in the James Stephens parish.

My eldest sister, Emer, was born in 1979. She may not know it but Emer is the rock of our family. She is the person everyone goes to for help and advice. She has a massive heart and would do anything for the family. I have two younger siblings, Mark and Sarah. Mark never played hurling but he was always fanatical about the game. He went into coaching early. He started with underage in the club and worked his way up, managing the James Stephens senior team for a couple of years. He managed Emeralds Urlingford in 2015.

Mark has always been very quiet and reserved. When he was younger, he was very overweight, which did affect his confidence. He carried that weight through his teens and into his early 20s but he has shed all those pounds now. Mark has always been a strong character in his own unique way but he has been a silent inspiration to me too in how he fought that battle with his weight, in how there was always such conviction about his character.

Mark is refreshing to be around. He is deep and honest and has a very simple and basic outlook on life. He is a huge hurling man but when we won the 2008 All-Ireland final, Mark left at half-time. He was on the motorway passing Carlow when the final whistle blew. We were annihilating Waterford but he didn't leave early to beat the traffic. His attitude was, 'This game is over, there's no point in hanging around.'

When I get tickets for big matches, Mark always takes his place in the defined seating plan Mam has drawn up, everyone taking their usual place in the line; my father, my brother-in-law Damien Dawson, Emer, Sarah and her boyfriend David, my mother, Clare, and my uncle, Father Jackie.

The seating plan is designed for a reason. My father is a raving lunatic at matches. Damien acts like a rampart beside him because he hardly opens his mouth. Emer doesn't get too excited either but Sarah is a hothead like my father. My mother doesn't even watch the games. Clare and David are completely relaxed while Father Jackie doesn't even know what's going on half the time.

Father Jackie is based in Borris-in-Ossory in Laois. He usually has to say a couple of masses before he can hit for Dublin. He normally arrives into the ground around 3.15pm, and then decides to talk to half of Croke Park before the game starts 15 minutes later. My father would be cursing and swearing at him under his breath for not being more tuned in but Father Jackie is always on a different wavelength anyway. He listens to the game on his headphones and often gives a delayed running commentary to the rest of the family. 'Marty Morrissey is after saying that Aidan Fogarty is about to come on,' Father Jackie would turn and say in the general direction of the group. And 'Taggy' could be on ten minutes and have bagged 1-2. It drives my father nuts.

Sarah isn't much better. She has always been my biggest supporter. She has always stood up for me any time someone has taken my name in vain, or cut the ground from under me with a nasty comment. She rounded on a Tipperary priest one time when he called me a tramp, scolding him for letting himself down in that manner as a member of the clergy.

Sarah only played camogie for a short time when she was younger but she was always crazy about hurling, and supporting me and Kilkenny.

On the day she made her Confirmation in 2003, I was playing a Fitzgibbon Cup quarter-final with CIT against UCC. Daddy and Emer went to the match in Cork. Mammy stayed back but it took Sarah a long time before she fully forgave her sister and my father for missing her special day. She soon understood. When she got older, she became more fanatical about hurling than anyone else in our family.

My mother's seat is always a waste of a ticket. She has seen very little of me hurling in Croke Park. She stays for the national anthem, blesses herself, and then walks around the back of the Hogan Stand. By now, all the maors and stewards know her routine. She smokes cigarettes. They give her tea. Eoin Larkin's mother, Lucy, sometimes joins her. All the while, Sarah keeps her updated on the game. The record for text messages sent to my mother was 48 during the 2014 All-Ireland final replay.

My mam can't handle the pressure but she would struggle to listen to my father too when all hell is breaking loose on the pitch and in the stands. He would be roaring and bawling but Sarah doesn't hold back either. Emer would be trying to keep both of them in check but she may as well be talking to the wall. Damien, or Deo as he is known, wouldn't say boo to a goose. Meanwhile, Father Jackie thinks he's Marty Morrissey. The women love him too because he looks like Sean Connery.

At times it sounds like a circus but at least you know that they are all hitting every ball with you. I look forward to the days when I can join that crew at matches, when my mam can sit down and enjoy supporting her county. But I hope that day won't come for a while yet.

All of the kids who hurled with James Stephens went to school in St Patrick's De la Salle. The club always tried to strengthen that connection by running a brilliant school-club tournament on a Sunday morning. One competition was for 1st, 2nd and 3rd classes, with another for 4th, 5th and 6th classes.

Seán Brennan and Micky Slattery ran the Sunday morning league. Seán would always referee the finals, dressing up in a full referee's kit, and carrying a tape recorder around with him that was blaring out the national anthem. They wanted to make us feel like it mattered, to make us feel important. And they always did.

St Patrick's was a nursery and an oasis for James Stephens and there were serious hurling men there to shepherd us along; Brian Cody, Matt Ruth, Noel Power and Paul Kinsella, who was Kilkenny county chairman for years.

Brian taught me in 4th, 5th and 6th classes but I had him for four years because I stayed back in 6th. The familiarity still didn't make any difference because I was really afraid of him. We all were. He had this wooden metre stick and he would lash it off a stool to get our attention. He never used it on us but if you were messing he would come down and leer over you like a shadow, jabbing his index finger into your chest, almost driving you back a yard with every poke.

He always exuded total control, supreme authority. Nobody was in any doubt as to who was the boss, the master, in St Patrick's. If fellas were messing while Brian was out of the room, he wouldn't let up until he found out who the culprits were. And when he did, there was hell to pay.

He used to frighten the life out of lads the way he would react. If there was any noise in the class while Brian was teaching, or writing on the board, he would grab the stick and lash it like a circus master using a whip to get the attention of his subjects. If the messers started up, he would go to town on them. He would put them under the table. If they were laughing or talking while they were down in that cooler, he would kick the table as a reminder that they were still being monitored.

Nobody ever tried anything major on with Brian but he had a way with the messers too. He knew how to get the best out of lads. He was an excellent teacher but his methods were still often old-school. He used to have this seating plan where he would sit you in order of your results. The brightest in the class always sat in the bottom left corner, with the weakest always planted right in front of his desk. Maybe it was Brian's way of having the messers or the weaker kids where he could see them, where he could get their attention, but it was a way of challenging guys too. Everyone wanted to be in the back row because there was a hierarchical status attached to the order. I was usually always in the middle row but the harder you worked, the more you moved closer towards the back of the room.

Brian was always like a psychologist in how he operated.

The Master

We were always mad to play hurling but if we had work to do and we didn't get it done, he would pull the plug. Matt Ruth would make those threats too. 'Right lads, I'm going down to photocopy these pages. And if there is any noise when I come back, we're not going hurling after lunch.'

Matt would come back and there could be lads swinging off the rafters but he still never carried out his threat. We would still be let out to play hurling. With Brian, you never got that dispensation or allowance. If you crossed the line, there was payback.

He was fair to everybody but the good hurlers still got the best jobs. We would sell the hurleys to anyone looking to buy one from the school. We would be sent on errands that might get you out of class for a while. We invariably got that additional break-time anyway through the goal-to-goal tournament Brian used to run. We would put up the names and the charts on the wall. At 11.30am, every day, he would give four cones and a ball to two players, and a whistle to a designated referee. We had a league going and it was serious stuff. It was highly competitive. Everybody was always zoned in but if Brian came out and fellas were fooling around, his raised big husky voice would send a shiver down your young spine.

Kilkenny weren't winning All-Irelands at the time but the hurling culture in the school was just all-encompassing. Matt and Brian had finished up hurling with Kilkenny by then but you knew that they would have still given anything to be playing. When Matt would give you work to do in class, he would be pucking the ball off the wall, the sliotar flying a couple of feet over your head as you were doing maths in your copy.

Matt never carried out his threat of stopping us from hurling because he would have missed that hour of enjoyment more than us. He had an amazing passion and love for the game. Matt had this saying that the first thing you should always do when you get a new hurley is shake hands with it. That was his way of telling us how to check the new stick for weight and balance, to see if that particular hurley suited you.

Matt had a big shock of grey hair. He was as grey as a badger when he was still playing for Kilkenny, whereas Brian was as bald as a coot. When you're young, you associate hair, or lack of it, with age so we hadn't a clue what age Brian was. We were all mad keen to find out. There was no Google at the time so I used to ask my dad. He would never tell me.

That added to the mystique and fascination around Brian. Even before he started teaching me, I knew full well who he was from listening to my dad, who would tell us stories about Brian, Matt and Joe Hennessy, and all the great Kilkenny players.

I didn't really know how many All-Irelands or All-Stars Brian had won. I just knew he was big. He almost felt bigger than the school. I went to my first All-Ireland final in 1991. There were big names on that team that went on to win successive All-Irelands in 1992 and 1993 but Brian still always felt bigger than all of them.

He just had this aura. I picked that up from the respectful way my father always spoke about Brian. I didn't know what an aura was but it almost sounded like a fear. And I felt I had to have that fear too.

At that time, Brian used to drive a gold Sierra car. I can still remember some of the numbers and letters from the registration. Every morning I went into school for the four years Brian taught me, the first thing I did was look to see if his car was parked in its usual spot. It was almost like a psychological check-point, the starting point of my day with the master. That added another shimmer to his aura but, even back then as a child, Brian had a presence in my subconscious, like he had with all of us throughout our time with Kilkenny. He was just always there, but in a good way. He was an excellent teacher, and excellent coach. You just knew you had to do things right, the way he wanted them done.

It was clear too how much he wanted to win. When I was in 5th class, we went down to play Ballyhale in a 7-a-side tournament. It was so intense that Brian got stuck into Liam Fennelly. The two were squaring up to one another like two prize-fighters before a big scrap. They didn't swing any punches but it felt like they were fighting. Brian certainly wasn't backing down. We all knew who Liam was because he had captained Kilkenny to the 1992 All-Ireland title but he seemed like an ordinary and mortal figure that day in the shadow of the master. I distinctly remember thinking afterwards, 'That's why I am afraid of Mr Cody.'

Any time we played a big schools match, Brian made us feel like it was an All-Ireland final. It wasn't fabricated to make us feel good about ourselves. It was genuine and authentic because that's how much it meant to Brian. It was so obvious. When I was in 6th class, we got to the Roinn A final against Kilmanagh. It was played in Nowlan Park on a Wednesday evening but the squad were called out of class at 2pm and brought to the lunch hall for a team meeting. You just knew that this was big, that it was big for Cody. That raging passion and emotion was all over his face. You could see how badly he wanted us to win. 'Put whatever part of your body in if you have to,' he said.

He almost felt a duty that if he was over that team, no matter the age or competition, that they had to win. We drew with Kilmanagh before beating them in a replay. Brian was absolutely ecstatic afterwards. He celebrated that success as much as he did after any of our All-Ireland finals.

When I watched the video of the game afterwards, I was taken aback by Brian's intensity. He was up and down the line like a lunatic. He was waving his arms around like a conductor. He was in the referee's ear. I remember thinking, 'Losing is not an option here with this man.' It wasn't.

Matt coached the team but Brian drove the operation. He drove everything to do with hurling in the school. When we were in 4th class, the school bought a plot of land on an adjoining site. It was as rough as a lunar surface but one afternoon, Brian told everyone in the class to bring in a garden utensil the following day. We all did. We spent the whole day picking stones from that field. Brian was stuck in the middle of us. That field became our school pitch.

When I think of Brian Cody, I often think that image is the best representation of who he is, of what the man stands for; roll up your sleeves, work hard, do your job properly, do it honestly, do it for your team-mates, for your future team-mates, for future generations.

All these years later, Brian Cody is still tilling the ground.

I was passing St Kieran's recently during the day when I decided to go in for a walk. The students were off on a week's holidays so I ambled into the main building. I met Adrian Finan, the school principal, and Ken Maher, the vice-principal. Adrian had coached me in St Kieran's. He managed James Stephens to the 2005 All-Ireland club title. It was nice to catch up. I ambled through the marble corridor, past all the old photographs of successful teams on the wall. I spotted myself and my bleached white head in the back row of the 2000 All-Ireland Colleges winning team. I continued down the large main corridor, before turning left down the glass hall, a long building with a line of windows and a slanted Perspex roof.

The building is lined with long benches. At the bottom corner of the building, where the glass house intersects with another corridor lined with classrooms, I used to sit there most mornings with Brian Dowling. We'd watch all the country lads streaming in from the buses, all carrying hurleys, pucking balls around on every corner of the school grounds. Hurling was only allowed in certain areas but the teachers always turned a blind eye.

At least 70% of the students carried hurleys with them every day. Some of them would bring their hurley to school before their schoolbag. The culture in the place just sucked you in. I knew lads who were absolute hurling fanatics in Kieran's and they hardly even hurled with their clubs when they left the place.

It was everywhere. Pat Murphy, a Carlow hurler, a St Mullin's man, used to teach us. He was a lovely guy, a fanatical hurling man, who was always mad keen to talk about Carlow hurling. We had no interest in Carlow's exploits but we knew that if we got Pat started that we could knock 20 minutes of hurling talk out of a 40-minute class. Tommy Walsh, who was in my class, used to even study Carlow hurling to get Pat going. He would read their match reports, even watching Eirtell on TV to try and find out the Carlow team named for that weekend's game.

When we were in 3rd year, we were in Pat's class one morning. Kieran's were playing Callan CBS in a big game that afternoon and Tommy kept trying to get Pat talking about the match. Pat wasn't biting but he still had his hurley and ball in the class and, while we were writing in our copies, Tommy chanced his arm. 'Sir, I betcha if you hit the ball off the wall, and then head it, that Kieran's will beat Callan today. It will be a good omen.'

Everyone started laughing but Pat wasn't buying it. A couple of weeks later though, Pat had the hurley and ball in class again. This time, when he did hit the ball off the wall, he – completely spontaneously – did head it when it came back. That was the unique culture in Kieran's, that symbiotic relationship between the game, the people and the place. It was what we did. It showed how we were all at one with the game.

Hurling just consumed us in the college. We trained so hard, at every level. We normally trained at lunchtime. A minute after the bell rang, you would be togged off and ready to go. We'd train for the guts of an hour, have a quick shower, and then run back into class trying to stuff sandwiches into our mouths.

We all loved the game but there was an aura about that black and white jersey. We all desperately wanted to wear it but you soon realised what it took to be given that privilege. The training was ten times harder than club training. You were competing with lads from everywhere; guys in clubs from all over Kilkenny, fellas from Tipperary, Waterford, Laois.

I made the U-14 team in 1st year and the U-16 team when I was in 3rd year. That helped my confidence but when a challenge was presented to me, it still took me a while to adapt. I loved hurling. I loved Kieran's. I had great friends but I didn't want to go back after the Junior Cert. I wasn't bright but I knew I had some academic potential. I did honours maths for the Junior Cert. I just hated studying. I found it difficult to concentrate. A great friend of mine, Micky Eardly, had left school early to take up a mechanic apprenticeship and I thought about going down that route as an electrician.

My dad wanted me to do my Leaving Cert so he played the smartest card he had in his deck. His friend, Peter Coogan, was an electrician and he asked him to take me on for a couple of weeks that summer. He also issued Peter with a directive. 'Dog the shite out of him and pay him shag all money.'

Peter was a lovely man but he carried out my father's request. My head was soon turned. I went back to Kieran's. I didn't think I had any business going for a trial for the senior team in 4th year but Adrian Finan said it to me one morning. I immediately dismissed it. 'Ah no,' I said to him, 'I'm not good enough for that level at all.'

'Go for it anyway,' said Adrian. 'The experience won't do you any harm.'

The first trial was the day we got our Junior Cert results. Even though I didn't drink at the time, a few of us went to an off-licence and bought a crate of cans. We went down to Coote's Lane and the lads polished them off. I had my gear with me so I headed off at 3.30pm for the trial. When it was over, I re-joined my buddies before ending up in a disco.

I made the Kieran's panel that season in 1999. I played all the league at corner-back. I played the first round of the Leinster championship against Good Counsel but James McDonald roasted me. A bad afternoon got worse when I got sent off. I cried my eyes out in the dressing room. I knew I had blown my chance but it was even more humiliating because players rarely got sent off for Kieran's. The only time I played again was the All-Ireland semi-final against the Combined Ulster Colleges because one of the corner-backs broke his finger. I was dropped for the final, which we lost to St Flannan's Ennis in Croke Park.

It was my first time in Croke Park as a player. I wanted more. We all did. We had a good team in 1999 but it got a whole lot stronger when Eoin Kelly from Tipperary came to the school as a boarder that September. It was a big statement from Eoin, and for us. Eoin came to Kieran's to win an All-Ireland. In April 2000, we won our All-Ireland, avenging the previous year's result by defeating Flannan's in the final in Nenagh.

Patrick Reid, TJ's brother, was on that team. At the time, they had a pub in Ballyhale and we ended up going down there for three days. The final was played in the middle of the Easter holidays so we cut loose. The house was like a youth hostel, bodies thrown and strewn everywhere.

God be good to Mary Reid, who passed away a few years later, she cooked a big fry-up for us every morning. I woke up one morning and there was a calf in the corner of the sitting room. The poor calf was unwell and was nestled beside a heater to keep warm.

We had our best team in 2001 but we were beaten by a Dublin Colleges team inspired by Stephen Hiney, Dotsie O'Callaghan and Conal Keaney. Getting beaten so early in Leinster forced me to put the head down and study harder than I intended to. I did a decent Leaving Cert. I got 320 points, and the course I wanted, but my overriding memory of my final year in Kieran's was of an opportunity missed, of an All-Ireland medal lost.

Hurling in Kieran's framed so much of our lives, and our futures. Just inside the front door of the main hall is a picture with two jerseys, a Kilkenny jersey and a St Kieran's jersey. Both are signed by the 18 past pupils of Kieran's involved in winning the three-in-a-row for Kilkenny in 2008. The names of every one of us are listed in two separate panels below each jersey.

Just around the corner, hanging on the wall outside the door of Ken Maher's office is another framed picture. It's a collage of images of Lester Ryan, who teaches in Kieran's, and a full printed version of his acceptance speech in Irish after the 2014 All-Ireland final replay.

Like so many of us, Lester knows Brother Damien. Lester made an agreement with Brother Damien before that year's Leinster final that if Kilkenny won the All-Ireland that he would deliver the full speech in Irish. Lester couldn't make the team that summer but he was determined to have that opportunity.

Given his position, as a captain not starting, two core themes formed the central plank of what he wanted to say, one of which was borrowed from an old Irish seanfhocal. Lester's words, 'Tá mise lán cinnte gur bhuamar inniú mar creidimid gur ar scáth a chéile a mhaireann na daoine,' translates into, 'We live in each other's shadow, we rely totally on each other.' His line, 'Tuigeann an panéal seo ach mbíonn an teorainn sa spéir, ach go mbíonn an teorainn san aigne,' means, 'limits are not set in the sky, but in the mind.'

It was beautifully worded but Lester encapsulated everything about our journey. We do live in each other's shadow. We rely on each other. Limits are set in your mind. My ambition is limitless now but I never thought I would win nine All-Ireland medals, especially when I was a young boy pucking around in that back-field in St Kieran's, hoping to play for the college, desperate to play for Kilkenny, and doubting if I ever would.

'We operated like a crazed army. We didn't give a shit about anyone. We were waging a war and anyone who stood in our path was just blown out of our way. The bigger the massacre, the better we felt.'

chapters
VI-X

No Boundaries

'My dream, I don't fear it, I work on it. I don't fear failure because I continually look forward to more success. I follow my heart, not my head. I am not trapped. I am not living by, or listening to, other people's rules. I make no apology for me. Others give up on themselves. I don't. My spirit, ambition, power, and daring to be my best, is impossible to kill.

Fear is not real. It's a choice. I risk to dare more, to explore how far I can go. My dream is real. Every day I wake, I step into it. I know what is possible. That's why I keep raising the bar.

Everything I do is a way of life, an obsession. I don't have a Plan B. It would only distract from Plan A. I test myself how far I can go, what I am capable of, how daring, ruthless and dangerous I can be in pursuit of excellence. Cogito Ergo Sum.'

– Diary entry, Monday February 22nd, 2016

MY dream is still real. Every day I wake, I really do step into it. I still know what is possible. Plan A is all that matters because the only plan I have is to be the best that I can be. We all go different ways and have different opportunities. We all have challenges and perceived obstacles. Finding your way depends on you, on what you're willing to do to be the absolute best version of yourself. If that only means being an impact substitute for Kilkenny in 2016, so be it. I'll be the best I can be in that role too.

I desperately want to play, but retaining that focus is important for me. I don't want to get lost in the year. I don't want to become disillusioned. I don't want my mind to become contaminated with frustration and anger. The easy option is to start pulling back, to get down and drag others down with me.

The last thing I want is to be seen to be here for the spin. I don't want people thinking, 'Ah he's only there for the gear and the glory of trying to chase Henry's record of ten All-Ireland medals.'

Fuck that. I want this All-Ireland medal as badly as any of the nine I already have. Numbers mean nothing. The ambition and hunger to still want more is everything.

I thought Brian might have played me against Tipperary in the league yesterday. He knows that Tipp always brings out the best in me but he and the rest of the management clearly still don't think I'm ready. I was disappointed because I love playing against Tipp. I love playing for Kilkenny more but February is nearly over now and I still don't know where I stand. Not having played since July 2015 is heightening my anxiety.

I was put out but I wasn't allowing my frustration to get the better of me. I wasn't thinking, 'Why isn't Cody trusting me more?' I knew I needed to be patient. I fully accepted that 2016 was going to be a different season and that being patient was going to be a key part of dealing with it.

Plan A is still the only plan I have.

Friday, February 26th, 2016

After getting the new power phase of our gym programme, we do a fitness test in IT Carlow. I missed the first fitness assessment before Christmas. I am the oldest on the panel now so this is a big moment for me. And I aim to make a big statement.

There was a big group in the hall. We were scheduled to run in groups of ten, when it probably should have been in packs of eight. I didn't mind. I went looking for young lads to test myself. I positioned myself between Chris Bolger and Paddy Deegan, both 21-year-olds. Facing off with a beep test and a couple of young lads – there's no better way to estimate your VO2 max.

The longer the test went on, the more frequent the beeps became, the more exhausted I became. When I hit level 20, my mind was gone. I was in so much oxygen debt I felt like passing out. Chris and Paddy were still going beside me but I could see they were only barely hanging on. By hell or high water, I wasn't dropping out before them. 'I'll show these boys,' I thought. 'I'll prove it to myself.'

I had burned them both off by 20.4. I had nothing left but I found something. When I eventually stopped, James McGarry told me that I had bailed at 20.8. I was slightly annoyed because I was convinced I'd hit 21.

Brother Damien set me a target of 19.11 but I'd say he knew I was capable of more. Yet he was still wise enough to make sure that if I didn't hit that target, I'd be close to it.

Damien is great at reading my body language. He is brilliant at contextualising everything. I was slightly pissed off a couple of weeks back when I was on the B team for a training match. 'You haven't played a competitive match in over six months,' he said. 'And you're annoyed because you're on the B team?'

Damien is great at grounding me; refocussing my thoughts. Subconsciously, I want to keep pushing myself. That's why I went into a group beside two young lads. I'll keep challenging myself but so will Brother D to ensure that I never become negative; that I never stray from Plan A.

The morning after the fitness test, I woke up with a chronic pain across the right cheek of my ass. Conor Fogarty told me one time that you should always turn a different side when you hit the line but I get more spring off my right foot. I was trying to spare every millisecond I had so I kept turning on the same foot. My right glute muscle was killing me but I didn't care.

I already have other targets set. Fogarty and Cillian Buckley hit level 23 on the fitness test. They are serious athletes but their standards are already in my sightline.

Sunday, February 28th 2016

My legs are heavy today. My body is tired as I put a lot into that fitness test, both physically and emotionally. I am very conscious that we are playing a match today. I mark Walter Walsh. I play well. I move well. I felt I played intelligently too. Bucks (Cillian Buckley) is hurt over not playing last week (against Tipperary) and you can see it in him but he is the best player on view today. I am happy with my contribution. My first touch needs to improve but that will come. After training I head to Brother D. He senses a comfort level in my attitude. He knows me so well, the way I think and act. He urges me not to dwell on a good performance today, and on the scores I hit at the fitness test on Friday. He tells me to push the boundaries more. To play on the edge. To take risks. Don't settle for good or very good. Strive for greatness.

Monday, February 29th 2016

We are having our one-on-one meetings with the management in Hotel Kilkenny this evening. My slot was down for 8.40pm. Joey Holden was in before me. As I waited outside, I heard this big laugh. Maybe it's just me but it sounded slightly strange. In my experience, these meetings are always about serious business.

The lads were there all evening. There were empty tea cups and crumb-covered plates strewn across the table. Just after I sat down, a waitress came in to take their food order. All the lads – Brian, Mick Dempsey, Derek Lyng and James McGarry – ordered steaks. I was asked if I wanted a steak too. We all laughed but it was an awkward laugh.

I always found these meetings awkward. I've known Brian most of my life but I've never felt easy enough in his company to relax. To me, our relationship has always been business. Soft banter has never been part of our conversation, or with the vast majority of players. Nobody really goes there.

The only one who ever did was John Hoyne. He was a character who loved his few pints and the craic. When himself and Brian chatted, it often ended up in a laugh. Hoyne was a huge character. He and his Graigue-Ballycallan clubmate James Ryall were freewheeling spirits who made some double-act. Hoyne's nickname, 'Dougal', came courtesy of the Father Ted character. Some of the stunts he pulled would have fitted right in on Craggy Island.

'Dougal' and Ryall were up in Dungannon one year presenting medals the night before a Walsh Cup match against Dublin in Parnell Park. Brian had signed off on the trip but they were instructed to be in the Burlington hotel for noon the next day. It was Ryall's first start for Kilkenny but at 4am that morning, Hoyne was belting out the 'The Rose of Mooncoin' up on the stage.

Ryall set his alarm for 8am but he and Hoyne collapsed into a coma. It was 11am by the time they woke up. They thought about coming clean to Cody until Ryall came up with a better idea. Hoyne rang and said that the front tyres had been slashed. It must have been the Free State registration. No garage was open. The Burlington was out. Brian said to head straight to Parnell Park.

They either hadn't time to eat, or they hadn't the stomach for food, so a bottle of Lucozade was their pre-match meal. The boys were dying. They survived. It was only a Walsh Cup game but Ryall and Hoyne had the neck and the balls to take a chance. Very few others did because it was never worth the risk.

Brian understands the group dynamic, the importance of proper chemistry and how it needs to be mixed with the correct blend of characters. Personalities who leaven that mix are critical to any group but Cody never wants somebody stirring the pot up too much.

John Mulhall was a great character, a guy who never conformed to expectations. He once had the distinction of representing Ireland in the World Series of Beer Pong in Las Vegas.

Mulhall was up for anything. At the homecoming for the 2011 All-Ireland, Brian handed him the microphone and Mulhall thought he was in the 3 Arena. He performed the song he'd written himself, 'G'wan the Super Cats' to the melody of KC & The Sunshine Band's 'Give It Up'. Every verse was loaded with enough classic lines for a stand-up comedy gig and we all belted out the chorus. Everything was going to plan until Mulhall came to the last verse. 'Now we've taken back our throne/Tipperary póg mo thóin/Liam MacCarthy's coming fucking home.'

Cody's body language immediately changed. When he took the microphone back off Mulhall, Brian told the crowd: 'You've witnessed a performance by a fella who is probably going to have the shortest inter-county career of all time.'

Brian may have only been joking but Mulhall was gone by the following spring.

Brian appreciates wit and fun but most guys suppress that part of their personality around him because nobody knows where they stand with him. That mystique about Cody and his personality means that the players never know how to take him. That is a strength of Brian's but he probably feels he needs that type of personality to be able to handle so many driven players.

Affection has never been a dynamic in his relationship with us. Cultivating such a distance between us and him adds to his mystique. He is nowhere near as severe in private as his public image suggests but nobody would dare cross him.

For him, it's just black and white. Nothing personal. Just business. Cody never believed that dropping big names, always keeping guys on edge, added up to ruthlessness but none of us were ever in any doubt as to how ruthless he could be.

Before the 2010 All-Ireland final, he pulled Paddy Hogan and team captain Eoin Guinan from the Kilkenny Intermediate team set to play in the All-Ireland final against Cork. The decision sparked some silent fury from the Intermediate management when neither featured on the senior team eight days later. Guinan's club were reportedly furious over denying their man the opportunity to captain his county in an All-Ireland final, which Kilkenny won.

Guinan was on the panel the following winter. After losing the 2010 final to Tipp, we went back training earlier than normal. We worked like animals over the winter. Eoin did all the hard training but after one desperately hard session in Mooncoin, Brian told him he was being released from the panel.

I remember afterwards wondering why Eoin had been dropped in such a callous manner. I think I asked him afterwards if he had done something during the session to piss Brian off. Eoin said he hadn't.

I didn't understand Brian's reason for bringing a fella down to the bottom of the county in Mooncoin, running the shit out of him in the muck and dirt, and then telling him he was gone. To us it was pointless. To Brian Cody, it clearly wasn't. Maybe he was put out by the criticism he got from the Kilkenny Intermediate management and from people in Eoin's club. If he was, that act of dropping him was Brian's way of letting everyone know who was the boss, and of who makes the big decisions in Kilkenny.

The players were disappointed for Eoin but none of us dared to question Cody's authority.

I'm sure players in other counties would have queried such a decision but other counties haven't had the success that we've had. None of us would look crooked at Cody because we all know the exact same thing could happen to any of us just as quickly.

I often hear stories of managers in other counties having a really good relationship with their manager, of that fun and relaxed dynamic that never existed between us and Brian. I often craved that kind of relationship with Brian but then when I'd hear stories of how cosy some players were with their manager, of some of the drinking and messing they'd do on holidays or during the off-season, I'm glad that Brian always kept that distance between us.

Nobody has a right to a jersey. We all appreciate that. Brian's methods have delivered us success beyond everyone's wildest dreams in Kilkenny. We appreciate and value the man so much. We don't expect to be mollycoddled but the lack of feedback is what drives most fellas mad.

Fellas with bags of All-Ireland medals have sometimes walked away bitter and angry. 'Cha' Fitzpatrick has never spoken out publicly about Brian but privately, I would say that he was frustrated and may have felt forced to walk away at just 26. You can still sometimes see that frustration in 'Cha'. He'll often have a go at Brian through some piss-take sketch. He once put up a team of 'Cody rejects'.

'Cha' was one of the most talented hurlers I ever played with, but I feel that Brian made up his mind about 'Cha' after that 2010 All-Ireland final. Physically he was blown out of it that day. He was playing some great stuff for us in 2011 but he couldn't cover the same ground any more and Cody didn't believe 'Cha' could survive in the combat zone the way he wanted him to. Brian let him stew on the bench and it played out just like Brian, 'Cha' and the rest of us probably felt it would – 'Cha' walked.

Brian was justified by winning another All-Ireland. He won another the year after 'Cha' walked. Brian's success immunises his methods from most forms of criticism but he still should have been more upfront with 'Cha' during 2011. If he had pointed out what he wanted from 'Cha', if he told him what he needed to improve on, maybe 'Cha' would have done what was asked of him, and would have given himself a chance of extending his Kilkenny career. Then again, if Cody loses faith in a player, there's no way back.

That lack of feedback can still be crippling. It depends on where you are in your career but it still drives some lads demented when they're not playing. I'm experiencing it now. It can make you crazy but you just have to accept that this is how Brian conducts his business. It works. It has always worked. He has already squeezed a fair career out of me.

Individualism is nothing. It's all about the team. The show will carry on without any one individual. He is so tunnel-visioned that players, personalities, egos, even feelings, don't come into the equation if he feels it means Kilkenny will become soft.

I don't even know if Brian recognises the frustration players have often felt. I'm sure he would if he sat down and thought about it but it's not on his radar at all. Players have got frustrated. They have left before their time was done but none of it seems to matter to Brian. You'd just wonder is it a standard test he sets for everyone — how long can you endure? How long can you stay here without knowing where you stand?

I'm lucky that I've had Brother Damien to lean on. We've

never been exposed to sports psychology under Brian, probably because he is the ultimate psychologist himself.

Brian completely understands the power of calculated instability, that tension he generates between hope and desperation. Brian might say to the group that five or six lads aren't pulling their weight and, no matter how well you're going, you'll still often think he is referring to you. That's the kind of stuff that continues to generate our relentless drive.

That's all that matters to Brian. He will not back down for anyone. He has his strong values, that Kilkenny hurling will keep rolling on, whoever is involved. That is the only focus he wants us to have. Nothing else matters. He is always afraid of outside influences contaminating the panel. That's why he has always been so distrustful of the media.

Some say it's paranoia. The majority of the stuff that has been written about Kilkenny over the years is positive but when Brian has no control, he gets edgy. His big fear is the insidious danger of complacency and softness creeping in and he always saw the media as a vehicle for creating those issues.

When Martin Fogarty was involved, he used to co-ordinate and organise all media requests but Brian always had the final decision. We were always told to say nothing. Seán Cummins, who was on the panel for a few years, came out with a comment once which encapsulated everything Brian thought, and wanted us to feel, about the media. 'Treat them like mushrooms; fill them with shit and keep them in the dark.'

We usually did but a few days after Dublin beat us in the 2011 League final, I was asked to attend a promotional event in LIT. We weren't back training until the Thursday and I went along without clearing it with management. When a journalist stuck a dictaphone under my nose, I just gave my honest opinion on what I felt had happened against Dublin.

I said it was the worst performance I was ever involved in with Kilkenny, which it was. I spoke about how our standards had slipped, which they had. The only thing I regretted was having a go at Eoin Larkin and John Dalton for indiscipline. Larks was sent off. Dalton was lucky he didn't walk because he should have. He hit Conor McCormack with his hurley before then kicking him off-the-ball. Dalton subsequently received an eight-week suspension over the two incidents.

When the story broke the next day, I knew there was a storm coming. Some of the headlines were suggesting a crisis and my name was smeared all over it. In the afternoon, a group text was sent out: 'Nobody, under any circumstances, is to speak to the media unless it is cleared by management first.'

The text was clearly directed straight at me. When we went back to training a couple of nights later, Brian admonished me before even saying a word about the issue. In front of all the players, he asked me to stay back afterwards, that management wanted to have a word with me. He could have pulled me aside in private but he wanted to make a point in front of the group.

I got grilled on not following the protocol. I said I forgot about it. LIT was my former college and I just went along to support the initiative they were launching. I didn't feel like I had done any wrong but Brian made me feel like shit. I just said what I felt. Brian knew I was speaking the truth but he still saw it as a betrayal of our code.

Any time we lost, he was always on high alert. After the 2012 Leinster final defeat to Galway, Cody went bananas. He had a veiled cut at some players for, what he felt, was an excessive public profile in the lead up to that game. I assumed one of those arrows was aimed at me because I did an interview to promote 'Opel Kits for Clubs' that week. I had no choice. I was driving a sponsored Opel car.

He went into complete siege mentality mode afterwards. At half-time in our All-Ireland quarter-final against Limerick in Thurles, I thought he was going to deck Richie Hogan. Richie was standing in the middle of the floor speaking to the group when Brian walked in. There was absolute venom in his tone when Cody told Richie to sit down as quickly as he could.

When Richie was sent off for striking Seánie Tobin with 12 minutes remaining, a Limerick supporter made his way towards the back of the Kilkenny dugout and began rapping on the Perspex covering before unleashing a string of expletives towards anyone from Kilkenny. As soon as Brian heard him, he didn't take it lying down. He reacted with an animated reply.

He was still like a lunatic after the game. He ran the county board out of the dressing room and then ate the shite out of us for a below-par performance. We were all afraid to piss sideways afterwards but Brian extracted one of our greatest performances from us in the All-Ireland semi-final against Tipp.

Cody had us playing like caged animals throughout the rest of that 2012 championship but one of his greatest achievements is consistently convincing us to play with the mentality of underdogs. We won the All-Ireland final after a replay against a Galway team which had beaten us by ten points in the Leinster final. That sweetened the taste but for Cody, and for us, the compulsion to win overshadows the sensation of winning.

Brian has had such success that none of us ever doubt him or his methods. With Brian and ourselves, the act of winning is greater than the titles and the glory that winning brings. Every performance, every win counts for something. The winning and glory never lasts long in Kilkenny because they are just part of the continuum that Brian has created. The next game, the next challenge, is all that matters.

That is the process which has always governed our approach and the process will always be king to Cody. That's why everything else is irrelevant to him. The media is something to be endured. Player endorsement requests are another unnecessary distraction but Brian knows they are inevitable.

He won't deny lads the opportunity to make a few quid but you know too that he'd prefer if you didn't. Most of the time you run a request by him, he will hit you with his stock reply.

'What do you think?'

It's a simple question but it's always highly loaded. And it's always followed by another wave of loaded questions.

'Where is it on?'

'Who is it for?'

'Who contacted you about that?'

'What will it entail?'

Brian is almost trying to make you feel so uneasy that you'll talk yourself out of the gig. 'Ah, no I don't really want to do it anyway. I'll leave it so.'

In my eyes, I'm still playing an amateur game. If I get asked to be a brand ambassador for some product, and I'd like to do it, I'll do it. When I go to clear it with Cody, I'm always firm.

'So you want to do it?'

'Yeah.'

You have to be smart about it. Brian has his standard question. And I have my standard and genuine reply. 'Brian you know this is my life. You know I want to get the best out of myself for you and the team. This is not going to be a distraction.'

Brian knew it wouldn't be an issue for me. He saw how much I was putting into my preparations, of how ready I would always be for the big matches. Other guys would have been just as well prepared as me but they wouldn't run any risks by doing a gig that they believed Cody didn't want them doing.

He just wants the best for Kilkenny and he doesn't care about anything that gets in the way. Brian knows I like playing football with the club. The senior football championship is always ran off during a short window during the spring but asking for permission to play is never easy. Brian just trots out his old familiar line, soft and gentle but as loaded as a stick of dynamite.

'What do you think of that, Jackie?'

On a couple of occasions, I was carrying knocks or slight injuries. The next question was inevitable. 'Will you get in enough recovery for training if you play that match?'

Then the switch goes off in your head, the one Brian is trying to flick, and just has. 'My hamstring is a little tight. If it does go, I'm in trouble. Jeez, I'll just pull out of the game.'

The perception often was that injury ruled me out, or that I pulled myself out in case of risking injury. The real truth often was that, while Brian didn't openly tell me not to play, he subliminally told me that it was in my interests not to.

And I'm not going to argue with that.

After sitting down in front of the lads for the management meeting, Brian handed over to Mick Dempsey to comment on my physical state. Mick said he thought my fitness levels, attitude and application had been excellent. Then he asked me how I felt.

'I'm great. My body and mind feel really fresh.'

Derek Lyng commented on how free I had been in my running over the past few weeks. James McGarry's advice was to play from the front, attack the ball and don't hold back.

That has always been my game since I fully established myself but Brian reiterated McGarry's point. From his experience, guys at the latter end of their careers tended to get cautious, hold back and do things differently.

'Do the things that made you who you are,' said Brian.

I nodded. I had Brother Damien's voice ringing in my head, his words about playing on the edge, on taking risks, bouncing around my mind.

Before the meeting finished up, Brian asked me something he hadn't asked over the previous six months.

'How's your foot, Jackie?'

'It's fine,' I said. 'I'm good to go.'

'Is it 100%?' he asked again.

'Brian, it's 100%, for sure.'

The way he asked the question left a nagging doubt in my head but I looked Cody in the eye and reaffirmed my reply.

'Brian, I'm ready to go.'

I am. All I need now is a chance to prove it.

If Only You Knew What Was Going On Inside My Head

THE weekend before Kilkenny played Galway in the 2006 All-Ireland quarter-final, we went to Monart Spa in Wexford on a training weekend. At a team meeting on the Saturday night, Brian laid it on hot and heavy. He wasn't happy with how some players were performing.

Then James Ryall suddenly interjected. 'Well Brian, if yere not getting it out of some players, and yere not happy with how they're performing, is it not time for ye to start looking at other lads?'

Brian didn't say anything. It was a ballsy comment from Ryall. I admired him for challenging Cody but I still thought it was directed at me. I was the team captain but I was struggling at the time. When the team was named for the Galway match later that week, I was dropped. Ryall was my replacement.

I was absolutely devastated. Martin Fogarty clearly noticed my distress. He asked me to meet him in the Springhill hotel the following day. We spoke in his car. I was happy with that arrangement because I didn't want to be seen among a Kilkenny public fully aware of my situation.

I appreciated Martin reaching out to me. I don't know if Brian asked him to speak to me. I'm not even sure if he knew about the meeting but I've no doubt he was aware of it afterwards because I was on the floor.

I knew I was under pressure to hold on to my place but getting dropped was still a hammer blow. Getting benched as captain was like a rabbit punch into my gut. I was sickened from the impact but I wasn't blindsided from the blow because I always suspected it could come.

And it just confirmed every fear I always had about the captaincy.

Brian absolutely loved Peter Barry. Of all the players he managed over the years, Peter was his favourite. It was more than just club loyalty because Peter was the ultimate expression of everything Cody believed in; honesty, animal work rate, supremely focussed, savagely determined, an abhorrence for the media, intensely committed to James Stephens as much as Kilkenny; an absolute dog.

Brian rarely referenced feats of courage or inspirational

leadership from the players. That was a standard expectation anyway from Brian but he often told the story of Peter's doggedness and bravery against Wexford in 2003 as an example to the rest of us. Peter got a belt in the balls. One of his testicles was as inflamed as a turnip. The doctor Tadhg Crowley wanted to bring him to the hospital but Peter refused to go off.

When James Stephens won the county title in 2004, Peter was the natural choice as Kilkenny captain in 2005. Peter lifted the Bob O'Keeffe Cup after we beat Wexford in the Leinster final but his Kilkenny career was over after the All-Ireland semi-final defeat to Galway. Brian hauled him off with 20 minutes still to play and Peter never came back.

When we retained the county title again in October 2005, the realisation suddenly hit me that I was now the most experienced player from the club on the Kilkenny squad. My initial reaction was pure terror. That subsided when I began to realise the honour I was likely to receive but any positive emotion contained a serious asterisk. 'Jeez, if it does happen,' I said to myself, 'it's going to put me under some pressure.'

It was confirmed shortly afterwards when Jimmy O'Brien, the club chairman at the time, rang me to say that they were proposing me as Kilkenny captain.

In his autobiography, Anthony Daly described the feeling of being asked to captain Clare for the first time in 1992. He said it was like being told 'some young wan fancies you.' I would love to have felt that way but I didn't. My overriding emotion was fear. 'What the fuck am I going to do now? How am I going to talk in front of all these lads?'

The fear was compounded by my instability within the panel. I wasn't sure of my place. My confidence as a Kilkenny hurler was fragile. The last thing I wanted, or needed, was more pressure. And now, here it was, albeit wrapped up in fancy paper and a bow, being dropped on my shoulders like an albatross.

I didn't want it.

I felt like a fraud. We won the league that May. I lifted the cup after we beat Limerick in the final but it wasn't an easy afternoon. Conor Fitzgerald took me for four points. After Henry, he was the highest scorer on the field from play. Fitzgerald turned me a couple of times and I couldn't get anywhere near him.

I just about survived. I just about got away without being completely exposed. It was great to captain Kilkenny to a national title but the manner of my performance siphoned a lot of the satisfaction from the experience. It also fed my doubts even more.

About a week later, I went to a media-championship launch in Croke Park. All the other captains were well established, respected inter-county players. I was genuinely wondering if any of them, or the media, actually knew who I was. I just nodded away. My conversation was loaded with small-talk. It was an uncomfortable experience. I really felt that I shouldn't have been there, that I wasn't entitled to be in those players' company.

Up to that point of my career, I had done nothing to earn that status. When I made my senior debut against Waterford in the opening round of the 2004 league, I got the run-around. I wasn't taken for 2-2 but I was so far off the pace that it wasn't funny. I remember chasing after John Mullane once and I felt like a snail trying to hunt down a hare. I got nowhere near him.

I started wing-back. The game was in Nowlan Park but a big crowd had travelled up from Waterford. I didn't expect to be playing the following weekend against Galway but Brian started me at midfield. I was gone by half-time. I was pure shite. I was on David Tierney before moving on to Fergal Healy. That was my year done and dusted.

I was like a ghost, nowhere to be seen. I trained away with the squad but I never expected to get near a starting spot. Being honest, I didn't want to be anywhere near it. If I couldn't cut it on a mucky field in February, what chance had I in Croke Park in the summer?

I just didn't think I was anywhere near that required level. Other players my own age, or younger, were passing me out. I knew I had to show something. I felt that pressure. At that stage, my only concern was getting a lower shirt number than I had for the previous match. Sometimes it was 28. We were carrying 34 players so they would often hand out two number 29 jerseys, and two number 30s. I got those jerseys a couple of times. You're just thinking, 'Holy fuck, I can't go any lower here'. That was my mindset.

I don't know if I even deserved to be on the panel. When I got my chance I was lost. I was slow. I got cleaned out. Twice. Kilkenny reached the All-Ireland final in that 2004 season but I didn't feel in any way part of the whole experience. I felt so completely detached that I wasn't even disappointed when we lost to Cork. I was looking at lads crying, fellas crumbled up in a heap of devastation. I was asking myself, 'Should I be more upset?' I certainly didn't feel any sense of loss.

I wasn't sure if I would be asked back in 2005 but I got a big break when James Stephens won the county title that October for the first time in 22 years. I had a decent season. I got pushed into midfield to mark Alan Geoghegan in the county semi-final replay against O'Loughlins. He was a big player for them at the time and I was steady. That lifted my confidence. So did winning the county title.

Still, I knew my level. When we reached the Leinster club final against UCD, I marked Brian Barry and I couldn't handle him. He was a serious athlete who I just couldn't keep up with. I was put back to wing-back for the All-Ireland semi-final but I was poor again against O'Donovan Rossa, the Antrim champions. I had a good game in the final against Athenry but I still didn't expect it to make any difference to my Kilkenny chances.

When James Stephens played a challenge game against Kilkenny before the All-Ireland club semi-final, Brian Barry cleaned me out again. I thought that was enough to get me canned but Brian started me wing-back against Dublin in Parnell Park the week after the club final. I went back into corner-back for the next game against Cork, which was my first match for Kilkenny at number four. We won the league, defeating Clare in the final, and I held onto my place for the championship. We annihilated Offaly in the semi-final before narrowly overcoming Wexford in the final. I missed the All-Ireland quarter-final against Limerick with a hamstring injury before coming on as a late substitute in the semi-final defeat to Galway. The game was gone lala by the time I entered the match, a nine-goal shootout which Galway won by three points.

Getting a starting Kilkenny jersey did lift my confidence but it didn't dilute the river of doubts streaming through my head. I didn't even feel in the top half-dozen players on the James Stephens team.

I felt my place was behind Peter Barry, Philly Larkin, Brian McEvoy, Eoin Larkin, Eoin McCormack and Donnacha Cody.

What's Going On Inside My Head

Larks had only come onto the panel after the club final. 'Mucky' McCormack and Donnacha wouldn't get a run with Kilkenny until the following season but they still seemed to often carry more value to the club team than I did.

When I somehow found myself as the most established James Stephens player on the panel at the end of 2005, I certainly didn't feel comfortable with that status. I felt I needed to be starring for James Stephens and I wasn't. We won another county title and a Leinster club at the end of 2005 but I went into 2006 with Kilkenny devoid of any real confidence. And the captaincy just heaped a burden on me that I carried around like an anchor.

When I look back on that whole experience now, I wished I could have enjoyed it more, that I could have embraced the challenge the way I should have. I just couldn't because my doubts continued to disarm and disable me.

I had minimal back-up in my locker to draw on. I had a decent league but my confidence was still on the floor. After the league final, I didn't know if I would start our first championship match against Westmeath. I was grateful to Brian that he handed me a starting jersey.

I did well but in the last ten minutes, my man caught three balls over my head.

I was like a lunatic because I knew Brian would focus on it. He had always been on to me about being more commanding under the dropping ball, of how he wanted our half-back line to be our launch-pad for attacks.

I was barely hanging on because teams were clearly targeting my weakness in the air. Against Wexford in the Leinster final, Damien Fitzhenry dropped his first three puckouts straight down on top of my head. I knew straight away that they were coming after me.

On that training weekend in Monart in Wexford, Cody spoke to me again about my struggles under the high ball, and of the urgent need to address that part of my game. Yet the more he drew attention to the problem, the more pressure I felt around it.

I struggled in the training game that weekend. Ryall played well as a wing-back on the B team. He was right to challenge Cody. He was doing it. I wasn't. Ryall was in. And I was out.

I'll never know if I'd have started the 2006 All-Ireland final against Cork if JJ Delaney hadn't torn his cruciate ligament in training beforehand.

Mick Kavanagh was JJ's actual replacement from the semi-final team but Mick was always more likely to get back in ahead of me. He was a specialist corner-back.

Mick had already played in six All-Ireland finals by then. I had only started one championship match in the corner. I had no All-Ireland final experience in Croke Park. If I'm being fully honest with myself, JJ's misfortune probably was the deciding factor in me starting.

The door had already reopened after the quarter-final. Brian clearly made his mind up about me as a wing-back and he fired me back into the corner in training. I did well enough to start the 2006 All-Ireland semi-final against Clare.

The first ball that came in between myself and Tony Griffin, I won it and drove it straight back down the pitch. It was only the first play but I was hyped up from getting a second chance. It was a release from the frustration of the previous few weeks. On my way back into the corner, I dug straight into Griffin.

He caught me up by the lapel. 'Hey boss,' he said, 'there's a long way to go yet.'

There was. Griffin cleaned me out. The next couple of balls that came in between us, he could have stuck both of them in the net. Griffin ended with four points from play but Brian released me from that Gethsemane at half-time, switching me to the wing, with Tommy Walsh going back in to try and sort out the full-back line.

I survived in the second half but playing All-Ireland finals has to be about more than just surviving.

Getting named to start the final was a relief but it still didn't suspend the worry or doubts rampant in my system. I was terrified of marking Ben O'Connor, who I knew could burn me for speed. When I looked around at the other names in our defence, I accepted that I was the weakest link. If Cork were as sharp as they claimed to be, I knew they would go after me.

What should have been the greatest experience of my life became a countdown to madness. It was like being trapped in a psychological torture chamber. And no matter where I turned, I couldn't escape that overbearing sense of trepidation, that underlying fear hardwired into my system.

Everything associated with the captaincy increased the stress levels within me. I didn't want to do the press day but I felt I had to speak. I wasn't talking in the dressing room; the least I could do as captain was speak to the media.

I wanted to keep my head down but my head was in such a mess that I didn't even know how to manage that much. The day before an All-Ireland final is normally a day players spend in a bunker but I managed to jump straight into the middle of all the hype. At 3pm, I decided to go for a stroll into the city centre.

A couple of lads from the Kilkenny Supporters Club were selling Kilkenny merchandise from a mobile van beside Kilkenny Castle, the busiest place in the city, and I sidled up to them for a chat. I stayed there about 20 minutes chewing the fat with them, about Cork, about our chances. All the while, streams of people were buying stuff. And there was me standing around like an idiot. I'd say if Brian knew, he'd have taken the head off me.

I think I was so uncomfortable with my position, and with the pressure of the captaincy, that I wasn't thinking rationally. I was acting in the complete opposite manner of what someone in my position should have been doing. It was crazy stuff but I was craving acceptance so much that I must have thought that a public appearance in Kilkenny city would somehow grant it to me.

I was so naïve that I left my phone on that night. I hadn't closed an eye by 3.30am when I heard the phone vibrating on the locker beside me. It was David Herity's number on the screen. Herro wasn't on the panel. He was living in Dublin at the time.

I obviously wasn't going to answer but I remember looking at the phone and thinking, 'He's outside Copper Face Jacks now. He's either met a friend of mine, or some doll, and he's telling them that he knows the Kilkenny captain and, sure, for the craic, he will ring him.'

Fucking hell.

For a few minutes afterwards, my head was trying to picture what Herity was really at. Was he trying to impress some doll? Had he met a clubmate of mine? Or did the phone just go off in his pocket? The last one definitely didn't happen but my head was in such a mess that that's what I was thinking of instead of trying to switch off and relax.

I'd say it was close to 5am before I closed an eye. When I did, I got about three-and-a-half hours of scrappy, broken, fitful sleep. When my alarm went off, there weren't those few drowsy seconds before I remembered myself. I was just glad that the day was finally here. And then strains of anxiety kicked in. 'Jeez, it's really coming now.'

That thought overpowered everything about the day. The build-up to the match was a nightmare. I was sick with nerves. I just wanted to be at the other side of the match. Even if we had lost, and I had acquitted myself okay, I would have been happy.

Everything was a blur. I don't remember who I was sitting beside on the bus. I can't even recall which hotel we went to beforehand. It was almost like the fear was suppressing every other emotion and thought I had.

I never said a word in the dressing room before we went out onto the pitch. I didn't want to but even if I had tried, I wasn't physically able. Even that was bothering me. I was thinking, 'You're captain, you should be talking.' Deep down though, I knew if I did, I'd only have embarrassed myself like a blabbering idiot.

I was down to mark Neil Ronan but as soon as I took up my position after the national anthem, Ben O'Connor arrived into my corner for company. Holy fuck. I was shitting myself.

Up to that point of my career, my most difficult days had

been on speedy players who could take me on. Ben O'Connor though, was a different level to anyone else I had marked in terms of speed. I was nowhere near quick enough to survive if he got possession ahead of me. If Ben turned me close to goal, I was totally fucked.

I didn't want to be anywhere near Ben but all my biggest fears crystalised in front of me. On the biggest day of my life, the ultimate nightmare which I had always dreaded was now a real possibility. I was thinking, 'Here I am, 80,000 people in Croke Park, millions more watching, and I'm going to get scorched alive. The whole world will see me exposed. And the whole world will laugh at me.'

I spotted Neil Ronan going to the wing. I was half-tempted to follow him out and let Tommy pick up Ben. I couldn't. That would have been an immediate admission of weakness. I stood my ground and just set out to stay alive.

The first two balls that arrived in between us were poor quality for a forward. I got a flick on one. I cleared the other. Cork were struggling to generate any decent level of possession out the field. They couldn't afford to have Ben on the periphery of the play so they moved him out the field after ten minutes.

The game was purely about me trying to make it through unscathed. At one stage of the second half, the ball broke to me through a thicket of players. Nine times out of ten in that situation, you'd pick the ball and drive it up the field. I just let fly and pulled on it. The sliotar pinged straight back into the melee of players, hitting someone's leg and ricocheting off to the side. That play summed up my mindset. 'Keep the ball away from me. I don't want to know about it. Just survive for as long as you can without someone running at you, or taking you on.'

Cork substituted Neil Ronan after 40 minutes but my anxiety levels only increased when I saw who they were bringing on – Kieran 'Fraggie' Murphy. 'Fraggie' is one of my best friends. He's a very intelligent player. He knows my game inside out. 'Fraggie' always had the measure of me at CIT training. He knew it. I knew it.

As soon as our eyes met, he smiled at me. 'Fraggie' started pinching my arse. He was trying to get inside my head and unsettle me but I was already rattled far worse than he, or anybody else, realised.

I was totally freaked out by the time the first ball arrived in between us. I jumped on 'Fraggie' and gave away a stupid free. He engineered a point from the next ball. I was on the backfoot but the game was being played on our terms by that stage. We were six points ahead with less than ten minutes to play. Our half-forwards and midfielders were dropping back into our defence. There were bodies and extra layers of protection all around me. Cork's forwards had no room to move.

When they took off 'Fraggie' with five minutes to go and replaced him with Cian O'Connor, I couldn't believe my luck. I couldn't believe Cork's decision but I was finally able to relax a little. O'Connor was primarily a defender. He didn't have scorching pace. We had extra bodies back. For the first time, I actually started to think, 'Jeez, we actually could win this. It could really happen for me.'

Reality soon knocked all that optimism out of me. Niall McCarthy won a ball in the corner of the Hogan/Davin Stands, waltzed in around me before passing to Ben O'Connor outside him. Ben rattled the net. The deficit was down to three points.

To me, it was the self-fulfilling prophesy I had expected all along. When you convince yourself that something bad is going to happen to you on a pitch, it more than likely will. 'There you go,' I said to myself. 'You knew you were going to get scorched. Well, you just did.'

If Kilkenny had lost, I'd have been burned alive at the stake but we held out. When the final whistle blew, I was the most relieved man in Croke Park. The overriding emotion was of pure relief. I was just so glad that I had survived, that I hadn't been completely exposed. It was only when the crowd started coming onto the pitch that reality hit me. 'Holy Jesus, I'm after captaining Kilkenny to win an All-Ireland.'

The only time I had ever put any thought into that possibility was when the prospect of having to make a speech crept into my head. I was too afraid to even think about a speech. I just never saw myself having to make one on All-Ireland final day.

I was walking up the steps when I heard Micky Walsh, Tommy's father, roaring and shouting to a steward.

'Let that man in. Let than man in, his son is after captaining Kilkenny to win an All-Ireland.'

Micky grabbed my father and literally just threw him in over the barrier and beyond a wall of stewards in orange bibs. I just caught my father and we both started crying. No words were said. There was no need for any.

When I met Brian afterwards, he wrapped me up in a big embrace. He was nearly as relieved as I was. I got that sense from Brian, 'Jeez, I can't believe we got through that with you. I can't believe we got away with it.'

If we had lost that game, and it had been on my head, it would have been Brian's head which would have rolled. Years later, a close friend told me about some of the stuff he had heard said about the two of us that day. 'What the hell is Tyrrell doing out there? The only reason he's there is because he's a James Stephens man like Cody.'

If that thought was circulating around Croke Park that day, I'm sure it was in every club in Kilkenny. I would have been aware of that perception of me, and of my club connection to Brian, but I had too much going on in my head to even go there. I was already a nervous wreck. I didn't want to make myself even worse.

Captaining Kilkenny to an All-Ireland title is dreamland stuff but the build-up of stress and worry quickly siphoned the emotion and satisfaction out of the experience. I didn't really enjoy myself afterwards because I was so emotionally wiped. My body had almost shut down from the relentless stress of the previous three weeks.

About two years later, we were on the beer one night when I finally got around to asking Herity what he was up to ringing me at 3.30am the morning of an All-Ireland final. Herro said he has no recollection of making that phone call.

I'm still convinced he was trying to impress some doll in Coppers.

Perfect

'After a short 40-minute session in bitter, cold conditions in Dunmore, we have a brief team meeting. James McGarry calls out the team. JT in at number four. I am thrilled. I head to Langton's for the meal buzzing, texting Clare and Mam when I get there. I can't wait to pull on that Kilkenny number four jersey again.'

– Diary entry, Friday March 4th, 2016

I DIDN'T see it coming but hearing my name being called out was something special.

My mind was racing for the rest of the evening. This will be my first game for Kilkenny in eight months. It's been a long and arduous journey but the road has still taken me back to where I feel I belong – playing with Kilkenny, with that sacred number four jersey on my back.

I slept soundly. I was awake at 8am and followed my usual Saturday routine before a Sunday game; eat well, plenty of carbohydrates, hydrate well, and chill out. I called at home for Mam's ritual Saturday pre-game dinner, which I love.

We have a club meeting at 5pm where our new manager, and one of my best friends, Niall 'Bobs' Tyrrell, talks about a new tactic we are going to use this season – bunch and break. It looks and sounds interesting but my mind is miles away. As I watched the lads train afterwards, Brian Cody, who is also a club selector this year, comes over to me.

'Don't be hanging around in the cold now, Jackie,' he said. 'Rest up for tomorrow but be confident. Attack everything. Be fearless.' It was nice to hear but I was surprised because Brian has never approached me in that manner before a game with Kilkenny.

I left and met Brother Damien in Callan at 7pm. My body is in good shape but my mind is even better. I am relaxed. I am enjoying everything about the day. 'Tomorrow is the start of a new journey, so enjoy it,' said Brother Damien. 'No matter what happens tomorrow, this is just the beginning.'

'I slept great. I headed to mass in Foulkstown and got a number of good luck wishes from the locals. It was nice but it was even nicer to get that real sense of community. Father Whearty wishes me good luck at the front door as I leave. 'I'll be watching you,' he says. It almost feels like a debut again. I'm relaxed but slightly nervous. I return home, get my gear-bag, change into my Kilkenny kit and head to the Newpark Hotel, where we meet at 11.50am. We eat and chat before heading to Nowlan Park. I stretch and get a rub. When I receive the number four jersey, I pause and

look at it for a few seconds, really soaking up that feeling again, before pulling it on. After a shaky first ten minutes, I grow into the game and exert an influence against Galway, marking Cathal Mannion and Conor Whelan, before finishing up on Richie Cummins. None of them troubled me. My hurling and sharpness needs work but I am happy with where I'm at. I go to Brother D's after Langton's. I am shattered, especially after the adrenaline wears off me. He said I was good, and he challenged me to always be in the top three Kilkenny defenders. He also tells me that there are areas for me to improve on.'

– Diary entry, Sunday March 6th, 2016

When I got the all-clear on my foot from the surgeon in December 2015, I still hadn't full peace of mind. Was there risk of a recurrence having pushed my body so hard? Would I really come back to the same level? Would I have the same confidence again at the top level?

After that Galway game, all those concerns faded away like a scent in the breeze.

The whole day felt celebratory. I played well but I soaked up absolutely everything about the weekend; going to my mother's for dinner on the Saturday; heading out to Brother Damien later in the evening; packing my bag that night; the warm-up the following day; the nervous energy and anticipation in the dressing room beforehand.

I had put on a Kilkenny jersey hundreds of times before but that feeling was never as sweet.

Brother Damien had ingrained those words in me from the

outset of the season, 'Don't go back unless you are going to enjoy the year.' This is what it's all about. These are the days to treasure. These are the days I live for.

I finally felt back. I was shattered after the match but I remember thinking to myself, 'I can't wait for my body to be in absolute ribbons tomorrow, knowing that I have played a game for Kilkenny again.'

'My body aches today but I feel a little better after a rub, some foam-rolling, and a dip in the pool. I meet Padraig Walsh in the pool and we chatted about the game and how much training we will do tomorrow. I am ready for it because I aspire, I desire, I achieve. My goals are realistic and nourished with hard work, smart work, courage, trust, honesty, will-power and determination, so that they become reality. My achievements and happiness are a journey, not a destination. Difficulties and challenges break some men but not me.'

– Diary entry, Monday March 7th, 2016

'Success doesn't come to you…you go to it and allow it to happen. Achievement is sprung from desire, insatiable desire. That fuels my energy to be, to achieve, to win. I am JT. I don't imitate. Mental toughness. Physical toughness. Success has a price tag and it reads:
Trust
Honesty
Self-belief
Being powerful
Ruthless

In control
Pushing boundaries
Taking risks
On the edge
Even dangerous
I get what I want because I write my own permission slips.'
– Diary entry, Monday March 14th, 2016

'Clare and I are off for a few days so we head to Lahinch in County Clare where Davy Fitzgerald has organised for us to stay in his beach house, which is very good of him. He is very generous and people do not see that side to him. We go for a massage and I do an active recovery session in the pool after to revitalise my tired body. We go for a lovely meal in the Atlantic Hotel before heading back to the beach house. I listen to the waves crash on the beach outside before heading to bed early. BIG DAY TOMORROW.'
– Diary entry, Wednesday March 16th, 2016

One of the first times I saw Davy Fitzgerald up close, I thought it was a phantom. I was training with the LIT Fitzgibbon Cup team in Cratloe Woods in Clare. We were going there to annihilate ourselves running. We got a bus out to the torture chamber, where we were dropped off at the foot of a narrow forest path before making our way into the woods to begin the hardship.

It was early morning, at some ungodly hour. I was half asleep. We were all trudging up to this starting point when I suddenly saw this small, hooded figure appearing out through the blackness of the trees. It frightened the shit out of me until I realised it was Fitzy. I remember thinking, 'This guy is fucking nuts.'

He ran us into the ground that morning. I never experienced anything like it. Fitzy was watching us like a hawk, roaring and bawling at lads who were lagging behind, pushing us to the absolute limit. Cratloe Woods was a favourite haunt of his but Davy had other training venues that would turn your stomach with their very mention; a hill in Broadford in East Clare; the infamous hill in Shannon where Ger Loughnane and Mike McNamara used to flog Clare hurlers like slaves. Davy ran us up and down those hills so often that we nearly flattened them into the landscape.

Fitzy was a serious operator but some of the stuff we did was off the wall; US Navy Seals wouldn't be put through it. Fergus Flynn from Clare was so mentally disorientated from the torture one morning that he decided to break for home. Instead of turning and heading back up one of the horrendous hills on the trail, he veered off the track and made for his car. Nobody knew where Gussy had disappeared to. One of the lads living with Gussy eventually spotted him later that day in their house; he was strewn asleep across a couch, his gear still on and half a chocolate cake on the coffee table beside him.

It was commando stuff. We often trained three times a day; a hurling session on the astro-turf at 5am; another field session at 1pm; back for a running session at 7pm. We hadn't time for college in January because when we weren't training, we were trying to sleep and recover.

I was on the Kilkenny panel by then but this was a completely new world. Everything was ultra-professional. When we turned up to training, all we had to bring was our boots. Everything else was laid out for us; socks, togs, a training top and windbreaker jacket, a towel. Four bottles of shampoo were provided for every session for us to share. It took some level of logistical organisation for a college team but it was no issue; the backroom team was bigger than Mike Tyson's entourage.

There was an element of madness to the whole operation. Wolfe Tones Rebel songs would be blaring out in the dressing rooms before matches, to the backing track of Fitzy roaring and shouting like a lunatic. When we played home games, the heating pump for the showers in the opposition dressing room would be turned off, just to piss them off even more, especially after we'd beaten them.

Certain guys in the operation had specific duties. One fella, known as Briars, would stand behind the opposition goal and verbally abuse the goalkeeper throughout the game. Another fella would take up station behind the opposition dugout, or subs, and lob verbal hand grenades at them throughout the match.

At times, it was a complete circus but it was still a really well-run operation. We had a dietician when some inter-county teams still hadn't one. We had a sponsored van for gear and logistics when no other college had that resource. Davy had game plans for every scenario. He had a structure in place to enable us to try and get the best out of ourselves but the atmosphere was always dictated by Davy's belief that the world and its mother was against us.

Kieran 'Fraggie' Murphy and I had gone to LIT from CIT in the autumn of 2004, and LIT won their first Fitzgibbon Cup title the following March. We had a better team in 2006 but

Fraggie and I got suspended for ineligibility. We were both out on work experience – I was studying construction economics – and weren't qualified to play Fitzgibbon hurling that year. We played the first few games of the season but our cover was blown when a journalist broke the story of how we were working, and were never in college. Davy went nuts. He blamed someone in IT Waterford for tipping off the journalist.

That gave him a cause to sicken IT Waterford but he could find a crusade anywhere. When we played Waterford in Dungarvan in the Waterford Crystal League in 2007, Mossie O'Brien and Dan Shanahan spent the first half beating the shite out of each other. When Dan arrived in on me, the two of us went at it. A fist fight broke out. Dan hit me a cracker of a shot into the nose. I got the line but there was still blood dripping off my nose when I was in the ice baths afterwards. When Davy saw me, he went off on a tirade.

'Who do those fuckers think they are? They think they can bully us around? No-one will bully us!'

The match was over. It was a nothing game anyway but Davy was roaring and ranting as if we were just about to go out on the pitch to play an All-Ireland final. A year later, when Davy was Waterford manager, he tried to get Waterford to bully us in the All-Ireland final.

Davy was very clever and astute but there were times when the red mist descended and it clouded his judgement. He used to go crazy on the sideline. He could literally go nuts four weeks out from a game. He was stone mad for confrontation and aggression. Roughing up the opposition was a baseline requirement. Bernard Gaffney from Clare was a huge man but Davy was always on to him about being too soft, about not being aggressive enough. He told Gaffney before one match that unless he hit someone and started a fight, the whole lot of us would be forced to go running. It wasn't in Gaffney's nature to hit a fly but he knew he had no choice. If he didn't, we would have all probably kicked the shit out of him for inflicting more torture on us. Gaffney levelled some poor fella for nothing and started a full-scale brawl.

It was chaos but the whole operation was often chaotic. Davy would tell you one thing. Another one of his coaches could tell you to do the complete opposite. At half-time, they would all line up and have their say. They could come out with anything. Cyril Farrell was the only one who was consistent because he used to say the same thing every time 'There's more in ye,' Cyril would say. 'Tyrrell, there's more in you.'

When 'Fraggie' and I went back for our final year in 2006-07, we lived with Austin 'Aussie' Murphy from Clara. 'Aussie' had been on the Kilkenny panel for the 2006 All-Ireland final but he was intent on living the good life as soon as he went back to college that autumn. 'Fraggie' was LIT captain that year but we couldn't get 'Aussie' motivated.

He wouldn't train in the morning so the 5am and 6am sessions were a non-starter. 'Fraggie' would repeatedly tell 'Aussie' that he was on his last warning with Davy but 'Aussie' would just sit back, curling his hair with his index finger, and laughing it off.

I was sharing a room with 'Aussie' and I managed to convince him one night that unless he got up for the 6am session the following morning, Davy was going to arrive at the house and bate him out the door. 'Aussie' went to bed with all his gear on, a woolly hat covering his head, and his boots at the bottom of the bed. As soon as the alarm went off, he pulled the duvet back, rolled out of the bed, slipped into the boots and was gone out the door. I think he was still in a trance but he didn't give himself time to think about it, or the hardship awaiting him.

We walked the Fitzgibbon in 2007. We had a super team which included four future All-Stars; myself, Joe Canning, Conor O'Mahony and Shane McGrath. The finals weekend that year was on in Carlow and we beat NUIG by eight points in the decider. As we were heading back to Limerick to celebrate, I rang Brian Cody to check in with him. Straight away, he started talking business.

Kilkenny had lost their opening two league games. We had lads out injured and were playing Limerick the following weekend in a must-win game. Brian said we were training the following morning at 11am. He didn't openly say he wanted me and 'Aussie' there but I was under no illusions that he did.

When I told 'Aussie', he went off the rails. 'Fuck that. We're going on the beer hard tonight. You may ring Cody and tell him to get lost.'

I couldn't. I didn't want to go back but I just had to turn up. I had no collateral to bargain with. Four months earlier, I was the only one of the Kilkenny team not to get nominated for an All-Star. When I told 'Aussie' I was going back for training the following morning, you could see the devastation on his face. He knew that if I turned up and he didn't, that he was gone off the panel.

We worked out a plan. Eddie O'Sullivan, one of Davy's backroom team, said that he wouldn't drink and that he'd drive us to Kilkenny. We had a whale of a night. We ended up back at a party at Shane McGrath's house. I didn't get to bed until around 5.30am. When Eddie started ringing me a couple of hours later, I was still in a coma. Eddie eventually tracked us down and loaded the two of us into the car like a couple of corpses.

We were so broke up that we stopped off in an off-licence and bought a couple of bottles of Buckfast. We wanted to down them on the spot but we were so ropey that we couldn't risk any more alcohol in our systems. We left the bottles in Eddie's car and spent the whole session with our tongues hanging out, craving the tonic wine to soothe the deep burn at the back of our throats.

I don't know how we got through the session but we did. The number one priority was to steer clear of Brian so he wouldn't smell the liquor off us.

As soon as we got back into the car, the party started again. I was sipping the Buckfast when my phone rang. It was the gang in Limerick. They had bad news. Enda Fenton was reportedly in hospital. 'Chippy' was set to undergo an emergency operation. I couldn't believe it.

At the house party the previous night, I started wrestling with 'Chippy'. I thought I was Stone Cold Steve Austin. I jumped off a couch and body slammed 'Chippy' straight into the ribs. I had supposedly punctured one of his lungs.

It was a stitch-up but the boys nailed me good. I was shitting myself. They all started texting 'Aussie' to let him in on the gag. He kept it rolling, using the texts as a subterfuge for regular updates on 'Chippy' and his worsening condition. A lung transplant might be necessary. He may need dialysis.

I wasn't long sobering up. I was out of my mind with worry. I rang 'Chippy' ten times but I couldn't get him. 'Aussie' told me that the surgeons were probably operating on him. I stopped drinking. 'Aussie' told me to keep necking the bottles, that it would numb the anxiety. I couldn't. I was thinking, 'I'll have to get a loan to cover his medical expenses.'

I wanted Eddie to drop me off at the hospital but 'Aussie' convinced me to go to the pub first, to sink a couple of vodkas for the shock. He said 'Fraggie' was there, and that he would drive me to the Regional Hospital in Dooradoyle. As soon as I walked in the door, the place erupted. 'Chippy' was at the bar sipping his pint.

'You bastard,' I said to him.

'The boys robbed my phone,' he said. 'I couldn't do anything.'

Three months after Clare McCarthy and I first started going out, we went to Castle Park in Kilkenny one afternoon for a walk. We were strolling in the gates when we met Henry Shefflin, his wife Deirdre and their kids. I introduced Clare to Henry and Deirdre and we had a brief conversation.

'Who are they?' Clare asked afterwards. 'They are nice people.'

'That's Henry Shefflin.'

'Who is he?' she enquired. 'Does he play hurling?'

The first hurling match Clare attended was the drawn All-Ireland final in 2012. I got Clare two tickets, for herself and her friend Joanna. They were prime seats, bang-centre of the Cusack Stand. Joanna couldn't get over the tickets. 'Jeez, did Jackie sell his granny for these seats?' she asked Clare.

Neither of them had a clue. They arrived into Croke Park ten minutes after the match had begun, disturbing and annoying everyone around them as they tried to find their seats. This big Galway fella ate the head off them. 'Will ye sit the fuck down,' he roared in disgust.

Clare worked in Glanbia, who sponsored Kilkenny. She knew that I hurled for the county but that was as far as her knowledge of my hurling career extended. Clare is from Dublin and her family's background is soccer but as we became closer, Clare began to understand me, and how much Kilkenny hurling meant to me. She immersed herself more in that world when Clare moved to Kilkenny in 2014.

I love Clare so much. I knew from an early stage that she was the girl I wanted to marry. I wanted to propose to her in a unique setting. I love Irish history. I was thinking of 'Giants Causeway' on the north Antrim coast, or the Cliffs of Moher in Clare. When I mentioned those options to 'Fraggie' Murphy, he told me to ask Davy Fitz if I could use his beach house in Lahinch, which is only a few miles down the road from the Cliffs. When I did, Davy was fully obliging.

I drove to Dublin to meet Clare's parents, Paul and Kay, and asked them for their daughter's hand in marriage. Then I did some research on O'Brien's Tower, near the highest point of the Cliffs, the spot where I planned to ask Clare to marry me.

When we went to the Atlantic Hotel for a meal the night beforehand, I gave Clare a present of a bracelet to throw her off the scent. The following morning was bright and sunny. Perfect. We had breakfast at a nearby café. We got some coffee to go and headed for the Cliffs. I had the ring in my pocket and was anxious.

As we approached O'Brien's Tower, I noticed a group of people around the viewing area so I stalled and began staring out across the vast expanse of Atlantic Ocean.

When the group had walked on, I moved quickly. We had to pay €2 each at the bottom of the hill to get access up to the viewing area but I could only rustle €3 out of my pocket.

I told your man at the gate that I'd pay him on the way back. I didn't want to miss this chance when the place was clear of people.

My heart was thumping as we hiked up the hill. My palms were sweating. I was more nervous than before any All-Ireland final but when the moment felt right, I bent down on one knee and asked Clare to marry me. She was stunned but thrilled. She immediately agreed. We kissed and hugged. We were both emotional but ecstatic.

When we returned to the bottom of the hill, the guy at the gate was smiling. 'Congratulations,' he said.

'Wha? Who told you?' I asked him.

'Nobody. We saw the whole thing on the CCTV camera.'

We had a good laugh. When I went rummaging for the one euro I owed him, he told me it was on the house.

Some house. Some view. Perfect. Everything was, and is, perfect.

'I wake up this morning and smile as our engagement is the first thing that comes to mind. I love Clare and she makes me so happy. My mam and I head to visit my granny. I head to Brother D before training. I love this as it refocusses me, and Damien challenges me in a way I wouldn't challenge myself. We only do 30 minutes of drills in training and afterwards, Brian questions the panel on

*our standard and work rate and intensity this year. When
the team is named for Sunday's game against Dublin, I am
listed at number 17.*

*'I believe and act as it was impossible to fail. I may not be
the best but I do things that others see as impossible, so that
I will be the best.'*

– Diary entry, Friday March 18th, 2016

*'The 21 living Kilkenny captains are invited to attend a
fund-raiser in Gowran Park today. It's a nice thing to be
a part of for the older lads as it has a reunion feel about
it. When I said it to Brian after training on Tuesday, he
dismissed it and said that it was the county board getting
carried away with themselves. It doesn't bother me as
I use it to dress up, and to look and feel great. I bring
Mam out for the day and further milk the engagement
congratulations. I head to Brother D afterwards and leave
there in great mental and physical shape after a busy but
brilliant week.'*

– Diary entry, Saturday March 20th, 2016

*'I arrive in the Newpark Hotel to find out that I am starting
against Dublin. Brian called me aside to give me the great
news. Paul Murphy has a crick in his neck. I was coughing
hard in the dressing room when Brian came over and asked
me if I was alright. I said I was, even though I wasn't. I
have a chest cold. I don't feel physically great but my mind
and attitude is in such a good place that it is a risk that I
want to take. I start well. After 15 minutes, they take Mark
Schutte off me and move their in-form forward, Eamonn
Dillon, on me. Although Padraig (Walsh) is in front of
me, and is the best player on the field, Dublin make a
clear attempt to try and expose me. They pepper my side*

of the field with balls but I handle it. I stand up and hold Dillon. He won a few balls off me and scored one point but, ten minutes into the second half, they moved Dillon into full-forward. I play well. I attack the ball and have a real presence in our defence. With ten minutes to go, I feel my left hamstring tighten. I signal to the sideline to take me off. Shane Prendergast replaces me to a huge ovation. I really enjoy the applause. Kilkenny fans really seem to have warmed to me. I feel that there is a real connection there because they appreciate me and my efforts. After Langton's, I head to Brother D for some work and some feedback, which is mainly positive. We don't have a match for two weeks now so Clare and I head to join up with my team-mates in Kytlers for celebratory drinks late into the night.'

– Diary entry, Sunday March 21st, 2016

We won. I performed well. It felt so good to be playing with Kilkenny again but, if I'm to be brutally honest, it was the first time I was half-hoping that I wouldn't have to wear the Kilkenny jersey.

My preparations weren't great coming into the game. It had obviously been an emotionally charged week. I'd had a few drinks on the Wednesday night. We spent the Thursday night celebrating with our families. They were drinking champagne. The house was buzzing. I was half-tempted to clear them out of the house as the clock ticked after 11pm but I couldn't. I was in bed by 12.30am, which is way past my normal routine, especially the week of a match. We had friends in again on Friday night.

So many late nights in succession, along with the emotion of the week, probably left my immune system slightly exposed, which surely contributed to me picking up the chest cold. It may have also been a factor in me twinging my hamstring.

For a few moments, the maniac inside my head started staring at me in the mirror. 'Did you overdo it? Could you have planned your engagement at a different time of the year, when Kilkenny didn't have a league game that week?'

I eyeballed him straight back. No. I wanted to get engaged this week. I wanted to do it this way. It was perfect. It was one of the best weeks of my life.

Ruthless Machine

'Bring out the best in me. Bring out the worst in me. Non-training day today so I do a ball-alley session. I update my food diary and email Noreen (Roche – dietician), who was looking for it. My body and mind feel good today. I am in good form as I head to the Newpark Hotel for a GPA (Gaelic Players Association) meeting.

Noel Connors, Seamus Hickey, Siobhan Early, Joey Holden, Bucks, Lester, Fog, Joycey and myself discuss current issues and discussions with the GAA about increased funding (5-10%). Hickey chairs a formal meeting. I sit and mainly observe. I take two things from it – the GPA do a lot of great work for GAA players; the second is that we are very well looked after in Kilkenny. Siobhan texted me later that evening thanking me for being there.'

– Diary entry, Thursday April 14th, 2016

EDDIE Brennan was brilliant in the 2005 All-Ireland semi-final against Galway. Kilkenny lost but Eddie almost rescued an impossible situation. He scored 2-4 from play. One of those points should have been another goal. He could have had two more points. He showcased the assassin mentality that later defined Eddie as one of the greatest goalscorers of his generation.

Eddie appeared set to take off after that Galway match but then he disappeared for the first six months of the 2006 season. Eddie did hard time on the bench during Kilkenny's seven-game march to that league title, only featuring against Antrim and Laois. When Kilkenny used 19 players in our Leinster semi-final win against Westmeath, Eddie wasn't one of them.

A few days later, he went to Brian and asked for a personal hearing. Cody was possibly playing mind games with him but he challenged Eddie with the prospect of a new role at half-forward. Eddie immediately re-invented himself as a hard-working wing-forward, totally reconstructing his game for the rest of that 2006 season.

Eddie went on to become one of the most productive forwards of his generation but Brian did more than just test him, and play mind games for the first six months; he was also teaching him, and everyone else, a lesson.

Brian walked into the dressing room during training one evening at the outset of 2006 and Eddie was handing out GPA forms for the players' union. Eddie was the Kilkenny GPA rep for years. He was only doing his job but it didn't sit well with Brian. Eddie was lucky that he was only benched for half a season because if Cody feels you are threatening the stability of the group, or tampering with the group dynamic, you're dicing with a life sentence as an inter-county player on his watch.

Brian was never sold on the GPA. He never came out and said it but he didn't need to. It was obvious to everyone else why Eddie had been sidelined. Lads quickly did the maths. It may have been the making of Eddie but it also transmitted a loud message to the rest of us that you didn't mess with Cody's authority.

The GAA and GPA operate under the same umbrella now but when they were separate bodies, Brian never went to the GPA All-Stars.

You'd always see most other inter-county managers at those banquets but Cody's consistent absence was his way of telling us that he had no time for the players body.

Any time you were talking to Paul Kinsella, when he was county board chairman, or Ned Quinn, the Kilkenny secretary, you were left in no doubt as to Cody's stance on the GPA. Similar to how he perceived the media, he viewed the GPA as a potential danger and risk to the stability of our ecosystem. And anything which threatened that harmony and spirit was ruthlessly policed.

Brian's first real experience with the GPA was before my time but it clearly left a mark on him. The GPA was still only in its infancy but was beginning to flex its muscles during the spring of 2002 when they went looking to make a symbolic gesture on the issue of players' rights and welfare. Before the league final in Thurles, it was suggested that Kilkenny and Cork would wear their jerseys hanging outside their shorts and socks down around their ankles during the pre-match parade. A lot of the Cork players were gung-ho on the protest but when the

Kilkenny squad had an internal debate on the issue the Friday night before the game, Cody buried it.

Andy Comerford was the only Kilkenny player who engaged in the harmless protest, along with half the Cork team. Nobody backed Andy. Lads were too afraid. It was natural for Cork to have felt isolated when it came to making the protest but that isolation hardened into criticism when Kilkenny won by one point.

The whole business left a sour taste in Cork's mouths towards Kilkenny afterwards. It never bothered us. We honestly didn't give a shite what Cork thought about us. We had plenty of other stuff to be focussing on.

We had no other choice. After Galway bullied Kilkenny in the 2001 All-Ireland semi-final, Brian thought the team had become soft after winning the 2000 All-Ireland. Cody swore that would never happen to one of his teams again. It never did.

Brian was a different animal in 2002. He became supremely focussed, more clinically and ruthlessly minded. That's how he always wanted Kilkenny to be. If Brian felt a protest was a distraction, nobody was going to question his approach.

That set the tone of the Kilkenny mindset towards the GPA but the route they were taking towards creating a better welfare state for players was largely irrelevant to us anyway.

We were happy with our lot. We were very well looked after by the Kilkenny County Board. We felt we had everything we needed. We recognised the GPA were there for the good of all players. Life did change for those players because of what Cork and the GPA did but we never bothered with that cause.

It was a selfish attitude but we didn't give a fuck. The only cause we had was to mow everyone down who stood in our way of winning more All-Irelands.

That is the selfish and single-minded mentality required to survive in Cody's Kilkenny. And it was the mindset which consistently kept us on top.

Because of our profile and success, many of us were still attractive, and necessary, brand ambassadors for the GPA. Some lads did well out of the players' body but, in our minds, we still felt that we only needed ourselves.

I'm sure Brian is more open to the GPA's ideas now given how well the organisation has developed. The GPA needed to adopt a certain attitude of militancy in those early days but hitching our carriage to that train was viewed as a potential obstacle to where we intended to go, where we wanted to go, and where we ultimately did go.

I was talking to a fella in work one afternoon in October 2009 when he asked me if I'd heard what Donal Óg Cusack had called Kilkenny in his book.

'The Stepford Wives,' he said.

'Wha'?' I asked. 'Who the hell are they?'

Nobody had iPhones at the time so I looked it up on the internet when I went home. It was a thriller satirical novel, the story based around a young mother who begins to suspect that the frighteningly submissive housewives in her new idyllic Connecticut neighbourhood may be robots created by their husbands. In Cusack's mind, we were all submissive robots controlled by Cody.

'The more strife we have in Cork, the more pointedly 'of the establishment' Kilkenny seem to become,' he wrote in his autobiography. 'The more disorder there is in Cork, the more Kilkenny likes to be thought of fondly as the land of milk, honey and contentment. The GAA's version of the Stepford Wives.'

Apart from Eddie, Donal Óg said he didn't like us. We didn't like Donal Óg and Cork. Deep down, we respected them because they were a good team but we always knew we were better than them after 2006.

The two groups had been on different journeys long before then. They had their reasons for going on strike but we still thought that they lost sight of what hurling was really all about. They had the balls to stand up to their county board but my attitude was, 'Have ye the balls to stand up to us?'

Some of them did but our mood and disposition towards Cork was still always cold and clinical. 'Ye can strike all ye want. Ye can do whatever the fuck ye want but this is about hurling. And we will show ye what that's all about.'

Even when they were in the trenches, we always skewed our attitude towards Cork to suit ourselves. Because those strikes were so high-profile and acrimonious, the Cork players were getting huge airtime. We would see some fella on TV and think, 'Who the fuck is this lad? What the hell has he ever done?'

We had lads with four or five All-Ireland medals and the general public wouldn't even know what they looked like. That was mostly our fault but we were happy to keep our army faceless once we kept trampling over everybody else on our relentless crusade.

It didn't take us long to blow Cork out of the water. We always felt they wanted to project this aura of ultimate professionalism, to propagate this myth that they were better prepared than anybody else. To us, it was just a mystique that we wanted to tear apart.

Seán Óg Ó hAilpín was their poster boy but was he really as professional as someone like Henry Shefflin? Did they all really have the balls for the battle once we started ramping up the physicality?

We had a chip on our shoulder towards Cork and the message they always wanted to transmit, of the image of elitism they were continually seeking to purport. When they started keeping to themselves on All-Stars trips, we were thinking, 'Who the hell do these lads think they are? Do they think they are better than everyone else? Do they really think they are better than us?'

They may not have intended to come across that way but that was our read on their collective personality. They had some great players but, if anything, we scorned how they went about their business. It suited us to believe that a lot of it was forced.

The morning after Cork won the 2005 All-Ireland final, Seán Óg went for a run. He happened to come across a pack of journalists in the hotel lobby, which was a convenient hook for their story when Seán Óg stopped for an interview. Seán Óg doesn't drink. He was a machine who trained every day of the year.

The day after an All-Ireland final was just another one of those days but to us it looked like another contrived attempt to market Cork as the brand leaders of all things professional.

We thought it was all bullshit. None of us felt the need to get up the morning after an All-Ireland final, put on our shorts and tell the world and its mother that we were going for a run. Some of us still probably hadn't yet seen a bed. Seán Óg was the ultimate athlete. Maybe he didn't anticipate the media being in the lobby but we portrayed it as another strand of the inflated picture Cork were painting of themselves.

I jumped on every opportunity. Brian Corcoran said he always intended to retire at the end of 2006. His club, Erins Own, reached that year's Munster club final but Corcoran said he was staying faithful to that promise, even if Erins Own won and advanced to an All-Ireland semi-final the following February. Corcoran didn't have to worry about any potential conflict when Erins Own narrowly lost to Toomevara.

Maybe he would have changed his mind if they had won but we went to town on the very fact of a potential decision in that situation. 'What do these lads really stand for?' I would rhetorically ask myself.

We played on all that stuff. If we got a chance to stick it to Cork, we'd give it to them harder than anyone else. They had been on top of us for a couple of years but once we took over from them in 2006, we made it our business to keep them down.

When we met them in the 2008 All-Ireland semi-final, we didn't just want to beat them – we wanted to set them back for a decade. They may have been getting notions about themselves but we weren't long putting those ambitions out of their heads.

They had some great men but we believed that a lot of their main leaders, Seán Óg, Donal Óg, Diarmuid O'Sullivan, Joe Deane, were finished by then. They were in their 30s by that stage. We were in our prime with a largely young team. When they couldn't take us down in 2006, they certainly weren't going to manage it in 2008.

We were never hung up on trying to find an edge in motivation on the opposition but we never had any trouble in sourcing that fuel before we met Cork. When they came with their running/ possession game in the 2000s, they were rightly playing to their strengths. They were tailoring their game to the players they had at their disposal but we never looked at it in those terms.

We had an attitude of, 'Why won't Cork come out and play us 15 on 15? Are ye that scared of us? Ye came up with this game because ye haven't got the balls to take us on man for man. And when it comes down to it, we will blow ye out of the water anyway.'

We did when we met them again in the 2010 championship. Donal Óg's comments weren't even a factor for us by then. It hardly even triggered a reaction from Kilkenny. Cork were gone, or were close to that team being finished. We had no need to get dragged into a verbal war over something that didn't even bother us. If we were robots, as Donal Óg suggested, we had no problem turning into Terminators and exterminating that team for good.

Brian never even brought that stuff into our dressing room. Even when Ger Loughnane often had a pop at us over the years, he never made an issue out of something he felt didn't deserve any airtime. There was no point, or need, for us to take offence with Donal Óg's comments in 2010 because we had already dished out the mother and father of all beatings to them the previous year.

By the time Cork rolled into Nowlan Park in March 2009, they had just emerged from their third players strike. I think it was more a collective Kilkenny mentality than just the mood within our camp but there was a genuine disdain by then for Cork and what those players stood for. We didn't just want to beat Cork that day – we wanted to trample them into the ground like dirt. Before we left the dressing room, someone encapsulated the cold-blooded and clinical feeling in our collective heart. 'If we get a chance, let's bury these fuckers.'

Once we got on top early, that impulse and desire to keep nailing them was propelled by the crowd who were baying for blood. They kept pushing us on for more and we gladly responded to the mood of the mob. Another county would have let up. We never would.

We took great satisfaction out of hammering Cork but we wanted to beat the shite out of everyone. We wanted to embarrass players. To mentally dominate them. A common phrase in our dressing room was, 'Let's put hurling out of these fellas' heads for a long time.' That basically translated into, 'Let's psychologically scar these fuckers so much that when they come up against us in the championship, they'll run from us.'

We had the mentality of assassins. We'd leather the living shite out of a team and it wouldn't even register with us. We'd be cold-blooded about the manner of the kill. All we were thinking was, 'Who have we next? Who is next up for the slaughter.'

We operated like a crazed army. We didn't give a shit about anyone. We were waging a war and anyone who stood in our path was just blown out of our way. The bigger the massacre, the better we felt. The more destruction we wreaked, the greater the high.

If we won by ten points this week, we'd want to win by 15 the following week. We wouldn't openly say it as a team but it was how we all felt. If we felt we had a team on the rack at half-time, we'd go out to murder them in the second half. 'Their heads are going now. Let's put hurling out of their heads.'

For sure, we did. Before the 2008 All-Ireland final, we had a beef with Waterford over how some of their players reacted after beating us in the 2007 League final. It was their first national title in decades. They were entitled to celebrate wildly afterwards. They didn't boisterously ram it down our throats but that's the way we contrived it.

I remember seeing John Mullane up on the podium without his jersey. That was just classic Mullane. He threw his jersey into the Waterford crowd after the 2002 Munster final. When I saw him bare-chested that day in 2007, I stored that image in my head for another day. 'The next time I run into Mullane, he will have his jersey off alright,' I said to myself. 'Because by the time we're finished with Waterford, Mullane will be too embarrassed to be wearing that jersey.'

They all were. When we met Waterford in the 2008 All-Ireland final, we put hurling out of the heads of some of their players for a long time. Ken McGrath said in his TG4 'Laochra Gael' programme that he was never the same player after that match. Ken was a superb hurler but he never recovered from that hiding. We did what we set out to achieve that day – to win and to psychologically scar in the process.

Before that game, a song was going around Waterford called 'Don't Stop Believin'. It was the same music and words to the original song of the same title by the US rock band 'Journey', interspersed with a series of player interviews and match-day commentaries.

That song was played everywhere but we were intent on playing a different tune. Everyone in Waterford, especially the players, had stopped believing after ten minutes when we already had them gutted like a fish.

We scored 3.30 that day, the same time the game began. And the same time the match finished.

Every year we came back after winning an All-Ireland, the same questions were always asked.

'Can Kilkenny have the same hunger this year?'

'How can they get any better than last year?'

'Are they regressing a small fraction?'

To us, those questions were always pointless. Irrelevant. Our attitude was always the same. 'That was last year; we will be even better this year. We will be stronger. Our younger players will be more experienced.'

When we were on a roll, we felt invincible. That buzz would course through your veins like a narcotic. And we all got off on it. I know I did.

Trouncing a big team, especially in Nowlan Park, was a euphoric sensation. And you just wanted more. We all wanted to be stuck right bang in the middle of it.

I never wanted to come off in league matches. I played as hard in the 65th minute as I did in the first minute. I wanted to play as many of those games as possible. We all did. Winning was the drug but hammering teams extended the high. And the starting jersey provided access to everything.

It was also the juice which kept the machine rolling at an obsessive and relentless rate. That day we hammered Cork in 2009, Henry only came on as a sub. If you were a peripheral player who had scored three or four points by the 55th minute, of course you were going to keep the pedal pressed to the accelerator for as long as you could. You couldn't think any other way given the names who were sitting on the bench.

Our forwards fed off that. They knew when a team was on the rack. They could sense when a defender was vulnerable. Other players would have backed off if their team was leading by 20 points. To us, it was another opportunity to cut loose, to maybe score seven or eight points to store some good form in the bank to impress Brian.

Goals killed teams and we were able to get goals so easily. Green flags were the poison in our bite. We ruthlessly pursued goals to kill teams early. In three successive All-Ireland finals between 2007 and 2009, we scored two goals inside two minutes. And on all three occasions, that two-goal burst effectively ended the game like the mark of an assassin; a bullet to the sternum, followed by one to the head to finish the job off.

Those devastating unanswered scoring bursts were the perfect emblem of our efficiency but we had serious assassins up front. As a set of defenders, we always had huge faith in our forwards, both in their capacity to kill, and to survive anyone trying to hunt them down. We didn't have to overthink our game and style of play. We had the luxury of thinking: 'Just get the ball down there, as long and as high as possible. It doesn't matter because those boys will win it.'

If they didn't secure possession cleanly, they'd all fight like dogs for the scraps on the ground. And if they didn't, they'd hook and block and tackle and torment the opposition defenders so much that it made it easy for us as defenders to deal with any ball coming our way.

We had the opposition on the run so often that games sometimes felt easy. I always believed I had much more in me. I remember being substituted once when we were ahead by about 15 points. I had played well but I couldn't bask in that enjoyment because my mentality wouldn't allow me to. I was worried that the guy who replaced me would play well. He might show Brian something that he liked. He might start ahead of me the next day.

There was no need for me to be thinking that way. I had played all the league games up to that point of the season. I was playing well but there was such a rich and decorated stock of defenders on the bench that I rarely had peace of mind.

I was never comfortable. I could never relax. I never felt able to take the foot off the gas. You'd look at other lads like JJ Delaney who could always take it in their stride but I could never bring my mind around to that way of thinking. If I did, I'd feel it signalled weakness.

I was always a thinker. I heavily analysed my own performance. There were times when that self-analysis, that constant unease, did mentally grind you but everything was overridden by winning. The enjoyment came from winning. And hammering teams made it even sweeter again.

When we were at our peak, and punishment beatings were a routine part of our ruthless operation, we felt that the pick of three or four teams wouldn't have beaten us. That stemmed from everyone; management, players. Every time we beat some team well, it just fed the monster even more. The thirst and craving for more blood became even greater. Some of the best hurlers in the game at the peak of their powers, brilliant lads on the bench, all fused with an unbreakable belief.

That indestructible combination was created by Brian. He knew we were the best and he galvanised us with that confidence and conviction in a subtle but convincing manner. 'Whoever is out there, we'll take them all on,' he would say. 'Any opposition, referees, Croke Park, whoever, we will beat them all.'

Brian said it with such conviction that we never doubted him for a second. If referees or the suits in committee rooms were looking for a way to take us down, or dilute our power in some way, we'd only ramp it up even more. Nobody, anywhere, was going to stop our crusade towards greatness.

We left so much collateral damage during that crusade that people often said we were bad for the game. Our domination was deemed to be destroying hurling. We mentally destroyed a player like Ken McGrath, and plenty more with him. That was a sad way for Ken to finish up but we didn't care about anyone, or anything. The opposition were our enemy and our enemy was there to be annihilated.

Ken's Waterford were a good team but they never won an All-Ireland. They still had something different about them. Many of their best players – John Mullane, Dan Shanahan, Eoin Kelly – expressed rather than suppressed their free-spirited tendencies. Their spontaneity summed up their uniqueness, their distinctive character. In time, hurling people will recall those qualities more so than their medals but medals were the only currency that ever mattered to us.

Does that chunk of metal dictate legacy and how a team will be remembered?

A bag load of them certainly does.

Were those Cork and Waterford players more recognisable, and more appealing, to the wider hurling public than the ruthless and faceless Kilkenny army that just wanted to kill and maim all around them?

We didn't care what anyone thought, or how they perceived us. If the media didn't like us, great. If referees wanted to see us beaten, we'd still find a way to win. If the whole GAA population are sick and tired of us and want to see us beaten, we couldn't have cared less. That was our attitude, full stop.

If people hated us, they hadn't the guts to come out and say it to any of us. If someone came up to me and said, 'Yere a boring shower of bastards, ye are ruining the game,' I would have nearly got off on it.

We had some great characters. We just never publicly revealed that character. That mystery and silence added more layers to our mystique as a team. We kinda loved the fact that everyone was pissed off with us. We loved it even more that we were going to keep pissing everyone off because we were going nowhere.

Our ambition was to take over hurling completely, to wipe the board with everyone. Enemies were lining up everywhere. And we just wanted to keep shooting until there was nobody left standing.

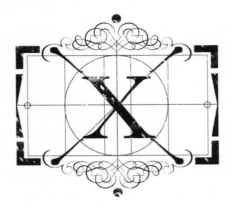

Our Way

'For the first time, Kilkenny start using GPS devices on players during training.'

– Diary entry, Tuesday April 26th, 2016

O N the Tuesday night before we played Waterford in the first round of the league in February 2016, the floodlights crashed in Dunmore during the warm-up. Mick Dempsey had told us beforehand of what he had planned for the session but the sheet with ball drills and possession games had to be ripped up. And we just went running.

Denis 'Rackard' Cody, our kit man, pulled up his van to the side of the pitch and turned on the lights as a backup. I was running beside Diarmuid Cody but I couldn't see where I was going half the time. When we went up to the top end of the pitch, away from 'Rackard's' generator, it was nearly like running with a blindfold on. 'Here we are,' I thought to myself, 'one of the most successful teams in Irish sport running around in the dark with car lights to guide us.'

In a unique kind of way though, it was a neat metaphor for who we are, for how we go about our business. In Kilkenny, nobody takes you by the hand, nobody guides you through the dark. You are always expected to find your own way.

The rawer and more primal the conditions are, the more Brian Cody likes it. Nobody is fed with a silver spoon on a gold platter. Our setup and approach is very basic. Much of that attitude may be driven by cost-saving but it suits Brian's methods. It is the culture and environment he wants to promote.

Mick Dempsey has cleverly constructed the professional apparatus around which much of our success has been framed but I'd say if Brian had his way, he probably wouldn't bother with half the paraphernalia attached to modern inter-county squads. I'm sure Mick often has to battle with Brian to introduce more modern methods. Most inter-county squads have been using GPS tracking data for years but we have finally only got around to using it now.

In the march towards a more professional outlook and appearance, Kilkenny always seem to be behind everyone else. We were the last county to wear a tight-fitting jersey. I'm sure we were the last county to get our initials on our training tops. We are only told to wear our training tops on a media evening, or an open night to the public. After that, you can wear whatever you want to training. Tommy Walsh often used to arrive out on the field with an auld woolly jumper. It was so thick it looked like it had been sheared straight off the back of a sheep.

We don't have our gear neatly laid out for us before training. Or a towel and a bottle of shampoo. Many inter-county teams now only have to show up with their boots and hurleys. I experienced that culture as far back as ten years ago with LIT. It's framed around the approach that players don't have to worry about anything else, only hurling, but I wouldn't want it that easy. I can wash my own gear. I can buy my own shampoo. I don't even know what some lads need shampoo for. A share of them only have a few ribs of hair left.

Brian has never had any truck with early morning sessions but our approach has always been steady and consistent. We always do the same warm-up drill in Croke Park. Lads pucking across the pitch in twos, before breaking into a first-touch drill in small groups. Unlike every other team in the country, we never do any small-sided conditioned games during our warm-up. You never see a bollard or a cone on our side of the pitch in Croke Park before we play the biggest game of the year. Some club junior teams look more sophisticated than us before matches but it works for us.

Personal discipline and personal responsibility is everything because feedback is always sporadic. After a body-screening test at the start of the year, the physios will tell you what areas you need to focus on to keep your body in shape. Our weight and body fat is regularly measured and monitored. We weigh in before and after training now. Urine samples are regularly taken. We go down to IT Waterford every six weeks for Dexa scans, where we lie on this bed for eight minutes as the arm of this scanning machine goes over our whole body to measure muscle mass, BMI and body-fat percentage.

The level of science and planning nutrition sky-rocketed over the course of my career. Noreen Roche, our dietician, has always been a key part of our setup but it still comes back to personal responsibility to get yourself in the shape required to play at this level for Kilkenny. Brian doesn't need the printout from a Dexa scan to tell him you're off the pace. He'll see that himself in the cauldron of Nowlan Park.

Our statistical analysis has really been stepped up in the last couple of years. Mick Dempsey brought in these two girls from Carlow IT, Emma and Louise, who collate and download the match data for us. They only recently introduced us to Hudl, a website where you can log on to view individual and team footage which the girls have gathered and uploaded.

It is far more professional than what we did in the past but Brian still has an ambivalent attitude towards stats. When he does look at data, the only real numbers he wants to see are our hooks-blocks-tackle count. In his eyes, that's the best measurement of the savagery and intensity he demands.

Most inter-county setups were kitted out with teams of statisticians and match analysts by the end of the last decade but Martin Fogarty first introduced us to the most basic concept of video analysis in 2011.

Three weeks before that year's All-Ireland final, Fogarty handed me a DVD of Lar Corbett. Lar went into that match as the hottest ticket in town but I used that 12 minutes of footage to forensically study the minutia of Lar's game; his movement, how he attacked the ball, how he liked the ball to be delivered into him.

The information was given to me but it wasn't rammed down my throat either. Martin's attitude almost was, 'Here's some footage on Lar, watch it if you want.' Martin or Brian never asked me afterwards if I did. Not too many other players were given that individual information either, primarily because our attitude was plain and simple. 'Man up and win your own battle.'

When we went man-for-man again in the 2012 drawn All-Ireland final against Galway, and got opened up in the first half, I knew I could have gone to Martin before the replay and asked him for footage to study Damien Hayes. I didn't bother. Fogarty never offered it. I knew I had to man up and get the job done.

That is what is expected of us. We don't feel we need video analysis as an instructional tool to tell us what is required. If anything, that was how Fogarty sometimes used video analysis – to publicly nail fellas. TJ Reid was completely pissed off after being taken off early in the 2012 Leinster final. When he was dropped for the All-Ireland quarter-final against Limerick, TJ was thinking of jacking it all in until Henry talked him out of it. On a training weekend in Carton House before the All-Ireland semi-final against Tipperary, Martin was taking us through some video clips when he told TJ he had picked one out specially for him. It showed TJ chasing back a Galway player in the first half of the Leinster final. TJ stuck with the player for five yards before he started drifting away in another direction. There was a big laugh in the room. TJ laughed too but it was only a front to conceal the embarrassment. Fogarty subtly delivered his message. TJ scored 2-2 from play against Tipperary. He ended the season with his first All-Star.

TJ manned up but that was just what was expected of him. Nobody else was going to take him by the hand. We have a ferocious team spirit but we all understand the importance of winning our own individual battle. We never bother with a huddle before the throw-in. We don't link arms in a line for the national anthem. Our management and subs don't group together on the sideline. We just never bought into this 'Band of Brothers' mentality that most teams seek to foster. We don't care about what anyone else is doing. We just do it our way.

Denis Cody has always been known as 'Rackard'. He has carried the nickname with him since scoring a goal in a schools match, when someone compared him to Nicky Rackard, the Wexford hurling legend of the 1950s.

I don't know what age he is but 'Rackard' could nearly have hurled with his namesake because he is almost 40 years in the job as Kilkenny kit man.

It's his life. Any evening we are training, you will always see 'Rackard' in his black van around the city from lunchtime. He will pick up hurleys from Dowlings. He'll stock up the van with water, energy drinks, protein bars and fruit. He has a place for everything; spare gear, training tops, hurling grips, Jaffa Cakes. He even has his own unique way of communicating. He calls me 'Pakie'. He calls other lads 'Snoz'. Don't ask me why.

'Rackard' guards everything with a disciplined frugality. He always has a box full of Karakal hurling grips but he minds them like a bag of gold coins. I got two new hurleys recently and I asked 'Rackard' for a couple of grips.

'Where are they?' 'Rackard' asked.

'They're at home.'

'No hurls, no grips, pal,' he replied.

That is the standard response from 'Rackard'. He has to see the ash in front of him before he parts with the goods. It's the same with the tubs of protein powder. You'd hear stories of lads from other counties stocking them up at home like a gym but 'Rackard' polices everything in Kilkenny with absolute efficiency and accountability.

If you request protein powder in our dressing room, you have to sign a sheet and write the date down, along with the serial number of the tub, before 'Rackard' hands it over. If you go looking for more of the powder again sooner than 'Rackard' expects, he'll ask you if you're taking too much of the stuff, just like our dietician Noreen Roche might investigate. You'd imagine that 'Rackard' was buying it out of his own pocket but that is how things are done in Kilkenny. Nobody gets anything easy. Nothing is wasted or casually frittered away. Everything is accounted for.

'Rackard' has always been Kilkenny's chief accountant on the ground, with everything. When we win the All-Ireland, he minds the Liam MacCarthy Cup. If you want to book the cup for an event, the booking invariably goes through 'Rackard'. When some of us are asked to present medals, 'Rackard' will often ferry us around so that we can have a few drinks. He is even prepared for crowd control. 'Rackard' has this flasher light on his van, for what I don't know. He plugs it into the cigarette lighter and off it goes.

He loves the status he has in Kilkenny. He is the man. A few years ago, he brought out a DVD entitled 'Rackard is the Man'. The song was written by a fellow Graignamanagh man, Seán Hoare, who was a member of the famous Barrow Boys band years ago. It was performed by the Celtic Cats, two of whom, Danny and Bob Grace, are also from Graignamanagh. The idea behind the DVD was to turn Kilkenny's All-Ireland successes of the last 15 years into a fundraiser for sick children in Our Lady's Hospital in Crumlin.

Featuring original behind-the-scenes footage from our All-Ireland wins, and the traditional visits to Crumlin Hospital the day afterwards, the song was especially poignant as it was written by Seán just three months before his death. Already, Rackard's DVD had raised up to €10,000 for Crumlin Hospital.

That says a lot about 'Rackard' but it also speaks volumes for the type of people Brian Cody wants around his setup, of the deep trust he has in key personnel.

As the game has become more professional, some backroom teams have swollen to more than 30, each with a specific logistical duty. Brian, though, has always kept a relatively tight support structure around the team. Key people perform more than one function but 'Rackard' performs multiple tasks. When we go away on training weekends, our whole logistical operation is 'Rackard' and his black van.

In 2006, we went to Monart Hotel and Spa in Wexford for a training weekend. We were all in the pool afterwards for a recovery session when we asked 'Rackard' to join us. He went out to the van and got a pair of 36" white togs. They had black and amber stripes down the sides but they were as see-through as a white paper bag.

There were a couple of girl lifeguards on duty and they were beside themselves laughing at how exposed 'Rackard' was. We were all trying to keep ourselves in check though because 'Rackard' was swanning around the place like Jay-Z at his own private pool.

We don't know where we'd be in Kilkenny without 'Rackard' because everyone loves him. When Tommy Walsh called time on his inter-county career at the end of 2014, he name-checked only one person from Kilkenny's backroom staff in his departing speech – 'Rackard' Cody.

'Rackard' is the Man.

Mick Dempsey is a football man from Laois. His mother was from Offaly. His five uncles hurled for Offaly. One of them, Matt, refereed All-Ireland hurling finals in 1958 and 1972. The family had a connection and interest in hurling but football was naturally Dempsey's game. He won six senior club championships with St Joseph's. He played for the Laois senior footballers for nearly 20 years, winning a league title in 1986.

Work brought him to Kilkenny. In 2000, he bought Shem Lawlor's, a long established and popular pub in John Street in the city. Mick had already built up an impressive CV as a football coach and as soon as he landed in Kilkenny, clubs began to seek out his services. He coached the Kilkenny minor footballers before Martin Fogarty recruited him as physical trainer for the Kilkenny U-21s, which won All-Irelands in 2003 and 2004. At the end of that season, Brian Cody came calling.

Brian may not have known what he was getting but nobody is in any doubt now as to the impact Dempsey has had on Kilkenny's success. His legacy continues to grow stronger all the time.

Mick O'Flynn, who had been fitness trainer with Kilkenny for years, was retained by Brian in 2005 but Micko was gone by 2006. I don't know whether he was let go, or he just moved on, but Dempsey became the main man entrusted with our fitness.

That season, he brought in Noel Richardson, who was the best fitness coach I ever trained under. Mick focussed more on weights but Noel, a former national champion over 5,000 and 10,000 metres and four-time Irish representative at the world cross-country championships, took us to another level.

Mick would tell us what to do whereas Noel was far more approachable, and much easier to talk to than Brian, Dempsey or Fogarty. Noel played a huge role in our four-in-a-row between 2006-09 but Mick has driven, strengthened and grown the culture to another level in the meantime.

His impact on Kilkenny has been all-encompassing. He set up the gym for us in Nowlan Park. Mick introduced proper weight training for the first time in 2005. After Galway blitzed us for five goals in that year's All-Ireland semi-final, the whole experience opened Kilkenny's eyes in terms of tactics. When Niall Healy beat John Tennyson for the fifth goal, the nearest Kilkenny defender was out beyond the 45-metre line. Kilkenny needed to get more streetwise and Mick's mindset and ideas were critical in altering Kilkenny's new world.

Football concepts and tactics have long been imported into hurling but much of that modern process began with Mick. It was subtle but effective. We placed more emphasis on collective defending but much of that tactical shift was still shaped from moulding our bodies into becoming effective and efficient human wrecking balls.

He coached us to get closer to the man in possession and block him with your body. The more bodies around the man, the better. Tracking runners and shutting down space around the D were basic principles of defending but Kilkenny were able to carry those duties out so effectively because Mick had us so well conditioned to do so. And the stronger we got, the easier we found it to savage the opposition in the tackle.

Mick's greatest strength was noticing something we were weak at and then devising a drill to ensure an improvement in that area. You could really see his football background in those drills. Our support play became an important part of our style. He always wanted more engagement in the play from players off the ball. He used to go to town on the forwards over their work rate, which was more ammunition for Cody. If Dempsey isolated a player over work rate, God help the lad when Brian turned his attention to him.

Mick always kept his distance from the players. I can only recall him being on one team holiday, when we were in San Francisco one year. He was only on that trip with us for a short period because he was going to, or had come from, New Zealand, where he was researching new training methods with some professional outfit.

His business interests, especially around Christmas, may have been a factor in him never coming away with us but he always seemed to spend that time travelling to educate himself more. Mick now heads up the Sports Academy and Sport and Exercise programme at IT Carlow and his sporting life has been a perfect study in self-made career progression.

With my job on the road, I'd often meet people who know Mick. 'How's that man keeping?' I'm regularly asked. 'Tell him I was asking for him.'

The connection is nearly always made through different types of sport because if an inch can be found, whatever the discipline, Mick will go looking for it. Brian has always had 100% faith in Mick. He constantly makes reference to us being 'the best physically prepared team in the country'. He would back that up by calling Mick the 'best fitness coach in the country'. He's probably right. If you look at all our success, we have always been physically at the perfect pitch.

Mick has always placed huge focus on physicality; on being big and strong and using every inch and ounce of that power. That was right up Brian's street because he always wanted lads trampling over other lads. The stronger you were, the quicker and easier it was for fellas to physically smash other lads to smithereens.

It's ironic that a football man has had such a big impact on one of the greatest hurling teams of all time but nobody in Kilkenny underestimates Mick's massive contribution. That is proven with Dempsey's status as the longest-serving backroom member in Cody's revolution.

He is like Brian in lots of ways; aloof and distant when he wants to be. I never had any real conversations with Mick. I wouldn't know what to say to him if we did speak. I think he always knew that I was looking after myself and he never felt the need to engage with me or speak about my preparation. But he would be on other fellas' cases if they weren't meeting targets or hitting standards that he and Brian demanded.

I often got the impression he was Brian's eyes and ears too. I cover Carlow in my job. There is an Applegreen service station on the road into the town. When I often stop off there, I'd regularly see Mick sitting up at one of the counters, drinking tea or coffee and reading reams of newspapers. He seems so engrossed in the detail that I often feel Mick is scanning those newspapers, diligently searching for anything negative that is written or said about us.

In a live TV interview with Mick, Brian and myself on the night of the 2014 All-Ireland final replay, Dempsey mentioned how one journalist compared me to a training cone earlier in the year, how a training cone would have more pace than me. What the journalist actually wrote was that a Dublin player had ran around me as easily as a training cone during that year's league. I wasn't even aware of the comparison but Mick certainly took note of it, construing the line the way he wanted it to appear, to sound. And I'm sure his most attentive ears were Brian Cody's.

The Saturday before the 2006 All-Ireland final, we had a barbecue in Hotel Kilkenny. When we sat down afterwards, we discussed how we would go about stopping Cork, and their running game which had been tearing teams apart for three years.

Our tactic was very simple – if your man got the ball, you were not to rush him, you were to focus more on the runner coming off that player. It was a very basic and simplistic tactic but as soon as the game began, that game plan went straight out the window. Instinct just took over. Any time a Cork player got possession that day, we all surrounded him like a pride of lions cornering a lame gazelle. And we savaged him.

That game, and how we played, is often referenced as the birthplace of modern hurling but our approach that day was completely unplanned. We did everything we said we wouldn't do. It was simply borne out of instinct and frustration and a collective impulse that we weren't putting up with this shit from Cork any more.

We saw early on the impact those turnovers were having on the game, which prompted everyone to hunt and scavenge like wild animals. Corner-forwards took it upon themselves to track back, purely out of a desire to win, to do what everyone else was doing. When James Ryall tore after Jerry O'Connor on one of his solo runs before flicking the ball off Jerry's hurley – a high-profile play because it stopped one of Cork's signature attacking plays – Richie Power picked up the sliotar 40 yards from our goal. Power was playing corner-forward but that willingness to work and dog fellas provided the clearest demonstration possible of those values which framed the game's future.

The future ultimately became ours but we never set out that day to pave the first slabs on the path to greater glory. We showed how Cork could be stopped. When Tipperary came on the scene shortly afterwards with a slick space-creation and stick-passing game, we took them down too in the 2009 final. Hurling was tactically evolving because teams were trying to think and work their way around us. Our only tactic was to wipe out everyone but that required a reassessment when Tipperary beat us in the 2010 final.

The first time Kilkenny openly used tactics, and properly executed what we had intended, was the 2011 All-Ireland final, when I was given a man-marking role on Lar Corbett, and we planned match-ups and covering roles around it. Apart from that game, tactics were never really directed or designed by management.

You knew that they would often target the weakest or most vulnerable member of the opposition defence. Eddie Brennan on Seamus Hickey in the 2007 All-Ireland final, and Henry on John O'Keeffe in the 2011 All-Ireland decider were pivotal match-ups carefully selected, and clinically executed, but management never openly discussed those key match-ups with the rest of us.

Most of any tactical communication came from the players. We spoke before the 2011 final about being cuter in how we used the ball, especially in the context of how Tipperary physically bossed us under high ball in the 2010 final. Richie Hogan spoke once about marking Waterford's Noel Connors and, how any time we launched the ball long, Connors would just hare straight back in around the D to either contest, or wait for the break. Our attitude always was any ball into our forwards is a good ball but, invariably against certain opposition, and how they were setting up, we knew we had to tailor or tweak our deliveries. Mick Dempsey and Martin Fogarty would have been more conscious than Brian of those subtle tweaks and alterations but most of the tactical suggestions or ideas would still have come through the players.

Brian's basic attitude towards tactics was to win your own ball. Management would talk about dropping back on opposition puckouts, particularly on getting five across the half-back line and forcing them to puck it long, but other tactical discussions were miniscule compared to other teams.

Protecting the D was never openly spoken about by management. Brian Hogan mostly played as an auxiliary full-back, and was the best in the business at it. He sat back deep on the D, and the opposition centre-forward was picked up – and regularly tormented – by deep-lying midfielders and forwards who found themselves in his air space. Yet that template wasn't preordained or specifically designed because most of our tactical organisation stemmed from how it was ingrained in us from our training games in Nowlan Park.

We had very intelligent players, especially Hogi, who were well able to see, and react, to what they were faced with. It may have come from a private word between Brian Hogan and Michael Fennelly beforehand, where Hogie would tell Feno to be conscious of picking up his man. In turn, Feno might say it to Eoin Larkin to drop deep into his zone, which would facilitate Feno's capacity to sit back as a human shield across the half-back line.

How we set up was a natural reaction or response to how we were conditioned. If Hogie was sitting back in a training match protecting the goal, and his man sniped a point from deep, the midfielders were fingered. If a midfielder was sitting back or tracking and covering, and the opposition midfielder rifled a point, Brian would be asking questions why the half-forwards hadn't got to him. All of us accepted that personal responsibility also meant collective responsibility. And that savage, relentless work rate meant exactly that. Savage. Relentless. Work rate.

A process was repeated so often during training matches that it honed and sharpened everyone's instincts. If a wing-forward saw one of our wing-backs being dragged up the pitch, he knew it was his duty to help out our wing-back by tracking that wing-forward, by hounding him, by making his life a misery when he won possession.

It was a completely selfless mindset, an attitude of, 'The ball is at the other end of the field but what can I still do to help out my team-mates?' That was the Cody philosophy.

His teachings became Kilkenny philosophy because that culture that Brian created, and the principles he espouses, have filtered down so deeply into the ground that they have enriched the soil like nutrients. The harvests may not be as bountiful any more but the culture will remain consistent.

Earlier in 2016, Ger Loughnane described Kilkenny as 'functional beyond belief.' He said: 'There is no way Kilkenny should be going for three in a row.' This team may not be at the same level as the four-in-a-row side but how could it be? The production line has slowed down at underage but we've still been dominant at senior level.

Loughnane may have been referring to the team but I didn't really understand the meaning of his comments anyway because Kilkenny's whole culture is based on a principle of functionalism; practical, operational, utilitarian.

The collective is everything. Everybody, no matter how small the link, is a part of the chain. St Kieran's won their third All-Ireland Colleges title in a row in March 2016 but every school in the county – primary and secondary – is looked after. Even schools in other bordering counties, which teach Kilkenny kids, get assistance from the county board. No other county sees the wider picture as clearly but we don't see ourselves like other counties.

We do it our way. Answers are always sought. Hard questions are always asked, at every level, in every club. The highest standards are the only benchmark. The whole county flourishes in a culture of professional management and accountability. That thinking frames everybody's approach, especially that of 'Rackard'. It's almost an attitude of 'What's the function of a grip if you don't have a hurley?'

Maybe we are functional but it works for us. Because it's our way.

'It doesn't matter how good a hurler you are, or how much of a reputation you have, they don't rate you in Kilkenny unless you have balls; unless you're a hard bastard who can make a difference when it matters.'

chapters
XI-XV

Damien

'We become what we continuously say we are, so the words we use are important. That is exactly me, and why honesty and trust are so important to me. It's also why I work so much with Damien, because he allows me to be me. I get what I want and am prepared to do absolutely anything to get it. I don't take no for an answer. Injuries don't hold me back, they only motivate me. The best is still to come from me.

I was excellent in training tonight. I pushed myself so hard that I lost 6lbs during the session. I felt I was the best player on view. I felt unreal afterwards. I feel that this is my best hurling spell in 4/5 years. I felt like I owned the pitch. I can't wait for this weekend to show what I am really about. I don't care about other people's rules or thinking. I want more competition. Those are the words I use about myself. And they are 100% true.'

– Diary entry, Wednesday May 25th, 2016

WHEN you enter the front of the main building of Coláiste Éamann Rís in Callan, two sets of double doors open into a small assembly area, kitted out with white floor tiles, grey lockers and framed by a high ceiling. At the bottom right of the assembly area, a small corridor leads to a Perspex side entrance. The last door on the left, just across from the career guidance room, is classroom number four.

It used to be Brother Damien's classroom before he became principal but the place is still smudged with his fingerprints everywhere. When the kids and staff have gone home, he clears the tables and chairs from the right corner of the room and opens out his physio table. When you lie on your back on that table, the roof directly above your eye-line is a gallery of pictures, slogans and sayings. There is a poster of myself about to clear a ball off my left side. JJ is there too. So is Richie Hogan and Henry Shefflin.

The pictures and library of quotes and sayings are the colour on a wall of white emulsion but my favourite one is from Muhammad Ali: 'He who is not courageous enough to take risks will accomplish nothing in life.'

For the first few years of my Kilkenny career, I was afraid to take risks. By the end of 2008, I won my third successive All-Ireland. I secured my second All-Star in a row. The doubts which had tormented me in 2006 had eased but they still hadn't subsided.

That 2008 final win against Waterford was the complete performance from Kilkenny. The opposition was irrelevant that day. Waterford hindered us about as much as cones in training as we secured the three-in-a-row and lay emphatic claim to immortality.

We scored 3-30. Waterford only managed five scores from play. We didn't concede a point from play for the first three quarters of an hour. It was the easiest afternoon we ever put down as a defence but I still wasn't happy with how I had played.

I spent most of the match on Eoin McGrath, who was substituted after 52 minutes. I did spend some time on John Mullane, who was Waterford's best player on the day. Mullane scored three points from play but only one of those was on my beat. Yet when I saw a newspaper report on the Monday about Mullane being the only Waterford player to win his individual battle – against me – I almost believed that he had.

I hadn't the confidence to convince myself otherwise, even though I knew Mullane hadn't done much damage to my name. But because someone else with a pen thought differently, I was more inclined to believe that person than myself.

I only hit the ball twice but that was more down to our absolute dominance than Waterford putting me, or our defence, under any real pressure. The team delivered an exhibition of power and greatness but the more I thought about my own individual contribution, the more I questioned it. Was two possessions really an acceptable contribution in an All-Ireland final, irrespective of the final score?

I still felt so inferior in my own skin that when I won that second All-Star a couple of months later, I was wondering if I really deserved the accolade. Was I just codding myself? Was Kilkenny's total dominance at that time shielding my limitations as a defender? Was I being carried to false glory on the coat-tails of our great players?

By that stage of my career, I had already accomplished a lot. I had four All-Ireland medals but I had won them without having taken any real risks. Was that really an accomplishment? Was that really living?

'Damien is not into mind games and I work with him to get the best out of myself. I trust him and I am totally honest about myself when I am with him, which I feel allows me to become more and more powerful. My honesty and trust allows me to go places that nobody else would go, which enables me to get the best out of myself. I strive to become more important, and more powerful, than anybody else. I don't want it to sound arrogant but when I reveal the real me to Damien, I get a sense of my own importance, and I practise it. There is a cut, an edge and a determination in me. Damien knows I will do anything to get my body and mind in the best possible shape I can. Damien never judges me and that's how we work at such a high level. I take risks with him. That is how I have become so powerful, and how I have increased my self-belief and confidence. It's my total honesty about myself which brings the best out in me. When I go to Damien, I come away feeling more powerful in body and mind. And I always take that with me into work, training sessions, matches. And my life.'

– Diary entry, Wednesday June 1st, 2016

A week before the 2009 league final against Tipperary, I was speaking to Brian Dowling, a good friend of mine from my days in St Kieran's. Brian had a good relationship with Brother Damien Brennan from Callan. He used to often go there for a chat and a rub. He was on the way to Callan to meet Brother Damien. I was intrigued. Who was this guy?

He comes from Arles in County Laois. He had spent some time as a principal in a school in James' Street in Dublin before moving to Callan CBS. Brother Damien had some background in counselling. He had worked with prisoners. He studied psychology. He had a qualification from UCD in fitness and injury-prevention. He had studied sports psychology but Dowlers didn't describe Brother Damien as a physio or some kind of head-guru. He seemed to be able to understand players, to be able to connect with them.

Brother Damien understood hurling too because he had coached Callan CBS to an All-Ireland B Colleges title in 1991, and a famous Leinster Colleges A title in 1998, when they beat Kieran's in the final. Brother Damien was Kilkenny minor manager for four years when the county won successive All-Ireland titles in 2002 and 2003. Many of those players continued to work with Damien afterwards because they swore by his ability to get them right for games.

I asked Brian to ask Brother Damien if I could call out to Callan with him. The invitation was immediately extended. I was nervous. I wouldn't have gone out there without Brian for company. We chatted in his school. Brother Damien was quietly spoken but there was an impressive authority and conviction to the way he spoke. After about an hour, we shook hands and left.

That Sunday in Thurles, Noel McGrath cleaned me out. The youngest player on the field took me for 1-3. I felt slow, lethargic and drained of confidence. I was still playing with fear. I needed something. Two days later, I rang Brother Damien.

We arranged to meet in the Edmund Rice Monastery in

Westcourt, just outside Callan, the place beside where Rice was born in 1762. It is a beautiful, peaceful spot but my mind was in a completely different, more chaotic world. I was still in a rage over Sunday. I couldn't relax. I didn't know where I was really going as a Kilkenny hurler. Could I keep going like this? Could I keep fooling myself, and everyone else around me?

Brother Damien could see that terror raging inside me before I even said a word to him. I needed help. He said he could take me on a journey to try and get there but there were three things he would ask of me if we were to work together: courage, honesty and trust. 'If you don't start there,' he said, 'you can't start anywhere.'

He told me to write down my goals. When I came back and handed Brother Damien the sheet of paper, he tore it up in front of me. I looked at him. He replied before I could even ask him the question. 'They are not goals,' he said. 'You can list your possibilities if you like. But the goal must be something you have 100% control over.'

He was forcing me to look at my goals differently, and how I could actually go about achieving them. Could I get fitter? Could I get stronger? I could because I had 100% control over that goal. And the goal makes the possibility a reality.

That was our starting point. One of the first questions Brother Damien asked me was did I think I could score a point in an All-Ireland final? If someone had asked me that before, I would have said no way. I thought it was a possibility. I wanted to make it happen but Damien checked me. 'You don't make things happen,' he said. 'You put yourself in the position to allow it to happen.'

I embraced that challenge immediately. Damien's approach is

completely holistic but much of it is also based on instinct. He knew I had become conditioned to looking over my shoulder. It was obvious to him how much my hurling was controlled by fear. I had no peace as a Kilkenny hurler. I wasn't enjoying my hurling life. The pressure and stress attached to trying to survive and perform was eating me alive but Damien began to instil the confidence that everybody else assumed I naturally had.

The more we met and worked together, the more I began to trust Brother Damien. I opened up to him. I relaxed more. I became more confident. I wasn't concerned about just surviving any more, about only minding my own corner. I wanted to liberate myself from those chains. I started going forward instead of retreating backwards. I was always a good striker. I had been scoring points for James Stephens at centre-back. Why shouldn't I get forward more with Kilkenny? Why couldn't I score a point in an All-Ireland final from corner-back?

And I began to put myself in a position to allow that to happen.

Once you exit through those Perspex doors at the side of Coláiste Éamann Rís, you're facing a huge car park. An open ball-alley stands out like a monument in the distance but once you veer to the left of the school building, the ground slopes down to a vast stretch of grass and two huge pitches, where the bottom field is separated from the line of houses behind it through a thick thatch of palm trees.

The first time Brother Damien brought me onto the pitch for a field session, he murdered me; speed work, footwork, striking, stamina work. Everything was done with a ball but it was relentless.

Mostly, Brother Damien would mark out cones in the number four position and call a series of drills I had to go through. Much of it was based on building speed and being quicker on the turn. Once we began to work on shooting for points, he would still incorporate those speed and stamina drills.

We mostly worked inside our own 45-metre line but if I was shooting for a point, as soon as I struck the ball, Brother Damien would begin strolling from Point A to Point B. It was around a 15-metre distance but I had to get to Point B before Brother Damien to stop him kicking a ball into an empty net. It was a crazy amount of ground to have to cover in a handful of seconds, especially when the drill was constantly repeated, but it improved my speed no end.

The more I started to shoot, the more accurate and confident I became. It was an uncontested drill but having to get to Point B before Brother D made it much harder to repeatedly execute.

I was brutal during those first few field sessions but the more my game improved, the more confident I started to become. Brother Damien began to evaluate my game. In all the years he has spent rating me since 2009, the highest number I ever got was seven. When he would ask me why he had subtracted three from my performance, I would excavate deep in my mind for the reasons. If I didn't, or couldn't, find them, Damien would instantly provide the answers.

His attention to detail fascinated me. He always had an issue with my feet. He never wanted to see me on the ground during a game. When I tire, I lean forward in my gait, especially when I am running. Body language was another key performance

Damien

indicator for him, especially if a forward had sniped a couple of points off me.

In the early stages of that 2009 championship, I had a couple of half-chances to shoot for a point, which I didn't attempt. We would study the footage, and examine the reasons why I didn't take on those scoring opportunities. I thought a few of them were Brother Damien only clutching at straws but he was constantly planting the seed in my head to start looking for scores. More than that, it was a complete change of mindset. It was as if he was trying to tell me: 'There's no more backing off here, no more playing it safe. Attack the ball. Attack your opponent. Take risks.'

I was. I did. I scored a point in the second half of the 2009 All-Ireland final. As soon as I struck the ball from distance, I knew it had gone over. As I was running back in to my position, the feeling was overwhelming. I thought to myself, 'I've arrived here, I have finally arrived. If I can score a point from corner-back in an All-Ireland final, I can fucking do anything.'

It was only the second point of my career but that score against Tipperary had real meaning. The point I hit against Wexford in the 2005 Leinster final was a pure fluke. I wasn't even going for a score. I won a ball near the '65 and was just looking to get rid of it. I turned and let fly. I was as surprised as anyone else when it flew over the bar.

The only people who weren't surprised in that 2009 final were myself and Brother Damien. When that ball broke, I know if we hadn't done all those drills, and if Damien hadn't challenged me to score, I wouldn't have even thought to shoot at the posts.

I had full control now. I just thought, 'If I do this right now, if I prepare as well as I can, if my mind is fully tuned, it won't matter who I'm marking, I'll fucking blow them out of the water.'

Even though I was the defender, I had always felt up to that point of my career that I was the hunted. I believed that the opposition were always coming after me, that I was an easy target. Well, from that moment on, I was the hunter.

For the first three or four years of my career, I never wanted to mark the opposition's top forward. If anything, I wanted to keep as far away from that player as possible in case I'd get scorched alive.

After 2009, I wanted the opposition's best player. I was looking for the Eoin Kelly, Lar Corbett, Damien Hayes. Brian had enough faith in me by then to hand me those briefs. I was carrying out those job requirements to the standard expected because I no longer had any fears or hang-ups of what those top forwards might do to me.

I rarely had off-days. I loved the big days, when the challenge was never greater. Before we played Tipperary in the 2010 All-Ireland final, I had absolutely no doubts about my capacity to perform in that arena.

When I saw Eoin Kelly up close in St Kieran's I always thought he was a genius. I never felt I'd be able to contain a player of that quality but by 2010, that's the company I was now able to keep. More importantly, it was the company I felt most comfortable in. Eoin had a good All-Ireland final in 2010 but so did I. Breaking even and holding my own on one of Tipp's best players was another endorsement of how far I had really come.

Lar Corbett was the difference between the teams in that 2010 final. He scored three goals but my motivation afterwards was to get a crack at Lar on a big day. And it only took me 12 months to get that chance.

Before the 2011 All-Ireland final, Lar was the hottest ticket in hurling, having scored 11 goals in his previous six championship matches. Ten months after nailing us with a hat-trick, Lar hit four goals in the Munster final against Waterford, a 21-point rout, the biggest winning Munster final margin in 29 years.

Two weeks before the final, we went to Carton House. On the Friday night, Brian called me to one side and said they were looking at a few potential match-ups. He asked me how I'd feel about picking up Lar. 'Bring it on,' I thought to myself.

Before we played an internal game the following day, Brian told me that they had instructed John Mulhall to rove all over the place, and that I was to follow him, and shut him down.

When I told Brother Damien my job-spec, he immediately turned my focus to my footwork and lateral movement. I needed every ounce of work he did with me out in Callan because Brian was stretching me to the max in training to get me ready for Lar. During matches, he would rotate Mulhall and Mark Bergin to just run me all over the place. The boys were fucked from ten minutes of running around like a greyhound but I had to sustain that pace and intensity for far longer.

I started to discipline my mind into what that duty required. The ball was often irrelevant because you had to track the man. Getting me into Forrest Gump mode was also conditioning the other defenders into understanding what my role meant for them. JJ Delaney knew I wasn't always going to be beside him. If the ball broke behind the number seven position, everyone else had to be aware that I may not be there to sweep it up. If a runner was haring into that space vacated in the left corner,

David Herity had to understand that I might be out on the far sideline, 70 metres away from normal sentry duty.

A week out from the game, Martin Fogarty handed me a DVD of Lar, a highlights package of his scores, plays and general movement off the ball. I was excited by the endorsement. 'Brian really has this much faith in me now,' I thought. 'Lar is their go-to guy. And Brian wants me to be the man to take him down.'

I became obsessed with carrying out that task. The Monday after we returned from that training weekend in Carton House, I put a photograph of Lar on the screensaver of my phone. Any time someone would ring, Lar's head would pop up on the screen.

When I was often in meetings or in other people's company, I would turn the phone in towards my body before I answered it. I didn't want them thinking I was a complete nut-job but the picture was there as a constant reminder to myself that something big was coming.

After about ten days, I finally removed the picture of Lar from my screensaver. I felt I was becoming too uptight about the task because Lar was completely dominating my thoughts. The last thing I wanted was to hit this fella down on top of the head and get the line after five minutes. By that stage anyway, I felt mentally ready. If Lar was going for a piss during the game, I would have been right there beside him.

For that final, we just had a completely fluid approach. Brian Hogan was to stay centre-back. JJ wasn't to move from full-back. I was to stick to Lar like a leech while everyone else just played wherever they ended up.

I tried to drive Lar mad. He always has his socks pulled up but I kept trying to pull them down. I was standing on his toes, kicking at his heels. I was never into verbals but I dialled up the heat that day. Nothing personal. Just business.

He didn't touch the ball in the first 15 minutes. A couple of the Tipp subs were warming up along the sideline at that stage. 'The boys are getting ready to come in now Lar,' I said to him. 'You'll be gone off soon.'

Then he'd shoot off. I'd just tear off after him. At one stage when he tried to dart away from me, I caught his helmet. My fingers edged through the bars on his faceguard and I scraped him below his eye with my fingernails. I'm not sure if I drew blood but when Lar started complaining to the referee, I just shrugged my shoulders.

I had noticed from studying the DVD that he would very rarely make a run when the ball was in that general vicinity. But if a ball was being pucked into a particular zone, or on top of another Tipperary forward, he'd look disinterested, try and lull you into a false sense of security, and then just take off like a hare. Most of the time, Lar was just taking a chance, hoping for a break. But if he secured possession, he had such a head of speed built up that it was curtains.

The game wasn't going well for Lar. I knew I had him completely frustrated when he started making these dashes. There was no purpose to what he was doing. I just interpreted it as Lar trying to get as far away from me as possible. I knew by then that he was in trouble. He was behaving erratically, different from normal.

I was sniping at him throughout the match. He probably couldn't hear me half the time because of the crowd and because he was running away from me but any time I got within earshot, I made sure he heard me.

'It's all over for you, Lar.'

'Not today, Lar. No way today.'

'Yere fucked. We have ye now.'

'Your Hurler-of-the-Year award is old news now.'

'Not today. Not today.'

I had never doled out verbals before. If a lad told me I was a bollocks, I'd tell him he was a bigger bollocks. Lar never said a word back to me but I just kept it going. It was more to drive home the point, 'There's no end to me today. There is just no end to me today.'

I tormented him. I don't know what he was thinking but I knew what I wanted Lar to be thinking. 'Ah for Christ's sake, this fucker again. Will he just leave me alone.'

When we emerged for the second half, we were kept waiting for almost two minutes by Tipperary. During that hiatus, groups of us drifted together, forming mini-conclaves all around the field. I was in discussion with JJ, Tommy and Brian Hogan when I suddenly switched back onto Lar mode. I sprinted towards the sideline. And waited. I had my eyes on the tunnel, not waiting for Tipperary, but for Lar. I looked like a hawk stalking his prey. I was.

If Lar was inside taking a piss, I was half-tempted to break down the door of the Tipp dressing room and just show up beside him at the urinal.

As soon as Lar ran onto the pitch, I matched him stride for stride, our hips almost touching like in a three-legged race at school sports day. As I escorted Lar back to his patch, I was burning his ear. 'Not today, Lar. Not today.'

I hardly touched the ball during the match, having just three possessions. Lar made just five plays but he never struck the ball once with his hurley. He got away from me once and tried to score a point but Colin Fennelly blocked the swing with his head.

I just wanted to keep the ball out Lar's hand but he still showed how dangerous he was when setting up Pa Bourke for a goal late on. That just focussed me even more as the finishing line loomed into view. I knew Lar hadn't the energy to keep trying to get away from me. I knew I had him by the throat but I also got off on the fear that he could slip me at any stage for a goal. He didn't. Lar had walked off Croke Park on All-Ireland final day the previous year with three goals. That day in 2011, I walked off the pitch knowing full well that I had won more than just a battle – I had also won the war.

Beforehand, I wanted to test myself, just to see how far I had really come. That day I felt more than I had just arrived. I felt bullet-proof. Almost invincible.

There were times when Brother Damien made me feel indestructible, that even a Panzer tank wouldn't knock me down. For so long in my career, I felt powerless, disarmed by what other people thought of me. Brother Damien enabled me to take the power back. He made me believe in myself. He also made me believe in the power of mental strength, of how anything realistic was possible, no matter how big the obstacle.

In the 2013 Leinster semi-final replay against Dublin, I tore my quad muscle. It was a grade three tear. That's normally a minimum of five weeks on the sideline. Yet Tipperary were coming down the tracks a week later and I couldn't countenance not playing.

I rang Brother Damien on the way back from Portlaoise. It was an evening game. I knew we would be back late but I asked Damien if he would meet me. It was close to 1am when I arrived at his place in Callan. 'What's the goal now?' was the first question he asked me. I knew if I said to play the following weekend, Brother Damien would tell me to go home. 'To put myself in the position that management can pick me,' I replied.

We chatted. I stretched. Brother Damien did some physical therapy on my leg. I didn't leave until 3am. I had planned to go to see The Coronas, Clare's favourite band, in concert in Waterford that Sunday evening but I was canning those plans. 'Why should you?' Brother Damien asked. 'Go to the concert. We will get some work done on this in the morning.'

We worked relentlessly all week, mostly two sessions a day. As the match drew closer, a seemingly impossible situation became possible. The medical team had initially ruled me out but I was now suddenly and almost miraculously back in the frame.

They planned a fitness test for the Friday night. Brother Damien told me to ask management to move it to Thursday. I was sceptical because that diluted 24 more hours from my recovery period. It didn't matter. I was passed fit to play. In the circumstances, my display against Tipperary that evening was probably the most satisfying of my career.

In life, if you can find someone who will work with you, and for you, where both people reach that special, symbiotic and selfless level, no obstacle is insurmountable. In Brother Damien Brennan, I found that person.

He knew I would do anything to get myself right. Since we had reached that level, I knew Brother Damien would do anything to help me get myself right.

It may have sounded selfish of me to be asking so much of this man. Was turning up on his door at 1am and keeping him from his bed until 3am really fair on the man? Was I eating up too much of his free time?

I never had to worry. Brother Damien had that trust and respect for me. He was so heavily invested in our friendship that he just wanted to help me maximise my full potential.

At the side of the Edmund Rice Memorial Chapel in Westcourt in Callan is the thatched house where he grew up. A path around the side of the house leads you through a line of ash and sycamore trees around the back to the monastery. In the small courtyard between the chapel and the monastery is a rectangular fish pond, packed with purple, orange and yellow fish, most of which are carp. The first fish went into that pond in 1971. The Brothers have never taken a fish out, or put one back in, ever since. The cycle of life just continues.

The path meanders through the garden, past glasshouses, shrubbery and flower beds. It's a beautiful, peaceful spot. I mostly meet Brother Damien in the school but we meet up every now and again in Westcourt. Any time I go there, it brings peace to my mind.

Even after I arrived, when I felt like the team – invincible – there were times when I did get a scutching from some hot-shot corner-forward. I was just far more mentally equipped to deal with those experiences because Brother Damien had provided me with the tools.

If I had what I perceived to be a bad day, I'd do something positive as soon as I could. I still am uptight about preparation and hurling but I have learned how to try and filter that emotion in a more constructive manner. Instead of allowing that negative emotion to eat me up, I just try and slowly flush it out of my system. That might be something as basic as going for a walk or just listening to some music.

Surviving at the top as an inter-county hurler is mostly a mental game. We are mentally strong in Kilkenny. That is the culture Brian Cody has created but most of us still have the same fears and anxieties as any other inter-county player. We have never had any access to a sports psychologist with Kilkenny. We don't really need one, partly because Brian is such a psychologist, but that doesn't mean we cannot lean on the practice to help us through difficult times. And so many of us, especially myself, are so lucky that Brother Damien has been there to help us become better players, and more importantly, better men.

In Brother Damien's old classroom in Callan, there is one saying close to the noticeboard that means a lot to me. 'To the world, you might just be one person. But to that one person, you might be the world.'

It's not from any great philosopher, poet, writer or former sports star. The quote isn't attributed to any one person but I have a sense that they are Brother Damien's own words.

At times in the middle of Croke Park, when it is filled to capacity, you can feel as if you are drowning, that you're out of breath, almost gasping to stay alive, to keep afloat. It's natural for players to often feel that kind of pressure in that cauldron but Brother Damien helped me to do more than just survive in that world. He enabled me to thrive in that environment.

And the man means the world to me.

Look at that face: *With my godparents Kevin and Maeve on my christening day*

Taking a sip: *Posing for the camera when I was two years old*

Sister in the middle: *Mark and I keep a close eye on Sarah*

The sacred cloth: *Wearing the Kilkenny colours with my neighbours Patrick and Johnny Savage*

First day at school: *Hair parted to the side as I prepare for my introduction to St Patrick's De La Salle*

Solid crew: *Me, Emer, my uncle, Fr Jackie, and Mark on Sarah's christening day*

Looking up to Granny: *With Granny Mini, wearing my favourite Ireland Italia '90 jersey*

The Master's report: *My conduct and attendance was always very good for Mr Cody, especially after I left De La Salle*

Black and white brigade: *A St Kieran's U-16 team. I'm at the far left in the back row*

Always got my back: *With Brian Cody on confirmation day*

Graduation day: *With Mam and Dad after receiving my degree from LIT in 2007*

Something I never thought possible: *Captaining Kilkenny to the 2003 All-Ireland U-21 title*

DJ ready to rock: *It was a privilege to be part of a Kilkenny team captained by DJ Carey in 2003. I'm second from the right in the back row*

If only you knew what was going on in my head: *Shaking hands with Pat Mulcahy before the 2006 All-Ireland final, tussling with my friend Kieran 'Fraggie' Murphy, and basking in the glory with Mam and Dad afterwards*

No way through: *Tackling Andrew O'Shaughnessy in the 2007 All-Ireland final, and celebrating with Brian Cody, Henry Shefflin, PJ Ryan and Eddie Brennan afterwards*

Village people: *Me and Eoin Larkin bask in the warm afterglow of Kilkenny's greatest performance, the 2008 All-Ireland final destruction of Waterford*

The oldest enemy and the sweetest feeling: *Beating Tipperary in an All-Ireland final in 2009 almost felt like winning two All-Irelands*

Redemption: *I felt like touching the heavens after we beat Tipperary in the 2011 All-Ireland final*

Brothers in arms: *Celebrating our 2012 All-Ireland final replay win against Galway with Eoin Larkin and JJ Delaney, and below with Henry Shefflin and Kieran Joyce*

An eternal evening: *Soaking up the purity and beauty of the sensation after beating Tipperary in the 2014 All-Ireland final replay alongside Kieran Joyce, Cillian Buckley, JJ Delaney, Eoin Murphy and Conor Fogarty*

You the man: *Brian Cody and I acknowledge each other after the 2015 All-Ireland final win against Galway*

Awards and tours: *Picking up All-Stars was always an honour. So was playing and captaining Super 11s hurling at Notre Dame College in Indiana*

School reunion: *Shaking hands with my old St Kieran's team-mate, Eoin Kelly, before the 2012 Interprovincial final*

Biblical plague: *I never played in worse conditions than the 2014 All-Ireland semi-final against Limerick. And I never felt more alive*

You cannot be serious? *Me and the Clare boys argue over a sideline decision during the 2014 league*

You wanna tango, Andy? *Facing off with Galway's Andy Smith during the 2014 Leinster semi-final*

What could have been: *Dejection after the 2016 All-Ireland final*

There is always a way: *Three Waterford players have me pinned down, but not locked down, during the 2011 All-Ireland semi-final*

'Rackard' is the man: *Filling Liam MacCarthy with Avonmore milk, with Denis 'Rackard' Cody and the boys*

Outjumping Hoggie: *Winning a ball over Patrick Horgan during the 2010 All-Ireland semi-final*

A night like no other: *The 2013 qualifier against Tipperary in Nowlan Park was the most electric, and tribal, atmosphere I ever experienced*

A mother's love: *Hugging Mam after the 2012 All-Ireland final*

The smile says it all: *Brian Cody celebrated our school's final win against Kilmanagh in Nowlan Park as much as any of our All-Irelands*

Muddied but unbowed: *After the 2011 drawn county final*

Hoisted high: *After getting sent off in the 2011 county final replay, I'll never forget the boys for ensuring I got to lift the cup*

No King's pardon: *Facing off with Henry in 2009*

Village pride: *With Mam and Dad after the 2011 final replay*

Beautiful: *Celebrating the 2011 county final win with friends I'd known all my life*

The Brother: *Br. Damien Brennan's friendship and influence has had a massive impact on my career and life*

Swimming with the big fish: *Spending a week with the Miami Marlins in 2015 was a super experience*

Sharp: *I always liked to dress and look good. Here I model some clothes for Littlewoods Ireland*

My future: *Clare and I enjoying life together*

Derek

HENRY Shefflin always wanted to referee every game he played. His status and standing in the game was so huge that referees were often intimidated by him. Henry naturally played that card whenever he could but before James Stephens met Ballyhale Shamrocks in the drawn 2011 county final, I was ready to knock every card in the deck completely out of his hand.

I knew that Henry would contest the first free that we were awarded. As soon as it was, I could see Henry making a beeline for the ref. I rattled him with a shoulder. 'You're not fucking refereeing this match today,' I said.

'Fuck off, you,' he replied.

He tried to get by me, to make his way to the referee, and I wouldn't let him pass. 'Not today, Henry,' I said. 'Not today.'

There was always a healthy respect between us but we often went at each other like stags in a glen during Kilkenny training.

It was often far more heated in club matches but in that county final, I was ready to rip the jugular out of Henry, and every other Ballyhale man's, throat.

After we won successive county titles in 2004 and 2005, Ballyhale took over in Kilkenny, winning four in a row, and beating us in two of those finals. O'Loughlin Gaels stopped Shamrocks winning five in a row but that wasn't much consolation to us. Carrickshock beat us in the quarter-final and O'Loughlins, our biggest rivals from across the city, beat Carrickshock in the final.

When 2011 rolled around, we were like men possessed. Only six players remained from the team which had won the 2005 All-Ireland club title but there was still a silent accusation attached to the team's name which incongruously sat beside our massive history and tradition. People in Kilkenny said we were a soft touch. And that drove me wild.

I was pumped for the drawn county final but I was even more psyched for the replay. I was doing well on TJ Reid. When Ballyhale switched Mick Fennelly to centre-forward on me, his first act was to dig me in the ribs. I gave it back to him just as hard but I got so stuck into Mick that I nearly forgot about hurling.

Ten minutes into the second half, we forced a huge turnover, where we bottled up Colin Fennelly. When Colin was pulled for over-carrying, the two of us squared up to one another. Before I knew what had happened, I drew back my head and stuck him with a head-butt. It was rash and crazy and I was sent packing on a straight red card.

The last 20 minutes of that game was a haze. I was beside myself with worry and anxiety that my actions could cost us the game. I was running up and down the sideline like a raving lunatic. My mind was gone. I still had my jersey on. When the linesman told me to go up to the stand, I told him to clear off. When a county board official told me that I had to get off the sideline, I ignored him and just turned the jersey inside out. I was lucky that Larks produced one of the greatest individual performances I have ever seen. He scored 1-11 and single-handedly pulled us through.

Winning that county title was a brilliant feeling but any time somebody mentions that final to me, that sending off is my dominant memory. I was captain. I should have shown more leadership. I was just happy to be allowed to accept the cup. I let myself down. I let my club down because I was suspended for the Leinster club quarter-final a week later, which we lost to Oulart-the-Ballagh. That defeat still hurts me as much as any other because I believe we would have had a better chance of winning if I was playing.

I was going to appeal the suspension. My helmet had been pulled in the scuffle and the club felt that they could build a case on my vision having being impaired. After meeting Brother Damien the following Thursday, he challenged me to look at the incident objectively. I knew my vision wasn't impaired. It was impulsive but I still knew exactly what I was doing when I nailed Colin. I needed to accept responsibility for my actions. I decided there would be no appeal. An appeal could have dragged on and impacted on the team. It hurt like hell to miss that game but it was my duty to take my suspension like a man.

The hurt was exacerbated because I felt I had ruined James Stephens' legacy in Leinster. Since the All-Ireland club championship had begun in 1970, the club had won a

Leinster title on four of the five occasions they had played in the province. The only time they didn't win Leinster was 1976, when they lost the final to Camross by one point.

When 'The Village' ended a 23-year wait for a county title in 2004, we were so elated afterwards that we wanted to celebrate for a month. Brendan Hennessy of KCLR came to the clubhouse on the Monday night to do a series of radio interviews and I remember Joe Hennessy saying that James Stephens never stopped after a county title, that there was a standard set, and that it was our responsibility to maintain it.

Joe was right. It focussed our minds straight away. We won Leinster six weeks later. We were haunted to beat UCD in that final. We scraped over the line by one point but UCD claimed that we were awarded two points that had actually gone wide. The TV evidence produced by TG4 clearly showed that the first of the controversial points had gone off the post and wide. UCD didn't lodge an appeal but 'Babs' Keating, the UCD manager, repeatedly called for us to offer his side a replay.

On the Monday evening, we were all drinking in Seamus Delaney's pub in Patrick Street when 'Babs' came on RTE Radio pleading with us to show some humanity. We were all pissing ourselves laughing. 'Shove that replay up your hole, 'Babs'' one of the lads shouted at the radio.

Our only focus was on driving on. The following March, we won an All-Ireland, the club's third. It was a day of days. Grown men were crying. Brian, Fan Larkin and Joe Hennessy were the first three men onto the field afterwards. One of the stewards tried to stop Joe but he made a break for it like a bold child. When the steward ran after him, Joe just grabbed onto Brian McEvoy and wouldn't let him go.

When we got back to the club that night, they set off fireworks in the ball-alley to greet us. The place was rammed with people. You couldn't even get near the bar for a drink so Adrian Harkin went down to a local off-licence and got a huge take-out. Adrian was always a step ahead of the rest of us but, sadly, Adrian was taken from us in 2012. AD was a very strong Village hurler. He won a county Minor title in 2003. In that year's semi-final, against a Carrickshock team going for three-in-a-row, AD did a serious man-marking job on John Tennyson. AD was a great player but, God be good to him, he was an even better character, someone we miss every day.

After AD arrived back that night with the carry-out, we sat outside on the street drinking. The party was still going as night segued into day. I don't know whether this fella was drunk out of his mind, or if he was a bandwagon crew member looking for a late piss up, but he shouted at the top of his voice: 'Come on St Stephens.' Jeez, it was a good job Brian Cody didn't hear him. He could have taken the head off your man.

'Dicksboro...1-12

James Stephens...0-11

Poor team performance. Our forwards were really poor. I had 18 possessions but I wasn't as strong in the second half as I was in the first. Still, at least my hamstring felt fine with it being my first full match in nine weeks. I didn't go out, and was surprised to hear that some Kilkenny players were out. FOCUS.'

– Diary entry, Saturday May 21st, 2016

The last few weeks have been a drag. A real drag. I pulled my hamstring after 15 minutes of the league semi-final against Clare in April. It was a Grade 1 tear. I rehabbed it and then tore it again. When I went for a second scan, I found out that I had a Grade 2 tear on my quad muscle. ARRGGHHH.

When I went to Brother Damien the night of the Clare game, he said to me that if I don't play championship in 2016, it will be because of circumstances outside my control. He gave me a sheet with the words: 'Between you and the goal you wish to achieve, there are a series of perceived obstacles, and the bigger the goal, the bigger the obstacle.'

I know the best way now to predict my future is to create it. I'm still in good shape. My body fat has gone from 14.7% down to 12.3%. My attitude and focus has ensured that I haven't lost any muscle mass but mentally, the last year has still been the most challenging of my career. Injury after injury after injury. Is my body just breaking down? Is it able for the grind and the punishment of the inter-county game any more?

I just feel like I'm constantly playing catch-up. We got a recent demo of our new gym session from Mick Dempsey and the sprinter Marcus Lawlor, most of which was explosive work. The frustration and anger was bubbling inside me because I knew I couldn't get stuck into it, which left me with more work to catch up on.

I missed our club game against Rower-Inistioge. We won by four points but I felt I needed to be playing more club games to push myself back into the frame with Kilkenny. I did return in time for the Dicksboro game but I know I'm still slightly off the pace.

It's been even more disappointing because Brian Cody

is a selector with 'The Village' in 2016, which I saw as an opportunity, a chance for me to show Brian, even more than usual, how much I still wanted it, how hard I was prepared to push myself every time I went onto a field. And I just haven't been able to do that consistently with persistent injury.

Brian has always been a massive club man, a massive Village man. Every year after the Leinster final, he would call us into the warm-up area in Croke Park and reiterate the importance of doing our stuff for our clubs. A round of matches was always fixed for the following weekend and Brian wanted to see lads dominating games, showing the leadership that our clubs expected of us. And anyone who wasn't, it was a black mark against them.

Brian always went to every club game in the county. In his eyes, showing good form there was an extension of our training games in Nowlan Park. If guys weren't doing it for their clubs, Brian often saw that as a mental slippage, that fellas were more concerned about the status of playing well for Kilkenny, than the duty and responsibility towards their clubs.

If some fella had been brilliant in a Leinster final and was benched for an All-Ireland semi-final, that decision could have been formed in Brian's mind as early as a club game three weeks beforehand.

There certainly isn't any hiding place for any lads on the James Stephens squad any more but, in all honesty, it has been strange to have Brian as a selector with 'The Village'. He never says much, which is highly unusual considering how vocal and domineering he is with Kilkenny.

He is an inspiration to everyone in the club but Brian's presence on the line has also probably been a little unnerving for fellas. His aura is so vast that guys are bound to be looking over their shoulder a little. It is inevitable for some lads to be thinking, 'How do you please this guy?'

I'm sure it has been challenging for the rest of the management as well. Brian obviously can't make all the training sessions, which makes it harder for him to form a consistent opinion on some fellas' real form. And I'm sure it can't be easy for Niall 'Bobs' Tyrrell and Joe Murray, who formed the other part of the management team, to argue against a point Brian might make too. Like, how do you tell Brian Cody what to do?

The only man I ever heard standing up to Brian was Fan Larkin. 'Ah, will you stop, Cody,' Fan would often say, 'sure didn't I put half those medals in your back pocket.'

If Brian made a decision during a game that Fan didn't agree with, Fan wouldn't be long telling him. 'You shouldn't have played that fella,' he'd say. 'He isn't good enough at all.'

Fan and Brian won a load of All-Ireland medals together but there is still that slight tension between them after how Brian treated his son Philly, with how Philly's career ended with Kilkenny. It's the same with Brian McEvoy, another club man, who left the panel in 2003. Many in 'The Village' may have felt he got a raw deal with Kilkenny. It can't have been easy for Brian to make those calls but making them against club-mates, against family he has deep rooted history with, underlines just how strong-minded the man really is.

I wouldn't think Fan holds it against Brian either because he is so easy going. He's the biggest character in the club. For years, we had an old photo of Fan on our WhatsApp club group. It looked like something out of d'Unbelievables but its longevity showed how highly regarded Fan is among the younger crew.

Derek

His little idiosyncrasies make Fan the unique character he is. Fan has his own language. He has his own distinct way of addressing fellas. When Joe Mernagh played for 'The Village', Fan used to call him either Joe Merner or Joe Mernaghan. I never once heard him call Joe by his proper name.

A chap from Bangladesh called Namouil Hossain was playing for us, a real hardy boyo. Fan used to call him Manoo. You could be at an underage match and you'd hear Fan's thick drawl carrying in the air. 'Manooooo, will you pick up your man.' When Fan and Philly were interviewed together during their TG4 Laochra Gael documentary, Fan detailed a game against Oulart-the-Ballagh where he called the club Oulart-the-Booly.

Fan couldn't care less about what he says or does. Opposite his house is a green which regularly used to host local soccer matches. Fan didn't give a shite. A match could be in full swing and he would walk straight across the pitch. It would have only taken him a few extra seconds to walk around the pitch but he wanted to make his point that he hated soccer.

When Ireland played Italy in the World Cup quarter-final in 1990, when the whole country was gone bananas on soccer, Fan and Georgie Leahy walked up through the town and sat in Castle Park for 90 minutes while the match was on.

Even when we were young, and we might be kicking a soccer ball around the pitch in Larchfield, Fan would clear us. He only wanted to see us with hurleys but everything he does is always skewed towards 'The Village' and improving the club. He wouldn't let my pal 'Bobs' Tyrrell back into the club until he changed his grip from left to right hand on top.

Any year he was a selector on Kilkenny underage teams, he would pack those squads with as many James Stephens fellas as he possibly could. One year, there were 11 Village lads on a Kilkenny minor panel by the end of the year. 'If a Village lad is going for a spot with another fella, and it's 50-50, a Village lad will get in,' Fan would say. 'And if it's 45-55, the Village fella will still get in.'

A lot of people don't like that attitude in 'The Village'. We're not a popular club. We never have been. Our supporters can be a bit mouthy. We are viewed as being arrogant. We have always seen ourselves as the best, even though we haven't always been deserving of that status. We have had huge underage success but we haven't dominated at senior level like Ballyhale have.

People don't like that we have such a big pick, that we are the largest club in Kilkenny city, but they're often looking for any reason to have a go at us. Now, Brian's involvement with our senior team has handed huge motivation to every other side in the county. Despite all Brian has achieved, there would still be a lot of jealousy towards him. And we know what everyone else in the country has desired for two decades – the chance to take down a team Brian Cody is involved with.

'We meet in the Newpark for breakfast before heading to Portlaoise to train. It's very warm so we do a short warm-up followed by 4 x 8-minute games. I perform very well throughout. I dominate Chris Bolger. I'm out in front of him, catching, blocking and delivering good ball into the forwards. Brian isn't happy with the effort and intensity, particularly our forwards. He feels their body language is poor and he lets them know about it. We finish strong in the last eight minutes. Before the session concludes, we

do a shooting drill but when I turn at 50% pace, I feel my hamstring tighten. FUCK.'

– Diary entry, Saturday June 4th, 2016

Ah, for the love of Jesus, here we go again. During the shooting drill, Conor Fogarty drove in a ball which I controlled but as soon as I turned and hit it over the bar, I felt a twinge. I suppressed the fear that it might be another tear in my hamstring but it was a lonely and agonising walk into the dressing room. One of our physios, Kevin Curran, did some acupuncture around the strain. He said that it felt like cramp but I've recognised this pain in my leg so often now over the last two months that I know that it isn't.

When we returned home, Kilkenny city was like a blue carnival. Dublin and Laois were playing a Leinster football quarter-final in Nowlan Park and the place was hopping. To try and take my mind off my hamstring, myself and Clare ambled up to the match, sipping coffees as we made our way through the blue Dublin hordes. It was interesting to watch the Dublin machine in full flow but I couldn't really appreciate it; my mind was blank; I was just vacant. I knew I had done damage to my leg again. The frustration was compounded because Shane Prendergast had also been out with a hamstring injury, which had further opened the door ahead of our first championship match against Dublin next week. And now, it looks like the door has been firmly shut again.

When I went to Brother Damien on the Saturday evening, the day of the injury, he reminded me of my decision at the beginning of the year not to go back in 2016 unless I was going to enjoy it. Was I now going to go back on that promise? I returned out to Callan again on the Bank Holiday Monday. On Wednesday, Tadhg Crowley organised a scan. A day later, he sent me on the report – a Grade 2 tear.

Holy shit. I couldn't believe it. I rang Tadhg immediately. He explained that it was probably a Grade 1, but with the needling, it could have shown up as a Grade 2. It didn't feel right, but it didn't feel like a Grade 2. The Dublin game was only two days away but fuckit, I decided to take a chance at training later that evening.

I didn't train with the group but I did 30 minutes running at 70-90% with Kevin. I was struggling a little inside but I still got a buzz from being able to run at that pace for that long on what was supposedly a serious hamstring strain. I clearly surprised Brian and the management too, who I could see talking together as they were looking over at me. It made no difference. They decided I wasn't fit. I was named at number four in the programme but Rob was starting instead of me.

It all just added to the frustration. At training three days before I picked up the injury, I felt like one of the best players on view. I was absolutely buzzing. When I went home afterwards, I wrote into my diary: 'I feel unreal. This is my best hurling spell in 4/5 years. I feel like a potent mix of power, ruthlessness, strength, agility, speed and fitness. And an insatiable desire to be the best, and to win, makes JT's progress unstoppable.'

And now it had come to a shuddering halt again. It almost rips away another part of your soul, especially when the door had opened up for me. Shane was out injured. I could see myself pulling on that sacred Kilkenny number four jersey again but the frustration now is compounded by the increasing uncertainty from every angle. Doubts attack your mind like a virus. I was completely on edge anyway but if I rehab my hamstring properly, and it goes again, how much longer is Brian going to put up with this? He wasn't going to drop me off the squad but could Brian really trust my body being right when I might need it most?

Brother Damien kept grounding me. 'Forget about Brian Cody, and what he is thinking,' he would say. 'Forget about everything else. This is all about you, what is possible and what is within your control.'

In theory, that's the way you have to programme yourself to think but it's still torture trying to clear the clutter and the anxiety from your mind. You're down in yourself. When you wake up in the morning, that feeling of being excited about going to training that evening is replaced by the misery of separation, like a bike rider being cut further and further adrift from the peleton.

That sense of detachment is crippling. You're at training but you're not really there. You could be jogging up and down the sideline with the physio but you may as well be running up the side of a mountain in Tibet. Deep down, you know you're not in management's plans.

This battle is driving me nuts. I'm not one of these people who can take a week or two off to rest; it's either 100mph or nothing. You'd wonder then are you killing that freshness, draining your energy, and becoming mentally jaded from not switching off?

The doubt and anxiety affects every part of your life; work, home, relationships. It's not fair on Clare to have to put up with my crankiness. I'd be gone completely off the reservation only for Brother Damien, but even his positivity is often only like wet sand against the constant tide of doubts flooding my mind.

It's eating me up. I'm eating myself up. I pulled my hamstring doing a shooting drill. What the fuck was the point in having me doing a shooting drill? 'If Kilkenny need me shooting against Dublin,' I said to myself, 'we're in big trouble.'

I was looking for blame everywhere. The pitch in Portlaoise was rock hard. The groundsman there got a pasting in my mind. I even started blaming the Dubs. 'If we were playing some other team, I'd have been down in Nowlan Park training on a proper surface, where this wouldn't have happened.'

It's all pointless. You know it's pointless but you still can't stop yourself when the battle is raging so relentlessly in your head. You repeatedly tell yourself to control the controlables but when you're pouring your whole life into this, it's only human nature that you'll try and second-guess everything.

The lack of communication from management makes it all even more head-wrecking. Everything is so tight-lipped. Nothing filters back to the players. The management team give the physiotherapists and doctors very little information. You could be on a massage table when one of the physios might mention that Brian rang today looking for an update on injuries. Your mind immediately goes into overdrive. 'Did he ask about me? Did he say anything positive or negative about my progress?'

You over-analyse everything when you have no idea where you stand. I always felt that I was one of Cody's men but now I'm wondering if I really am any more? Maybe Brian now sees me as one of his men in the dressing room but not on the pitch. Or am I just a back-up for ten minutes? If Brian even said to me that my role from now on was being a dressing room leader, maybe I would accept it. It wouldn't be easy but at least it would have taken the torturous double-guessing out of my head.

The real terror is the fear of where all of this is really heading. We've all seen this before. Brian doesn't always let lads go; he lets them drift before the rocks eventually loom into view. Michael Rice was let drift for a while before he was eventually let go in late April 2016. Ricey is a great friend, a brilliant leader. He was a huge loss to our setup but none of that matters if Brian Cody doesn't believe you have something to offer. And now I'm wondering, 'Is Brian letting me drift? Am I heading for the rocks?'

For years, I never really had to worry about my position on the Kilkenny team. I never took it for granted. I always kept myself on edge but I still knew that once I remained focussed, and my attitude was right, I was nailed down at number four. I always thought that the biggest challenge was trying to keep your starting place but the challenge of trying to get it back when your body is breaking down is a whole different world. That test is even harder again when you're trying to get something back which you're not sure is even there for you any more.

This has been an extremely challenging year in my career but I won't be broken. I won't give up. I am 34 now. Time is moving on but I have so much more to give, so much more to look forward to, something which was taken from my first-cousin Derek Tyrrell when he was the same age as I am now.

One morning in January 2015, I got a call from my mam. Derek was missing. He had fallen into the River Nore in Thomastown at 2am. I was shocked but we had training in Dunmore at 10.30. I don't know what I was thinking but I went.

Padraig Walsh was a first-cousin of Derek's too. He wasn't at training. I had no sooner togged out when I asked myself, 'What the hell am I doing here?'

When the session had finished, I went straight down to Thomastown. The heart-breaking and soul-destroying process had already begun; teams of volunteers painstakingly pacing the river bank looking for a body. The river is 50 metres wide along that stretch in Thomastown but the water level was high and the current was strong and fast as usual in mid-January.

The devastating pattern was repeated for four days; down at the river at first light, walking up and down in groups of threes until it was dark. You'd be emotionally shattered every night but it was almost impossible to sleep.

Volunteers came from everywhere; James Stephens, other local hurling and soccer clubs, other people who just wanted to help in the search. Paul Murphy texted me after Kilkenny training on the day the news broke and arrived in Thomastown ready to help that afternoon.

Davy Mulcahy, who Derek and my father worked for, organised and choreographed the search. Davy used to send out a group-text every morning: 'Today is the day we are going to find Derek and bring him home.' My mam and my sisters sat with Derek's mother, Mary, and his brother, Tommy, every day. My mother would always ring me at 3pm but I never had good news to give her.

Mary just wanted her son back so she could bury him beside her husband, Tommy, my father's late brother. The anxiety was increased because we knew if Derek's body wasn't recovered soon that the current could take him out to sea and his body might never be found.

Derek

On the fourth day, thank God, the divers eventually located Derek's body, about 200 metres from where he fell in, just beyond a bridge where he had become entangled by the loose roots of a tree. He was down so low, and the water was so cold, that Derek's body was perfectly preserved.

It was so sad to see him being hauled out of the river that day but it was also a huge relief. I wrapped my father up in a big hug. It hit Dad hard. He had worked with Derek. He was very close with him. Dad felt like a father-figure to Derek because cancer had claimed Tommy when Derek was just 27. When my grandfather passed away, Derek moved in to live with my granny.

I often think of Derek. We were the same age. He had a unique uncle-nephew relationship with my father. Derek never played hurling but he had the same passion about his trade – carpentry – as I have about my sport. He should have had his whole life ahead of him but God had a different plan for Derek.

Seeing the effect his death had on Mary and Tommy, my father, and my granny, stayed with me for a long time. I won't say it changed my perspective but it gave me a greater appreciation of everything I have in life, especially the glorious opportunity I have had with Kilkenny.

I won't lie. There have been times so far in 2016 when frustration poisoned my perspective. The inferno of ambition and desire within me raged in the wrong direction. That burning passion quenched in me a little.

Mentally, I switched off a fraction. Maybe I was just disillusioned from not knowing where I stood but I haven't lost faith. I will keep going and keep trying, until I can't go or try any more.

What Drives You On Can Drive You Crazy

IN the early days when we would go drinking after a Leinster final, one of the standout moments of the day would arrive when we'd get Tommy Walsh and John 'Dougal' Hoyne to start up about Tullaroan and Graigue-Ballycallan. It was like something out of a sketch from d'Unbelievables.

There is a fierce rivalry between the clubs because they are neighbouring parishes.

Tommy always called the Graigue-Ballycallan boys bluebottles. When he'd be drunk, he'd say, 'All I want to do is squish bluebottles.' Any time he'd pass Dougal, he'd say 'bluebottle', before stomping his feet on the ground like he was squashing a fly with his shoe.

Tommy's home address is actually Ballycallan, which Dougal always played up on. 'G'way to fuck Walsh, what are you talking about, sure you're a Ballycallan man.'

Tommy was never having any of it. 'Me father,' – Tommy would begin a lot of sentences mentioning his father – 'told me that when they were building the house at home, they built the main part of the house in Tullaroan, but they built the toilet in Ballycallan. So we eat and sleep in Tullaroan. But we go to the jacks in Ballycallan.'

And then the roof would lift off the pub. Tommy would be so into it. 'Dougal' and Ryall would just be sitting back, sipping their pints and smiling, silently trying to think up ways of how they could nail Tommy in return.

Some of the best craic we ever had was the couple of days after a Leinster final. Apart from an All-Ireland final, you'd only go drinking for one day after most games but success in a Leinster final was usually an excuse to go on the beer for at least two days. After all the hard training over the few previous months, it was a chance for lads to cut loose. And we did.

If you weren't in Billy Byrne's pub at the top of John Street by 12pm, you were chasing the day. In later years of the last decade, we used to go to Shem O'Hara's pub in Thomastown. We'd do a good bit of boozing out there before heading back into town but we'd all be scuttered drunk by 4 or 5 o'clock. Everyone was always in the one place and the craic was deadly. The lads from the south of the county try and wind up the boys from the north. The lads from the north would put on that drawl southern accent and completely go to town on the boys from down there. Nobody was spared. Nobody spared themselves with liquor. If Henry was langered, and was dancing above on tables, lads would take that as a licence to get more drunk than they already were. They'd go swinging off the chandelier.

You always look forward to celebrating after a big win but the whole scene has changed big-time too in the last few years. Lads are on phones now the whole time, on Snapchat, or else trying to impress dolls on Tinder. Different groups would be in different pubs. That is probably a reflection of society in general but group culture has changed dramatically, to the point that the feeling has been siphoned out of the moment through the communication of technology. In the past, the only time lads would take out phones was to text some other fella to see where the hell he was, or to ring some other lad who had gone up to Apache Pizza and tell him to bring back a few bags of chips.

You don't want to be looking back too far but a Leinster medal, and the craic afterwards, meant a lot more in the 2000s than it does now. I've stopped counting Leinster medals by this stage. That might sound disrespectful to fellas who would kill for just one Leinster medal but, to us, winning a Leinster title is seen as the quickest route to an All-Ireland title. It's also a statement of confidence to ourselves, as if to remind ourselves that we are on track, that we just have two more games to go and we will be All-Ireland champions again.

When we won the last two Leinsters, we went on and won the All-Irelands. That is always our plan. Even though the whole feeling around a Leinster title is almost meaningless, we still feel that the Bob O'Keeffe Cup is ours, that it is almost an insult for somebody to take it off us. Any time some team did – Galway in 2012, Dublin in 2013 – we visited severe retribution when we played them again.

The backing track was always the same. 'These boyos have

fucked up our year. They've put us through the back door.' It was only an extra match but we used it like a personal vendetta against them for having the audacity to take something off us which we felt they had no right to do. We believe the Bob O'Keeffe Cup is rightfully ours. We believe we should be winning it every year.

And that's the plan again for the 2016 Leinster final.

'We meet in Nowlan Park at 8.45am and head off for training in Dr Cullen Park (Carlow). They hand out blue and green jerseys before we play an internal match and I'm on the blue team, the weaker team. I lose all my power, focus and what I am all about. My mind is only looking for the answer to one question. 'Why am I not on the A team?' Rob Lennon is in ahead of me. Why the hell isn't Cody trusting me? My focus should be about me, showing what I am capable of, and just enjoying the day. I try and turn my attitude around during the warm-up but it's too late. We play four seven-minute games and I'm only average. My body language, attitude and mindset is all wrong. I'm too consumed by worrying. We finish training and I am completely pissed off. I get on the bus and don't engage with anyone. I drift off into my feeling sorry for myself world.'

- Diary entry, Saturday June 25th, 2016

On the bus journey to Carlow, I thought I would start on the A team. I felt I was better than Rob Lennon. I was injured for the Dublin game but now that I was back, I believed that the management would recognise that too. But as soon as that blue jersey was handed to me, I wanted to go home. I just thought, 'Fuck this, have they zero faith in me any more?'

I was so thick with myself for losing it. It was a surreal place to be because I had never felt like that before. I tried to snap myself out of that funk. 'You've got to play unbelievable now to start in this Leinster final,' I thought. I needed to be positive but I couldn't alter my mindset. I had allowed all the negativity to flood my mind and poison everything.

I was raging. My mental state was scandalous. Chris Bolger was marking Rob Lennon at the other end of the field. At one stage, he went around him. All I was thinking was, 'Take it in and stitch it, show Rob up.' I was like an antichrist when Chris drove it over the bar.

My head was so all over the place that I just basically gave up. I couldn't channel the rage properly so I started pulling wild on anything that moved. I swung so dangerously on Larks at one stage that if I had connected, I'd have cut him in two.

I lost control of everything. John Joe Farrell cleaned me out. I was so tuned out that when Eoin Murphy took a long puckout during the first half, I never moved. I didn't think the ball would reach the full-forward line but when it dropped behind the half-back line, John Joe trotted out, picked it up and drove the sliotar over the bar.

During one altercation, I pulled the helmet clean off John Joe. He buried me with a hurley. If I had tried that move before, it would have been more calculated, where I would be trying to get into John Joe's head. His head was crystal clear because he was doing a number on me. My head was spinning like a tumble drier. Part of me wanted to break the hurley across John Joe but I hadn't even the inclination to hit him a shoulder. I was only a ghost by then.

I couldn't handle it. The questions came at me in droves. 'Why have I mentally collapsed over the colour of a jersey?'

'Have I gone that mentally weak?'

'Am I that frustrated?'

As soon as I got back onto the bus, I put on my headphones and effectively put up the sign: 'Do not disturb. Dangerous animal within.'

I went out to Brother Damien in Callan the following day. As soon as I arrived in the door, he knew I was pissed off. He could see I was feeling sorry for myself. He laid into me straight away.

'You're feeling sorry for yourself because you were given a blue jersey? You're upset because you were named on the B team? What have we been speaking about? What about this being the most enjoyable year of your career, about you being the best version of JT? Where has all that gone? Where is your mental state now?'

I didn't want to hear about it. I hated that he was so right on everything he said. Part of me wanted to pick holes in a couple of his points but I had nothing on him. Brother Damien knew it too. And I had to sit and take it.

The more I listened to him, the more I accepted that he was right, that his words were what I needed to hear. Because of the honesty between us, Brother D was the only one who could snap me out of that funk. As soon as I walked out the door, I accepted that I wouldn't be starting the 2016 Leinster final.

My mind and my attitude changed immediately. I felt more comfortable in myself. Still, I was a little anxious too. I thought I was mentally stronger. I was surprised by how mentally exposed I felt in that position.

I need to pull myself together quick.

'We have a meeting tonight in Nowlan Park. We watch the first half of the 2015 All-Ireland final because Brian wants to remind us of what Galway are capable off. He also shows us an 'antics clip' of their off-the-ball shit, fist-pumping, Andy Smith kind of stuff. Brian doesn't speak but he asks Mick (Dempsey) to talk. He more or less repeats what he said in Carton House before the Dublin game, that we were never gone for people to say we were back, but that we need to build on the Dublin performance, especially in terms of work rate and intensity. Mick also says that when real team-work is shown in big games, that these are the best moments. I feel much better today. My attitude and mindset are different. I feel far more positive.'

- Diary entry, Monday June 27th, 2016

That fist-pumping shit has always driven me crazy. We hate it. We hate teams and players who showboat like that. We see lads who have won nothing, who we don't rate, dancing around like Premiership players after scoring a handy point or making a routine clearance. What planet do they think they're on?

You'll never see a Kilkenny fella at that shite. If a fella started to behave like that, nothing would be said to him but the first chance one of us would get, we'd cleave him. It wouldn't take him long to get the message. And that message is quite clear.

'That is not how we do things here. That crap will not be tolerated.'

We nearly had a hit list of guys we wanted to nail but Shane McGrath from Tipperary was always at the top of that list. I went to college with Shane in LIT. I always found him to be a great fella but when we'd see him fist-pumping after winning a free, it used to drive us all wild.

We had no great love for Andy Smith and his on-field antics but at least Andy was a hardy boy who tried to mix that edge to his game with the other shaping. More lads from other counties were all show but they had no depth when it came down to it. 'When it comes down to those guys,' Cody would often say about certain individual players from various teams, 'they just don't cut it. They'll dance around at the start but they'll be gone off the pitch by the 50th minute.'

Our attitude towards Galway has always been consistent. We believe we can get at them. We always felt that if we were right, we'd do them. And if they did beat us, which they managed in the 2012 Leinster final, we'd say, 'They won't beat us again to win the All-Ireland.'

When they came into Leinster first in 2009, we did see Galway as a threat to our provincial superiority. We never wanted to give them a foothold in Leinster. We didn't want them getting any momentum from a run in the province because they had been craving momentum after years of isolation. We wanted them wondering why they ever bothered their arses coming over from Connacht. We wanted to nail them, to send Galway a loud message in those early years at the turn of the decade. Now that they were in Leinster, we wanted to get them thinking about more than just isolation. Our aim was to give them more than just a challenge; we wanted to send them back into the wilderness.

Galway have taken us out in some big games over the years. Along with Cork, they are the only county to have beaten Kilkenny three times under Cody. Still, we never felt there was any consistency to Galway. When we came up against certain counties, you'd nearly mark the same fella the whole time. With Galway, it was always someone new, someone different. 'Here is the latest hot-shot coming now,' I'd say to myself. 'I'll send him off with his tail between his legs, like the rest of them.'

We never felt Galway could back up two or three good performances in a row but we still knew they were dangerous on any given day. We also knew that they were capable of blitzing us with goals, that when they got that scent of blood in their nostrils, they had the ability to make the kill.

They did it to us in the 2012 Leinster final. They annihilated us in the first half but we were all over the place that day. Especially myself. A couple of minutes in, Iarla Tannian had possession in the middle and instead of going for a long-range point, he dropped the ball in right on top of me and Joe Canning on the edge of the square. I hate when a forward is in behind me. I knew Canning was going to catch it and bury it, which he did.

Galway went for the jugular early that day. Tannian could have taken his point to settle him down but he aimed for Joe in the spot where he could do most damage. Galway had clearly decided that the first chance they got, they were going to bury us. We came to play that day. Galway came for war. And we were blown away.

Brian learned a lot from the 2001 All-Ireland semi-final, when Kilkenny were casual and they sleepwalked into a Galway haymaker. We all absorbed a similar lesson after that 2012 provincial final.

When we broke it down afterwards, we knew our problems stemmed from coming with the wrong mindset. We had the wrong attitude. Without saying it, we had it in our heads that we've played Galway a load of times and we always beat them in the end. We had nothing to prove and nothing to fear. Nobody was on edge that week, not properly anyway, when we should have been.

I remember one of the county board officials remarking early on in the week that ticket sales were slow. There was word it was going to rain on Sunday as well.

The public wasn't up for it because they thought it was a foregone conclusion. There was a casualness to it all.

That usually wouldn't matter when you were properly focussed, when you were in a constant state of preparation the week of a game. It was about being in a constant state of unease, of making sure that every facet of my life was on edge so that I wouldn't be flat on the day, so that I would let nothing slip come Sunday.

Casualness is only a problem if you let it be a problem and we allowed it to be an issue that day in the first half. When we were at the height of our powers, we had to almost have a 24/7 mental shield in our daily routine in Kilkenny. We had to learn that anywhere we went, in our day-to-day jobs or everyday lives, we had to protect ourselves from that loose talk, that bullshit. But we're only human. Some of it seeps in, no matter how mentally strong you are.

Brian wasn't long trying to snap us out of that mentality at half-time. We were down 14 points but Cody laid it on the line.

'If anyone thinks we're beat, go into the showers because we're going to war in the second half.'

I was nearly looking for my shampoo. I didn't think we could win but Brian wanted to make it a different game in the second half. He told all the defenders to pick your man and follow him everywhere, try and dog him into submission. It showed us how much Brian still believed in us. We still lost but we outscored Galway in the second half. That was where the road to winning that 2012 All-Ireland, against Galway, began.

Even though we were in desperate straits that day, there is never any panic in a Kilkenny dressing room, especially at half-time. You trust Brian. He trusts you. You know you're going to get a whole new lease of life for the second half.

We believe if we are in striking distance of a team at half-time, even if we are down a few points, we always feel in a better position than we felt before the match started. Then the confidence really kicks in. We all know that everyone is going to ramp it up by 10 or 15%. We know too that the opposition are going to be expecting that onslaught. Most of the time, when it comes, they get submerged beneath that tide, as if they knew all along anyway that the tide was going to wash them away like a self-fulfilling prophesy. And once we saw any weakness, we went to town on it, opening up a crevice of doubt into a canyon of misery in their minds.

'A short session is followed by a brief meeting, where Brian was the only one to speak. He spoke about what Galway bring and the hatred they must have for us. He urged us

to meet that fire, intensity and savagery. And to better it. It was a good meeting and lads really seem up for it. It is the same team as the Dublin match. I am disappointed not to be playing but I feel I will be needed at some stage. My mind is great now. So is my body. I will be ready.'

– Diary entry, Friday July 1st, 2016

Galway should hate us because we have beaten them so often at this stage. Apart from the perception we have of them, and how we view Galway, I think much of our attitude towards them stems from an incident back in 2003. Leinster played Connacht in the Interprovincial final that year in Rome. I wasn't there but I'm sure it was the usual craic with those trips – a match and then a big piss-up.

On one of the nights out, a gang of lads were getting into a taxi outside a pub. Tommy Walsh was already in the back seat beside a few Galway fellas. Tommy asked the taxi driver to wait for John Hoyne, who was still outside. One of the Galway lads instructed the taxi driver to keep going. 'Leave him there,' he said. 'He's only a Kilkenny fucker.'

Of course drink was involved. The same fella who came out with the comment was never much good himself. He was only on the panel for a year or two, without ever really starting on the team. He may not have been speaking for the rest of the Galway lads in that taxi, or on that trip, but we didn't see it that way. Kilkenny had won three of the previous four All-Irelands. Galway hadn't won anything for 15 years at that stage. The team at the top is always there to be taken down but what right

222

had that Galway lad to show one of our players such little respect? And especially with a Kilkenny player already in the car. Was that telling us what they really thought of us all?

Galway seem a different team in 2016 under Micheál Donoghue. They appear more solid, more grounded. You don't really see them fist-pumping any more but for years, that shit made our blood boil. 'Ye can bring it every now and again,' we would say to ourselves. 'But have ye the balls to bring it to us when it really matters? Can ye back it up?'

It doesn't matter how good a hurler you are, or how much of a reputation you have, they don't rate you in Kilkenny unless you have balls; unless you're a hard bastard who can make a difference when it matters.

That's the stuff Brian constantly preaches. Being manly, being brave, is a baseline requirement. When Brian changed his backroom team a few years back, he brought in Derek Lyng. I felt there was a message there straight away. Brian loved Derek. He was a savage warrior, a guy Brian always wanted in the middle of the battle. Cody could have brought in someone with more of a coaching background than Derek, someone laden down with more All-Irelands than Derek. He brought in Lyng because he represented everything Brian believed in.

Derek wasn't a flashy player but the flashy players weren't always the highest rated players in the county. The fancy plays didn't always register in Kilkenny. The raw, savage, dogged stuff did; winning a dirty ball; catching a puckout among a forest of hurleys and winning a free; putting your leg in the way, getting it reddened from a loose hurley, and winning a free; dragging your team out of a difficult situation from just being a pain in the hole and not giving in. It was mostly about being a man, having real backbone when your team needed you most. That's what they rate you for in Kilkenny.

They are the Cody values. It is not all about skill. He always had plenty of those fellas but he always wanted those lads to become dogs. Brian loved those fellas who had that awkward hardness, like 'Taggy' Fogarty, more than anyone else. Brian sees that hardness and relentlessness in fellas and he gets them to bring it every day they play. Even if their hurling let them down, Brian always believed we had enough good hurlers around them to compensate for that deficit and get the job done.

The guys we rated in Kilkenny were not the guys who were rated everywhere else. I was talking to Martin Fogarty one day and he was raving about Limerick's Wayne McNamara. 'We'd love to have him up here,' said Fogarty. Wayne was an average hurler but Fogarty saw something in him which appealed to him, and what we stood for in Kilkenny.

Tony Óg Regan was another guy who was highly valued in Kilkenny. We felt he was a serious operator but they blamed him in Galway for letting Shefflin cut loose in the second half of the 2012 drawn All-Ireland final and the Galway management effectively got rid of Tony Óg the following season.

Tipperary's Paul Curran was another fella whose stock was highly valued down here. Padraic Maher was always respected and rated but he went down a lot in our estimation after breaking Michael Rice's hand in the 2012 All-Ireland semi-final. We were never afraid to drop the blade but I don't think any of our lads would have pulled a stroke like that. It was a desperate pull and Maher was never forgiven in Kilkenny for crossing that line.

Dublin's Conal Keaney was very highly thought of. So were

some of the less heralded Cork lads; Niall McCarthy, Timmy McCarthy, Wayne Sherlock. Ronan Curran was a warrior we rated big-time.

I always had great regard for Eoin Cadogan. I met Cads at LIT in 2007 when we won a Fitzgibbon together. I always felt Eoin had something about him. He carried himself with an air of confidence, an edge, a swagger. I wasn't surprised to see him take over from 'The Rock' O'Sullivan in 2010, and having a great year that season. I still keep in contact with Cads and feel that the best might still be to come from him.

Lads had good respect for Brendan Bugler in Clare and the aggression he brought to his game. Joe Deane was very fondly received in Kilkenny but you can see a trend here with most other lads – hard men who would get the job done. We could relate to those lads because we saw so much of ourselves in them.

The player Brian probably rates more than any other fella on the Galway team – Johnny Glynn – isn't around in 2016. He's gone off to New York.

He came on as a sub in the 2012 All-Ireland final replay. He was only 19 at the time, just out of minor, and the first thing Johnny did was level me with a shoulder. He knocked me straight onto my arse. I knew nothing about him but I remember thinking, 'This guy is a hard bastard.' The same day, he ended up scoring the best goal of the match, which he stitched into the top corner.

Glynn brought that hardness and ball-winning ability that few teams possess but he's not around now. And Galway will miss him.

'We pulled away late on yesterday but we never looked like losing. We won by seven points for a finish. The match was so similar to the 2015 All-Ireland final. I thought they would have learned from it. They hadn't. I expected Galway to bring it to us but they just fell away again. I don't know what the hell it is with them. Is it lack of leadership? (Iarla) Tannian and (James) Skehill came up for a chat afterwards on the pitch. I swapped jerseys with Skehill.

I partied well into the night afterwards. This morning, I headed to Brother Damien to nurse my hangover and to do some work on my body. We spoke about the game, how I looked and felt. We set our next challenge to be 25% better (5% every week) before the All-Ireland semi-final. We speak about where that improvement will come from, both physically and mentally. Am I disappointed not to have played on Sunday? No. Why? Because 2016 is going to be my best year yet. I am in a great position. There is a great future ahead of me if I am courageous enough to go there. It is all down to trust, honesty, real honesty now. I want to surprise myself with how honest I can be with the person I trust. I know the best is yet to come. As I head off out the door to go on the beer again, I have one dominant thought in my head. 'Let's go get this 10th All-Ireland medal.'

– Diary entry, Monday July 4th, 2016

Sharp

BEFORE I went to Kilkenny training one evening in 2010, I was conversing with a few friends on Facebook. I closed down my laptop but I never logged out from my account. I was living with two of my closest friends, Niall Tyrrell and Micky Eardly, at the time. When the two lads noticed the laptop on the table and realised that my Facebook page was still active, they spotted an opportunity. And went for it.

Pretending to be me, they started tapping on my keyboard and writing all sorts of shite. I was friends with this guy on Facebook. He was gay. I didn't know it at the time. I'm not sure if the two lads knew it either but they struck up this conversation with him. It was purely a piss-take but when this guy asked me to meet up, the lads freaked out. They closed the laptop but the damage had been done. Your man clearly started talking to people about my advances. Before I knew it, the whole of Kilkenny was rife with rumours that I was gay.

People were finding it easy to join the dots. I had grown my hair long at the time, down to my shoulders, where I brushed my fringe to one side along my forehead, tucking it in behind my ears. I'm not saying that long hair suggests anything to do with your sexuality but some people may have thought that my appearance reflected my sexual orientation.

My sister texted me shortly afterwards to say that she had heard the rumours. She was very upset. I was too because the GAA community often has the mindset of a village and the thunder was spreading. A friend who lives in Limerick told me some time afterwards that he heard that I was about to come out publicly in an interview and announce that I was gay. I started to panic. Was some newspaper going to run with a story that I was gay?

It had an effect on me. I was getting frustrated with the rumours. They weren't going away. I completely respect the gay and lesbian community but the last thing I am is gay.

It took me a while to discover how the rumours had started but I was driven demented to find out how they could. One of the lads still on the Kilkenny panel is an awful messer when he is drunk. He would often sneak up to you on a night out and kiss you on the lips when you weren't looking. I was wondering if someone had seen that interaction between us one night and come to the conclusion that I was the instigator.

Was it the hair? I knew my mane had nothing to do with it but I was so paranoid and insecure that the day after we hammered Dublin in the 2010 Leinster championship, I went in to town and shaved it all off. I thought cutting my hair might trim the rumours but they didn't.

Despite my confidence having gone to another level during

that time, the side effects of that rumour reminded me of how far I still had to travel mentally. My family were telling me to laugh it off, to treat it for what it was – a rumour. But I just couldn't.

Despite the openness of my relationship with Brother Damien, I could never bring myself to tell him about it. I don't know why. He always said to me that I could talk to him about anything. I desperately wanted to talk to him but I just didn't feel comfortable telling a Christian Brother about stories that I was gay.

Eventually, in the summer of 2011, I did. I was walking out the door one day when I just left a piece of paper on the table beside him and kept going. I wrote down what I wanted to say, of how there were rumours circulating about me, and of how they were affecting me mentally.

An hour later, a text message beeped on my phone. 'You are continuing to liberate yourself. You still have great things to achieve. And we haven't seen the best of JT yet.'

I felt so much better after that text message from Brother Damien. It was like someone had erased all the anxiety from my mind as easily as someone wiping chalk off a board with a duster. I never thought about it again.

I wasn't even slightly embarrassed the next time I met Brother D. We actually had a big laugh about the whole thing. He started pulling the piss out of me because he knew all about the rumours. He had to because everybody else in Kilkenny was talking about it.

By then, it didn't matter any more. I felt liberated. I knew I still had great things to achieve. I was convinced that there was far more to come from JT.

The Warrior's Code

In any walk of life, the only thing more powerful than reality is perception. In the GAA world, though, perception can often be a particularly poisonous strain of that reality. Difference sometimes represents a code for cockiness. It creates a suspicion of arrogance. Ambivalence. Bravado. Self-indulgence. That is not how some GAA players see or seek to portray themselves but the perception is often out of their control.

Labels are convenient. A less than conservative image is often a more convenient topic of conversation than a GAA player's hurling or football skills. That image never makes up the whole truth but exceptional performances are often those players' only means of immunising the suspicion. On the bad days, those players are always the first ones condemned.

I have often struggled to understand that mentality in the GAA. Why hide that latent swagger of expression? Why conform to the usual stereotype? Most GAA players who are different, or who look different, don't go on a crusade to say they are different. How they look, how they carry themselves, is often just an extension of their personality.

For years, I was afraid to express myself. When I wasn't comfortable in my skin as a Kilkenny hurler, I wasn't fully content in myself as a person. People didn't rate me. I didn't rate myself but my perception of myself as an inter-county hurler had to change first before anybody else would see me differently.

When I became more confident, I started to express myself more. The long hair was just an example. When I bleached my hair before that U-21 game against Wexford in 2002, I associated it with being a mistake because I linked it to my performance. I sank into an abyss of embarrassment and self-pity afterwards. A tub of bleach hadn't slowed me down but I hadn't the confidence to believe otherwise.

From an image perspective, I always liked to think of myself as different. My mother nearly killed me when I dyed my hair blond before the 2000 All-Ireland Colleges final against St Flannan's. St Kieran's players and Kilkenny hurlers didn't dye their hair. It wasn't seen as the manly or respectful thing to do but I didn't care. Why shouldn't I colour my hair? What harm was I causing?

When I struggled during the early part of my senior career, though, I wouldn't have dreamed of pulling that kind of a stunt. I was afraid to piss crooked. I didn't feel I had the collateral to back it up. I was a nobody on the panel. I was lucky to even be there. Even when I was captain in 2006, I knew a lot of people in the county didn't want me on the team.

The Kilkenny hurling public are highly critical and conservative at the best of times. I won't say they are narrow minded but they have a narrow minded view of how Kilkenny hurlers should behave, of how they should carry themselves.

They demand high standards. That is the culture Brian has created but the general persona and personality of the Kilkenny hurling public is framed on humility. They don't get carried away. They don't expect the Kilkenny hurlers to get carried away.

From the county board right down to the grassroots, we like to keep everything very simplistic. We're very slow to change. We don't care what other counties are doing; what we are doing in Kilkenny works for us. That feeds into the whole public persona and perception. 'This is how we produce our hurlers. This is how our hurlers are going to be, how they are going to act, and carry themselves.'

There are no guys on the sun bed before training. Nobody wears white boots. TJ Reid came into training one evening around 2011 with a pair of green Predator F50s. They weren't even that flashy. You might get away with them now but Cody wouldn't entertain the sight of them back then. 'Don't ever let me see you with those in here again,' he told TJ.

Everything is low-key. Down-played. Some of the suits we have worn over the years for the All Ireland finals left a lot to be desired. Some of the shirts were so dated that you would see my dad eyeing them up each year. His wardrobe is bulging with them. I don't know who picks those suits and shirts. I'd love if they consulted the players but they wouldn't dream of it.

They would see it as a distraction. They certainly wouldn't ask me anyway. They'd be afraid that we'd end up looking like the Liverpool FC Spice Boys, dressed from head to toe in cream-coloured suits before the 1996 FA Cup final. I wouldn't go that far. Maybe white pants, though. Just for the craic. Just to see people's reactions in Kilkenny.

You could understand Brian's reasons for never taking us away on a foreign training camp. We always got enough done in plush spots like Carton House. Our success always backed up Brian's approach but it was always laced with that consistent understated tone for a reason. He probably felt that a training camp in Vilamoura may have given lads notions that we were more important than he wanted us to believe.

You have to admire how Brian always kept us so grounded in the face of such unprecedented success. One of his greatest achievements was to continually get us to play with the mindset and attitude of underdogs but I don't think that was ever a problem for Brian. That humility is just ingrained in us. It's almost governed by an attitude that if you start thinking you are bigger than you are, you've gone mentally soft. And every single one of us has been institutionalised by that culture.

When we had drink is us, of course we lightened up and talked ourselves up. Why wouldn't we? At times, we felt entitled to that much.

I remember being at Michael Rice's stag a few years back. A lot of us there were still playing for Kilkenny. We had this running joke about writing a book on our success, and what we were going to title the tome. We even had a WhatsApp group called 'Whatwegoingtocallthebook'. I was only looking at it there recently. One of the mock titles was, 'They said it wasn't going to be easy. But it was.'

We're not completely humble but, fuckit, we're entitled at times to bask in what we have achieved. We'd just make sure that Cody wouldn't hear about us mouthing off, or having the craic about our success. We knew if he did that we'd all be in trouble.

All of that stuff anyway would take place in the off-season but it never lasted long. We'd win the All-Ireland, cut loose for a week, then reset to club duty, and when that was all over, we'd be back thinking about winning the following year's All-Ireland.

That humility and grounded attitude ensured that our success made us stronger, not weaker. If I won an All-Ireland, and an All-Star, that ensured a whale of a winter. A team holiday. Maybe an All-Stars trip to the far side of the world as well. But as soon as I went back training in January, I'd be looking around at other lads on the panel thinking, 'These boys will take my head off to get what I have just had.'

Straight away, I felt I had a point to prove again. That is humility but it is also just reality in Kilkenny. You just go again. You keep going. We never get soft because we have built up such a tolerance and resilience that when we match that with the belief we have in ourselves, we know that if we are right, physically and mentally, nobody will live with us.

You are always inspired too by the humility of the men who went before you, the guys who began paving the path to greater glory when that picture of greater glory and domination was still far off in the distance. I remember Peter Barry and Andy Comerford saying to us, 'There's a lot more to being a Kilkenny hurler than putting on a Kilkenny top and swanning around the town thinking you're better than you are. If any of ye here think that, off out the door with ye.'

We never verbalised it but we'd like to think that we have continued that culture with the younger players. We never said much because we didn't have to. All lads had to do was look at Henry Shefflin, JJ Delaney, Brian Hogan and Tommy Walsh, at how hard they trained, at how they carried themselves. After all they had achieved in their careers, how the hell could any young lad get carried away with himself?

No matter how many All-Ireland medals or All-Stars you had, you couldn't get ahead of yourself. Brian Cody's greatest achievement is getting lads to believe that we need Kilkenny more than Kilkenny needs us.

And he is right. No matter what you have done, you're dispensable in Cody's eyes. He knows it. He knows that we desperately need and want Kilkenny hurling.

I like that humility to our approach but I also don't see anything wrong with being a little different, while still abiding by those principles. As far as I've always been concerned, I can do and say whatever I want. I can project whatever image I want to portray of myself, as long as I keep backing it up on the pitch.

I always took pride in my appearance. I always liked fashion and good clothes. I always liked different hairstyles but my confidence was so low for so long that I was afraid any altered appearance would be deemed unacceptable to the Kilkenny hurling public. And to Brian.

It was only when I finally started to believe in myself as a hurler that I began to express myself more as a person, to promote my image more. I wanted to present that image of being a confident, suave, well-presented and well-dressed modern young man.

When I would wear something off the wall, the boys would take the piss out of me. I'd just tell them that they'd all be wearing the same gear in six months' time, that their girlfriends would be buying them the exact same stuff for Christmas.

I'm sure there were plenty of times when people around the city looked at what I was wearing and wondered if I was on a different planet. I didn't care but you could detect that attitude. For someone to express themselves in Kilkenny, the eyebrows are raised higher here than they would be in plenty of other counties, many of whom would be perceived to have a more diverse culture than what we have in Kilkenny.

On the other hand, when you are backing it up on a hurling pitch, some people will recognise you for that diversity. A father came up to me on the pitch one day after a game and told me that his young son wanted to wear skinny jeans because he saw me wearing them. But if I had played poorly that day, I'm sure plenty of others would have been privately saying, 'Look at that fucking eejit. He must think he's in the boy band One Direction.'

Irish guys are less inhibited now about expressing themselves through their clothes but for years, attitudes within the GAA almost seemed to portray fashion as being soft and unmanly. Paul Galvin changed a lot of those attitudes and I always liked his approach. He felt fashion could change how you feel and how others feel about you. Galvin also sees fashion as a form of expression. And I could always relate to that. I liked looking well. I liked to express myself because what I wore was an extension of my personality beyond a Kilkenny jersey.

I like fashion. I like shopping. I often spend a day in Dublin, Kildare or Newbridge just browsing around shops, looking at new clothes, checking out different brands and new labels. I often did it on the week of a big game. It might not have been ideal to be on my feet for so long but I viewed it as the perfect way to reset my mind to a pedestrian pace before it accelerated on game day. Nobody would have bothered me. There aren't too many hurling fanatics floating around Kildare Village or Dundrum Shopping Centre.

Brian didn't want us in the spotlight but I liked it. I believed that appearance and attention could help you get ahead in life. Of course there were monetary rewards from those appearances but I also liked the way it all fed into my ego.

By raising my profile, I also acted accordingly. If I was in the spotlight more often than most Kilkenny players, I had to back up that profile with my performances on the pitch. I had to be in the optimum mental and physical state to be the person I was projecting myself to be.

I felt I was constantly raising the bar personally by giving myself those opportunities. Most of the Kilkenny guys were happy to melt into the background but I liked the public recognition. I also felt it was a reward for my hard work, an acknowledgement of the standards I repeatedly set, and met, on the pitch.

I also viewed it as part of my overall development, both as a player and person. The recognition, that self-promotion, gave me confidence. It boosted my ego. Other players ran from that fear of over-exposure. They didn't want to take the risk it might entail if a public appearance was followed up by a poor performance. I just embraced it.

Henry got most of those endorsement deals but if the opportunity ever came up, and I wanted to do something, I would. You'd know the gigs you could do, and the ones you wouldn't bother with. Brian was very good to me but you had to play the game with him too. I knew I'd only be pissing him off if I went with a request every second week. But if I fancied something, I'd do it.

The hardest request I ever had to square with Brian was for the first screening of the now annual TV series, 'The Toughest Trade'. Ciarán O'Hara, the TV producer, rang me with the idea. It was an opportunity to spend a week playing baseball with the Miami Marlins while All-Star baseball player Brian Schneider swapped his bat for a hurley to spend time in Kilkenny and line out with James Stephens.

I know for a fact that a lot of lads in Kilkenny would have

ran a mile from that request. They would have seen it as a distraction. They wouldn't have even broached it with Brian but as soon as Ciaran had the words out of his mouth, I wanted to be on that plane to Miami.

I was just firm with Brian. The plan was to fly out on the Monday morning after playing Dublin in the 2015 league. I would be back by the Saturday, which meant only missing two collective training sessions. I told Brian that it wouldn't make any difference to my overall focus but I left him in no doubt as to how much I wanted to avail of the opportunity. He agreed.

I had a camera crew and production team trailing me every day, which was extremely draining in such heat, but I loved being involved in a professional environment. And I enjoyed being on camera.

The first day I was out there, a group of Latino players approached me and asked which sport I played.

'Hurling.'

'Curling?'

'Hurling,' I repeated.

'Hireling?'

'Google it,' I said.

They obviously did. The next day I spotted them, they were all over to me straight away. 'Holy shit man, that game is fucking nuts.'

When we were doing catching drills later that day, I ditched the catching glove and just started using my left hand to field baseballs flying around the place. Trying to connect on a 90mph baseball though, was a whole different ball game. Luis Alicea, who won a World Series as a coach with the Boston Red Sox tried to teach me the basics of the technique. Hurlers mostly strike on the front foot, which is the complete opposite of how they hit in baseball. I was completely naïve. I thought I'd walk up, get my feet right, and just smash the thing out of the park. I was way out of my league. I had to alter my stance so that everything was aligned from my ankles to hips to knees to chin.

I immersed myself in the culture of the Marlins for the four days I was there. It was a different world. One afternoon at practice, I got chatting to Giancarlo Stanton, who had just signed a 13-year contract worth $325 million, the richest contract in US sports history. Each of the 30 teams in Major League Baseball play 162 games over a six-month season. It's a crazy and attritional schedule but I'd love to see how Giancarlo would have survived if he was pitched into the Nowlan Park cauldron and had lads leathering the shite out of him from every angle.

He was a right fielder in baseball but Brian would probably have used Stanton as a half-back because he was an animal striker. A couple of months after I left, Stanton hit a 466-foot home run, the longest in the history of Citi Field, home of the New York Mets. That's crazy shit considering the pace the ball is coming at from the pitcher.

That was my challenge – to line out in a college game and hit a 90mph pitch coming from a Major League pitcher who had retired that week. It wasn't easy. You basically have to start swinging before the ball even comes near you but you only get three attempts.

The morning of the game, I was shitting myself. I expressed my concerns to Ronan, one of the producers. 'This whole thing hinges on me clocking this yoke,' I said to him.

He instantly put my mind at ease. 'Don't worry Jackie,' he

said. 'We're staying here all night if we have to until you hit one.'

I actually hit the third ball. The first two flew past me. There were two foul balls called as well before I wound up and made the connection. I was so surprised that I actually stood for a couple of seconds, not realising the ball had zipped down the field.

It was a great experience but the whole week was some craic. We hired this flash red sports car. We were filming one morning down on South Beach Miami and I just ditched the car as close as I could to the promenade. Over there, you're not allowed to park on the opposite side of the street but I thought I was in Kilkenny city and I just pulled into the first parking place I spotted. We were in the middle of the interview and I looked over and saw the car being towed away.

On the night the programme was aired, the sponsors AIB had a launch night in Dublin. I would love to have gone but Kilkenny were training that evening and I didn't want to push it any more with Brian. He might have thought my head was up my hole. There were other times when I'm sure he did but I took up the opportunity anyway.

Three weeks before the 2015 All-Ireland final, I got asked to appear in a TV advert for Electric Ireland, who sponsor the All-Ireland minor championships. I wanted to do it but initially, I didn't think it was possible. I was still hobbling around on crutches. I couldn't drive. Given that I was pouring nearly every minute of every day into trying to be right for the All-Ireland final, I didn't think I could afford to waste a day at a TV shoot in Dublin. And on top of all that, what the hell would Cody think?

Yet the more I thought about the opportunity, I said to myself, 'Why not?' A break from the relentlessness of the grind might not do me any harm. Plus, being asked was also justification for my efforts, and for me pushing the boundaries as far as I was in an attempt to get what I wanted. I just asked myself, 'Irrespective of what Brian thinks, why shouldn't I do it?'

Opel were kind enough to loan me an automatic car for the day so I could drive to Dublin. Myself and Dublin footballer Michael Dara Macauley did two separate shoots under the same theme, 'This is Major'. We set the scene by making it look and sound as if we were reminiscing about our first inter-county minor championship game when we were really talking about our Debs night. Macauley was busting moves on the dance-floor and sipping from a piña colada through a fancy straw. I was dolled up in a light-blue three-piece suit, flashing a cheesy mile at the camera while holding a bunch of flowers and a box of Milk Tray chocolates.

I wonder what Cody thought of that one?

The Sweetest

ONE weekend in November 2013, a load of us travelled down to Wexford for Brian Dowling's stag. We were all well juiced up on the Friday night, especially Tommy Walsh. He approached me with that glint in his eye, shining with a mad fusion of craziness and intent.

'Who do you want?'

'Wha?'

'I want Tony Kelly anyway.'

'What the hell are you raving about, Tommy?'

'You can have Podge (Collins) if you want him.'

Then he looked over at JJ Delaney. 'JJ, you can take Conor McGrath.'

The whole night, he kept it going. 'I can't wait to get Tony Kelly next year,' he was repeating.

Then he'd look over at me again. 'Hey Jackie, you better make sure you sort out Podge Collins.'

The following morning, Tommy was up at 8am. He got one of the lads who was on the stag, but who wasn't drinking, to drive him out to the beach in Wexford. He was still drunk when he jumped into the freezing Irish Sea. 'Tony Kelly isn't training in the sea in the middle of November,' he was roaring. 'So I'll be ready for him next year.'

It was crazy shit but it was the theme for the weekend because the boys kept winding Tommy up. And, like one of those wind-up toys, Tommy kept it going.

'I want Tony Kelly next year. I'll be ready for him.'

'No, Tommy, I'll take Kelly,' I repeated on numerous occasions, just to get him going.

'No way Jackie. He's mine. I want him.'

Kelly had still to turn 21 but he'd already been named Hurler of the Year and Young Hurler of the Year. Podge had been runner-up in both categories. They were both the face of a new, young and exciting Clare team which had won a brilliant All-Ireland against Cork. Ten of the Clare players which featured in the All-Ireland final replay were under 22. They were after winning successive All-Ireland U-21 titles. The general feeling around the hurling world was that, now that Clare had arrived, they were going to take over.

That was the challenge to us and, in Tommy's mind, he was already getting ready for it. That was how his mind always worked. After we beat Waterford in the 2011 All-Ireland semi-final, we were in Christy Morrison's in Kilkenny City on the beer on the Monday. The previous year, Patrick 'Bonner' Maher had done a job on Tommy in the All-Ireland final. He didn't really clean Tommy out but he limited his influence on the match and Tommy was still stewing from it. Tommy picked up a stool and took off out the door. We took no notice of him until he arrived back a minute later and put the stool above his head. 'This is Bonner Maher,' he said. 'And I'm going to eat him alive in the All-Ireland.' Then he threw the stool on the ground and a big roar went up.

None of us had any doubts that Tommy would take care of 'Bonner' in 2011. We were mad keen for a crack at Tipperary in that final. We swore retribution after 2010, and we got it. After being beaten twice in the 2013 championship, we were even more demented to prove to ourselves, and to everyone else, that we weren't finished. But we weren't sure that we would. We didn't know whether we had reached the end of the line.

We knew we would be seriously competitive but there was certainly some anxiety among us, especially myself, about how fast these Clare lads were, and of how much pace, athleticism and mobility had seemed to dominate that 2013 summer. Clare were like a crowd of Olympic sprinters. Cork weren't far behind them. Dublin had serious mobility and athleticism too.

I forced myself to go to that 2013 All-Ireland final, the drawn game, just to see the pace up close. I was in the front row in the Cusack Stand. Clare was at one side of me, Martin Walsh, Tommy's brother, was at the other side. Podge Collins took off on a solo run down the sideline in the second half like Usain Bolt. When it looked like he'd been cornered, he flicked the ball over some lad's head, before popping it over the bar. 'Holy fuck,' I thought to myself, 'this has gone to another level.'

Then I was looking across the pitch and seeing acres and acres of free space. I was picturing myself out there, JJ beside me, and wondering how we would shut down those channels, how we would deal with those runners coming at us like steam trains. The competitor in me was saying, 'We would survive; I would survive.'

But I had to ask myself deep down, 'Is that just the warrior coming out in me? Would I really cope with that pace? Would I really survive in that heat?'

I nearly started to have nightmares about it all. I almost had this Tom & Jerry cartoon vision of Podge running between my legs and scoring a point off me. And like in the famous cartoon, everyone laughing at me, and everyone silently cheering for Jerry who had just done a number on Tom, the big, bad cat. Again.

It also reignited memories of the terror I felt when marking Ben O'Connor in 2006, and the mental torment that went with it. I was more experienced in 2014. I had far more confidence. I had a worldliness about me that I would have wished for in 2006. But I was eight years older too. The miles on the clock had added up. Would I be ready for the pace of Podge now?

I knew there were going to be changes, especially in the defence. I was 32. JJ was 32. So was Tommy. Brian Hogan was 33. Cody was never going to play all four of us at the same time, especially the way the game had gone. There was a fear that the game had just caught up on us, that teams like Clare and Cork were speeding past us.

We accepted that reality but we also knew Clare or Cork, or Tipperary or whoever, would face a different reality from us.

Brian Murphy was the Cork centre-back in the 2013 replay but he was man-marking Podge and was chasing him around like a hare. Podge and Murphy were inside in the corner when Pat Donnellan charged 50 yards straight up the middle to set up Shane O'Donnell for his first goal. I was thinking, 'If Hogie

The Sweetest

hadn't nailed him, JJ would. And if JJ had missed him, I'd have buried him. And if all of us had missed Donnellan, Tommy would have taken him out.'

So when we looked at it coldly and more clinically, we were all thinking, 'These boys are not as good as they think, or as good as everyone else is making them out to be.'

When we went back at the end of 2013, there was a completely different feel about things from the very start. We went back training early but the older players were given some time off from that collective training over the winter because Brian wanted us fresher for the long haul. Derek Lyng and James McGarry were brought in as selectors. It was never verbalised by the older crew but we knew that this was one last hurrah for the majority of that group.

The fact that Tommy was talking about facing it in November, when he was on a stag, when hurling should nearly have been the last thing on his mind, showed how intent we all were in embracing, and meeting, that challenge head on.

At the end of the 2013 All-Ireland quarter-final, one of the Cork players turned to 'Taggy' Fogarty, shook his hand and said, 'Enjoy the concert tonight.'

He knew all about our plans because the whole country did. Bruce Springsteen was performing that evening in Nowlan Park and we had a Garda escort booked to ferry us back there in time for the show. I live in Kilkenny city so I was going home first but all the other lads had their glad-rags with them in Thurles. We were nearly thinking more about what classics 'The Boss' was

247

going to perform than focussing on the heat Cork were going to bring.

I couldn't have been 100% tuned in. Only a handful of us were. After losing to Dublin in a replay, we stumbled into a qualifier against Tipperary a week later but we still summoned the resolve to beat them. We overcame Waterford the following week in another savage battle, which we won after extra-time. We thought we were back on track. We thought we had got over the hump, that the road to an All-Ireland final had cleared for us. We expected to beat Cork but they blew us out of the water that day in Thurles.

It was only a few days later I realised how much all of us in Kilkenny were off our normal page of preparation. I was driving past Nowlan Park when I spotted these huge trucks entering through the gates. They were still dismantling the stage and gathering up all the concert gear. The pitch was in shite. The first All-Ireland semi-final was the following week. 'Where the hell would we have trained if we had got there?' I asked myself. 'If we wanted to work on tactics, where could we have gone where the public, or spies from another county, couldn't see us?'

There was a festival atmosphere in the county with Bruce coming to town but we got completely side-tracked by it. You couldn't blame the county board, or anyone else. They were making good money out of the concert. It boosted the profile of the city but it galled me that we still couldn't work our way around the distractions of the concert. I blame us the players. I was trying to organise a ticket for the concert for a friend a few days before the match. That might seem harmless but tickets were normally the last thing on my mind leading up to a game.

It was a unique occasion. The Boss wasn't going to be in town any time soon again but as far as I was concerned, I never wanted to see or hear about Springsteen again after that night. After coming on stage, he launched into a three-and-a-half-hour set of pure rock 'n' roll. He played all his old classics. The catchy 'Death To My Hometown' was the most up-tempo song of the set. Shortly afterwards, he performed 'Wrecking Ball'.

To me, those two songs summed that whole day up. Kilkenny was rocking that night but I knew that all of us, and most of the county, would feel like the place was shrouded in death the following day. Because Bruce had taken a wrecking ball to the players' heads.

Tommy was always the soundest, most level-headed and decent guy you'd ever meet but he was some craic with drink in him. In 2009, our All-Ireland medals presentation clashed with the GPA All-Stars. There was a good few of us getting awards and the GPA didn't want our absence to compromise the event so Dessie Farrell, the GPA executive, brokered a deal with us. We would come to the ceremony, and they would present the hurling awards early, at 8pm. They would book a fleet of taxis immediately afterwards and fill them up with drink for us. We would be back in Kilkenny by 10pm.

We were flaming before we even left the CityWest hotel. Tommy was so merry that he took Conor O'Mahony's award instead of his own. Even though the Kilkenny people were waiting on our arrival for the night to fully kick off in Langton's, we got the taxi to stop at Paddy's pub in Clara. Mam and Dad were texting to find out where we were but we literally didn't know. We hardly knew whether it was night or day.

There were two auld fellas at the bar, quietly sipping their pints. Tommy went to the jacks and when he arrived back, he pretended to be a young bull who had just been let out onto a field for the first time. A young bull wouldn't have been as wild – Tommy was leaping around like a demented leprechaun.

Then he decided to play a game. 'You've to disappear around the corner,' he said. 'And you've to come back as an animal. And we have to guess what kind of a beast you are.'

We were roaring and lewing like calves, snorting like pigs, kicking like horses. This was all going on while we were suited up to the nines in Tuxedos. The two auld fellas at the bar knew who we were but they were looking at us like we were aliens who had landed from Mars. The phones were hopping by that stage. We jumped into a taxi and were back in Langton's within 20 minutes. We were all hammered. You could see Brian looking over at us but we didn't give a shite.

When Tommy was called up to collect his medal, he grabbed the microphone off Mícheál Ó Muircheartaigh, who was the MC. He started talking all sorts of stuff. It had zero context to the night but he went on about Tullaroan, and their rich history as a club. 'Me father always says, 'You think you're great with all your All-Irelands but you don't have a county medal with the sash.'' Then he looked down at his father. 'I don't have one now Da. But I'll have one some day.'

Then he turned his attention to Brian. 'And where's the other lad – Buddha.'

Holy fuck. I nearly collapsed. We all did. A few months earlier, the comedian John Kenny had done a piss-take sketch on Brian, where he referred to him as Buddha. Now, Tommy thought he was John Kenny. It was like something Kenny and Pat Shortt would pull off with d'Unbelievables, only it was better.

'Ah Buddha,' said Tommy, 'the best of them all.'

I looked over at Brian, who in fairness took it in good spirit. When Ó Muircheartaigh tried to put an end to the circus and take the microphone off Tommy, he pushed him away. He went on for another ten minutes.

James Ryall knew the camera man who was recording the event. He tried everything to get a copy of Tommy's stunt but the county board had got to him first. He was warned to make sure that part of the evening was deleted. Can you imagine if that sketch somehow made its way onto YouTube? It would have got more hits than Justin Bieber.

The weather conditions during the second half of the 2014 All-Ireland semi-final against Limerick were like something out of a biblical downpour, borrowed from the end of the world. It was primal. Feral. The rain storm was raw and relentless. The floodlights were on but you could hardly see anything at times. They were unimaginable conditions for hurling but I loved it.

We were hanging on by our fingertips but I never felt as alive in my life. It almost felt transcendent. We were all so desperately trying to stay alive, to keep afloat. Everything was underpinned by a relentless expectancy that anything could happen next, that one fatal error could sink us. It was so breathless that it almost felt like a dream. And yet we were living so much on the edge that we were living in the fullest sense.

It was all kind of magical. It felt like there was 120,000 at the game. We didn't think Limerick would bring it but they brought absolute war to Croke Park that day. They had us on the rack. They should have beaten us. We were on the brink but Limerick couldn't push us over the precipice.

I found myself in places of the field that day that I never saw before. I was up supporting Henry on one occasion for a scoring chance. It was a mad, crazy experience but we had that strange but warm feeling walking off the field afterwards, half-giggling, knowing that we probably should have been beaten, but acknowledging and appreciating that, despite everything, we weren't defeated.

Up to that point of the season, we had answered all the questions asked of us. We annihilated Offaly. We beat Galway well after a replay. We hammered Dublin in the Leinster final but we were only really forced to dig into our resources of willpower and motivation when Limerick charged at us like a rhinoceros in that third quarter when outscoring us by 0-6 to 0-1. We repelled the charge and flattened them with a run of late scores.

We knew we were fully back but the doubts resurfaced after the drawn All-Ireland final against Tipperary. I wasn't great. I had a virus two weeks beforehand. It was out of my system the week of the final but it had drained my energy levels. It wasn't an excuse, because there are no excuses when you go out there in Croke Park, but I had nothing in me. James Woodlock took off past me at one stage of the first half and left me for dead.

I was detailed to mark Noel McGrath. He was playing very deep. I was following him everywhere but Mick Dempsey arrived onto the field after about 15 minutes and told me to go back into the corner. I did but I was all over the shop. We all were because we couldn't get a handle on the movement of the Tipp attack. Noel McGrath came back in on me again because Tipp felt he had my number that day. He had because he took me for four points from play. Seamus Callanan took JJ for five points. 'Bubbles' O'Dwyer hit five points from play. 'Bonner' Maher scored one goal and should have had another. Lar Corbett rattled a chance off the post. We saved two Seamus Callanan penalties. Tipp had a late chance from a 'Bubbles' long range free to win the game that drifted a fraction wide.

We had a recovery session the following Tuesday night, but all the goalkeepers, defenders and midfielders were asked to stay behind. It was almost like an inquisition into what had gone wrong. Opinions were sought. When David Herity mentioned something about puckouts, Brian nailed him, more or less telling him to shut the fuck up. Puckouts weren't the issue.

When Brian asked me what I thought, I took the opportunity to question him and management for their approach beforehand. We were only told an hour before the game, in the dressing room, who we were marking, who we were matching up with. 'To me, that was completely naïve of management,' I said. 'I needed to know a couple of weeks in advance who I was supposed to be picking up so I could mentally prepare for that player, and that challenge.'

Brian may have been thick with me for calling him naïve, but I didn't care. He couldn't argue with the numbers. Tipp hit 1-28. They could have scored 5-30.

Brian may have accepted as much but he wasn't slow in reminding us that we had failed too. One of our tactics was for our forwards to press hard on their defenders for short puckouts.

The Tipp goalkeeper Darren Gleeson is an excellent striker and we wanted to force him to go long. We did but we still didn't dominate on those long, high puckouts. 'Bonner' Maher's goal came from a long ball that broke through our half back line. Brian wasn't happy with us as a defensive unit. I knew there and then that there would be changes to the defence for the replay.

There were. Kieran Joyce was named at centre-back. Padraig Walsh came in at wing-back. We settled on different match-ups, ones we had spoken about, and which we were comfortable with. I knew if we, as a defence, played well, that we had a chance. And when I heard Brian Gavin was named referee for the replay, I knew we had a right chance.

The Wednesday after the 2011 All-Ireland final, I ended up in Dublin on the piss. The lads who were teaching in the capital had to be back at work on the Thursday so we decided to join them as they attempted to drain the last drop out of the celebrations.

I was loaded. Myself and Richie Power got dislocated from the main group and we arrived into Flannery's on Camden Street around 9pm. Brian Gavin, who had refereed the final the previous Sunday, was standing at the bar drinking on his own. He still had a plaster across his nose, covering the cut he suffered when Tommy Walsh started swinging his hurley like a sword among a group of players. Tommy was trying to hit one of the Tipp lads but he clipped Gavin and his nose started pumping blood.

We had a right laugh about it. We had a right few Jägerbombs with Gavin as we drank with him into the night. We completely took the piss out of him but Gavin took it all in good spirits.

When we were on the All-Stars trip to San Francisco in 2012, there was a sizeable Kilkenny contingent on that tour. A group of about 15 of us went to a college American football match, most of which were Kilkenny lads, plus a handful of others, including Gavin. We had a whale of a time. We were throwing American footballs around the car park. We all got on well with Gavin. I felt there was a connection there. Tommy sent him a jersey after that incident in 2011 and I know Gavin appreciated the gesture. I got the impression that he liked us; that he admired what we had achieved.

Gavin could have sent Tommy off that day in 2011. He might not have seen Tommy swing the hurley but plenty of other referees would have gone looking for the culprit and wouldn't have been happy until he had been punished.

To us, that sent out a message. Gavin liked the game played on more physical terms anyway than most referees. As defenders, we felt that we would be able to dial up the heat on Tipp forwards for the replay, that we had more of a licence to cut loose than we had under Barry Kelly, who refereed the draw.

We'd long had an issue with Kelly. When Dublin beat us in the 2013 replayed Leinster semi-final, one of our lads was within earshot of Kelly after 'Dotsy' O'Callaghan scored a point. 'Great point, Dotsy,' Kelly said to him. It may have only been a harmless acknowledgement of a great score but to us, Kelly encroached past a barrier he shouldn't have breached.

In the All-Ireland quarter-final a month later, Kelly dismissed Henry on a second yellow card. The same afternoon, Cork's Shane O'Neill escaped with what should have been a red card. In May of that year, Kelly aggravated the locals with his handling of our league final victory over Tipperary in Nowlan Park. That was a bad-tempered match. Eight yellow cards and two reds were evenly split between the teams, but we felt that we didn't get full justice that day.

When Setanta Sports filmed a series on referees that season titled, 'Men in Black', Kelly was wired with a microphone for a couple of matches, including that Cork-Kilkenny All-Ireland quarter-final. At one stage of that match, after Henry had been sent off, there was a loaded exchange between Kelly and Tommy Walsh.

As he was running back into position, Tommy pulled up beside Kelly, and sniped at him. 'What's gone wrong with you against us?' he said, before disappearing out of the camera shot.

Kelly took five or six seconds to compose his reply before putting himself within Tommy's earshot: 'Be very careful,' he said. 'Be very careful [number] five.'

Barry lost his wife a few months later in 2013, who passed away after a short illness. We respected how hard it must have been for him to return to refereeing in 2014, and to listen to us mouthing off to him, but we still believed that he had it in for us. And that year's drawn All-Ireland final confirmed our theory. In our minds, the late free Kelly awarded to Tipperary, which 'Bubbles' missed, was not a free.

If it had gone over, God only knows how Cody and Ned Quinn would have reacted to Kelly.

Gavin is a top class referee but we knew we could push our physicality levels more to the extreme for the replay. We knew that if we got in Tipperary's faces, if we roughed them up more than we had in the drawn game, that we'd have them where we wanted them. We knew that when we put on the squeeze that they wouldn't have the balls to respond.

As soon as the ball was thrown in, we were like wild animals. The game was only on a handful of seconds when 'Bubbles' got a ball and I blocked him down. Lar Corbett picked up the break and Paul Murphy blocked him down. The ball was turned over and that pattern continued.

In the increased hostility of the environment, Tipperary couldn't find any fluidity or rhythm. We hounded them out of their stride. We never let them get any energy or momentum. The game was played on our terms. We squeezed the play much better than we had in the drawn game. I was marking 'Bubbles' because we changed our match-ups. He scored a couple of points but we all won our individual battles. Our defence was never dragged, disorientated and discomfited like it had been three weeks earlier. For a finish, we swallowed up that Tipp attack whole, like a boa constrictor snake.

The final whistle that day was something else. We had won plenty of All-Irelands before but the explosion of emotion was so primal that it felt like our first. JJ and I were on our knees as we saluted the Kilkenny crowd behind the Canal End. It was hard to make sense of such a magical day, of an All-Ireland final win that was probably the sweetest ever for that group.

Deep down, we knew that group of players would never be together again. JJ, Tommy, Brian Hogan, David Herity and 'Taggy' walked away that winter. Henry finished the following March after Ballyhale's All-Ireland club triumph.

The tribe was still moving on but it was fitting that some of our greatest warriors departed the battlefield shrouded in the greatest glory imaginable.

'It's hard to describe the feeling of winning an All-Ireland. It's an inner happiness that lasts for months but the main hit for me was immediately after the final whistle. It was euphoric, the ultimate high.
Motivation or hunger were never an issue for any of us. For most guys, those feelings were 95% of the reason why they kept coming back for more. For me, it was always 100%. I was completely addicted to it.'

chapters
XVI-XX

Savagery

'We meet in the Newpark (hotel) at 10am for breakfast.
Larks collected me. Afterwards, we headed to Carton
House. We get the schedule for the day along the way; food,
train, food, ice-baths, pool/recovery, physio, meal, and then
time to ourselves from 8pm onwards. Training begins at
1.30pm and I am mentally and physically tuned in, mad
for road. We go straight into 4x10 minute games. The
teams are continually mixed up. I marked Mick Malone,
Wally (Walter Walsh) and Colin (Fennelly). I do very
well. I dominate my position. I am on the ball a lot. I felt
I had a great presence out there. Afterwards, I headed to
the pool for recovery. Then I head back to the room, which
I am sharing with Larks. I am wrecked. All the lads are
either playing pool or getting rubs but I fit in a one-hour
nap. I feel great afterwards. After our meal, Paul Murphy
organises a soccer penalties tournament, €10 a man, which
turns out to be great fun. The lads then break into a North
v South soccer game but I only watch on as I am too tired

*after the day. Brian soon gets wind of it and shuts it down,
but not before Kevin Kelly smacks a volley and hits Cody. It
was very funny.'*

– Diary entry, Friday July 22nd, 2016

I DON'T know what it was about Carton House but the
place always brought out the animal in me. I used to get
so excited by being in that professional environment that
it almost took me over. The whole weekend was normally built
around an internal training game, where I considered my own
safety, or the safety of anyone I was marking, irrelevant. I got
so pumped up for those matches that I'd turn into Darth Vader
in a bad mood.

We were all always psyched on those training weekends.
Tommy Walsh once said that one of his favourite wins was
the B team's result against the A team before the 2014 drawn
All-Ireland final. The B team's half-forward line that afternoon
was Tommy, Henry Shefflin and Richie Power. They were
pissed off to have been relegated to the bench that summer and
you could see the venom and anger steaming out through their
pores.

All of the B team dialled up the heat that afternoon. Willie
Phelan manhandled TJ Reid for the whole game. Tommy spent
most of the match leathering his brother, Padraig. The A team
responded. Cillian Buckley went to war on Power. I hit anything
that moved. It was an absolutely savage battle. The B team
walked off elated. The A team were like demented lunatics. Any
time our defenders were angry and upset after one of those big
internal training games, I knew we were ready.

The success of those training weekends usually hinged on the match because everything was geared towards it. We'd normally have a team meeting the night before and Brian would always re-emphasise what was at stake, how places were up for grabs. He was always so true to his word that 21 or 22 fellas would go to bed believing they had a chance of playing in an upcoming All-Ireland semi-final or final. The core of the team was nailed down but lads on the periphery believed that if they took out one of Brian's main men that they could move themselves from the margin into the centre of the picture. In truth, that was often a licence for anarchy.

Those games weren't always played for regular, sustained time periods. They could be broken up into three 15-minute segments, or four tens. Mick Dempsey had it worked out that the ball was normally in play for an average of 80 seconds. In those matches, that average usually went through the roof. The forwards would get such a hammering that there would hardly be any scores. There were times when they didn't even want to score. Forwards would often get away from you but if you made any attempt to get close, they'd nearly turn back and engage you for a reason. They wanted to pull across you. They wanted retribution.

They often had every right. Before the 2011 All-Ireland final, I was marking Colin Fennelly in a training game in Carton House. It was Colin's first year on the panel. He was flaky enough at the time and I knew I could rough him up. A ball came in between us at one stage but it was going five yards over our heads. I was nowhere near it but I just pulled straight down on Colin's head, like an executioner would swing an axe. You could have heard the bang in Maynooth town nearly a mile away.

The Warrior's Code

I just turned and ran. Colin was holding his head. Then he put his arms out in the air, like an exclamation mark as to why there had been no free. If I pulled that stroke in a match, I'd have been suspended for six months.

Brian raised his voice. 'JACKIE, don't do it.'

'Colin,' said Brian then in the same sentence, 'get used to it.'

The same afternoon, there was a big mill at the other end of the field. Tommy Walsh went for John Mulhall and nearly killed him. Nobody batted an eyelid. It was just another standard Kilkenny training match.

Anything went. Anything. In a training game between the 2014 All-Ireland final draw and replay, a row broke out between Eoin Larkin and Padraig Walsh. Larks and Tommy Walsh are the best of friends but Tommy wasn't impressed with the punishment he was dishing out to his brother. When a melee ensued and Larks fell to the ground, Tommy wired into Larks, and let him have it.

Tommy was always uncompromising on a pitch but I had never seen him lose the cool like that before.

Larks got up and made a run for him. Lads had to hold him back but Tommy wasn't backing off either. Brian came in and tried to smother the blaze but it was still raging because Larks was spitting fire. He blew up the match and Larks stormed off the pitch. Brian roared at him to come back. When he eventually did, the blood was streaming down Larks' face from this big cut over his eye.

Tommy was standing up for his brother but you could sense the tension in the air afterwards. Tommy knew the issue had to be addressed. He left Langton's and called straight up to Larks' house. His daughter, Holly, answered the door.

264

'Is your father there?' Tommy asked. When Larks cooled down, the two boys squared their differences.

Brian was probably delighted with the row. The two boys showed the fight that evening that we hadn't shown against Tipperary in the drawn All-Ireland final. He knew if we brought that fight to the table for the replay that Tipperary wouldn't live with us. We did. And Tipperary couldn't handle it.

Nobody carried over grudges or stored spite from those training games because if they did, we wouldn't have had a team. There could have been multiple court cases for GBH or aggravated assault but that was what you signed up for. You just took the punishment and got on with your business.

We were so tight that nothing got out of hand. When Richie Hogan came into the panel first, he got some going over. He came in with a huge underage profile but we soon cut him down to size. On his first night in, he marked Tommy in a training game. The second evening he marked me. The third evening he marked Noel Hickey. We all descended on Richie like a pack of wild dogs and ate him alive.

Young lads got a savage education, just like all of us did. Before the 2014 drawn All-Ireland final, myself and Ger Aylward went to war on each other. We pucked the heads off one another. During one altercation, I pulled the helmet off him. Ger had the ball in his hand and he just lashed it straight at me. I stepped out of the way and the ball flew over the bar.

'Puck it out,' roared Cody. Next ball. That's all that ever mattered. A lot of the time when the ball was in the air, lads would be rolling around on the ground leathering the shit out of one another. The ball could land beside something resembling an MMA scene and lads would just play on as normal, as if the two lads resembling cage fighters were invisible. When they'd eventually get up, the jerseys could be half ripped off them.

When Brian paid no heed, you knew you had a licence to ramp up the heat. Even if you got the head chopped off you, Brian wouldn't entertain any bitching or moaning.

Nobody looked for frees because Brian didn't give them. Protection was non-existent. If some fella was beating the living shite out of you, on and off the ball, you had to sort it out yourself. Nobody else was going to step in. We all had enough to be worrying about trying to survive and hold on to our own jersey.

The only fella I ever heard looking for a free was Henry, which happened about twice in the 12 years we were on the panel together. Henry took some fair hardship during those sessions but he never voiced his frustration loud enough for Cody to hear it. Maybe Brian did but it made no difference.

The only time he might blow for a free was if someone was stupidly pulling a jersey or if a player blatantly pushed someone into the back. Brian hated those unnecessary indiscretions, those cheap frees, but you could decapitate someone and he wouldn't even notice. He, and we, knew we wouldn't get away with that lawlessness in Croke Park but we all knew that if we could survive in Nowlan Park, nothing would shock us anywhere else. And it never did.

I never had any issue with someone hitting me a really bad belt because I dished enough of them out myself. But if someone hit me a sneaky or sly slap, I'd want payback. 'I'll remember that,' I'd say to myself. Invariably, I'd get retribution.

We all did. If you clipped someone during our last hard training match before an All-Ireland final, the victim would jokingly remind you of it during the warm-down. 'You bollocks, I'll have to wait until next year now to get you back.'

That was the culture. The club rivalry never carried over into Nowlan Park. If some fella from O'Loughlin Gaels or Ballyhale nearly took your life during a club game, it never registered. You were probably trying to do the same to him.

The names changed over the years but the culture never did. There were always hard boyos knocking around. Willie O'Dwyer. Derek Lyng. 'Gorta' Comerford was a rugged detail. John Hoyne was another coil of raw hardness, one of those guys that you may as well have been hitting an oak tree.

The harder lads were though, the more other fellas tried to chop them down.

Some lads were pure filthy. Tommy Walsh was no saint. He'd be waving the hurley around like a sword. He'd have two or three fellas hit before they'd even know what had happened. I wasn't much better. Neither was JJ. He was desperate for flicking across the wrists. JJ didn't have a name or reputation for the loose strokes or dark arts but he was a master at concealing the practice. He'd have a lad hit four times before the ball would even land near him but JJ married that edge to his game with pure class because he was the greatest defender I ever played with. He had everything. JJ was a joy to play with, a pleasure to soldier alongside, because we had such a telepathic under-standing. The toughest and hardest of all, though, was Noel Hickey. He would be bating lads up and down the field like he was walloping cattle with a stick to herd them into a field. I loved playing beside Noel because if someone got past me, there was no way they'd get past Hickey. He'd cut them in two without a second thought.

The Warrior's Code

Noel always seemed to have a licence to do anything. He could pull strokes far more vicious than I would and Brian would never say a word to him. I used to genuinely feel sorry for Martin Comerford when he marked Hickey. Because 'Gorta' was so tall and he had an aerial advantage on Noel for high balls, Hickey only had one option – pull first. And by God, did he play that card. 'Gorta' would catch the odd ball but the punishment he took, you wouldn't see it in Guantanamo Bay. Noel used to blacken him. 'Gorta' wore an ash-guard protection glove to try and limit the torture but it made little or no difference. When 'Gorta' broke his hand once, the x-ray showed up multiple other little fractures. I'm sure Hickey was responsible for most of them.

He had the same ruthless attitude towards everyone but God help anyone who pissed him off. We were in Langton's drinking on the Monday after the 2006 All-Ireland final. We weren't drunk but we were getting there when Hickey mentioned something about Brian Corcoran. He didn't go into much detail but he referenced Corcoran's symbolic gesture to the Cork crowd, when Corcoran was on his knees after scoring a brilliant point, the last score of the 2004 All-Ireland final. You could just imagine how much that image hurt Noel, of how much that hurt stewed in his head while he was on his own on his farm throughout that winter. His career looked to be over in 2005 when he was diagnosed with a virus that had attached itself to the muscle around the wall of his heart. He wasn't around for that year's All-Ireland semi-final, when we shipped five goals against Galway, but he returned in 2006 like a man possessed.

When we met Cork in the All-Ireland final, Corcoran hadn't a chance. Noel tied him up like an invisible straitjacket but he got his retribution too. When Hickey fired Corcoran out over the sideline once in the first half, it was his way of telling Corcoran that he wouldn't be celebrating on his knees again. On another occasion in that first half, Noel pulled wildly on a dropping ball between him and Corcoran. Cork scored the resultant free but Hickey had laid down another marker that this time, it was going to be different.

As a defender, Noel always had a killer instinct. He exuded a menacing and aggressive body language. You, and the opposition, just always knew that Hickey was going to do whatever had to be done to get the job done.

In the 2007 All-Ireland final against Limerick, Mike Fitzgerald got the ball about 10 minutes before half-time and took on Noel at the Hill 16 end near the Cusack Stand side. I was less than ten yards away. The ball hopped up between the two of them and as Noel went for it, he tore his hamstring. You could see straight away his day was over.

Mike Fitz had the ball though and as he turned, it looked as if he was in around Noel and had a straight run in along the endline to goal. Hickey decided in a split second that he wasn't getting in on goal. He let fly with his hurley and pulled across him. I could hear the crack of the hurl across Mike's hand. As Noel hobbled off the pitch, Barry Kelly raised a fully-deserved yellow card. Noel didn't care – the goal wasn't breached and he did what had to be done. That's a killer instinct.

That moment stayed with me for my whole career. I thought about it several times afterwards. Hickey pulled that stroke so quickly and instinctively that you'd hardly even see it but it brought home to me what he was willing to do. He was in agony. His All-Ireland final was over. But without even thinking, he was doing anything he could to stop a goal. Mind the house. Nothing else matters. Ruthless. That was our identity.

Brian didn't play Noel much in his last season in 2013 but he still had plenty of use for him, like a car-testing mechanism at a vehicle inspection programme. If Brian wasn't convinced a lad was fully ready before a big game, he'd throw him in on top of Hickey to find out.

We had those cards to play, which nobody else did. Savage warriors. Men who would do whatever it took, whatever was required, to get fellas ready and primed for the battle, to get the team over the line. You saw that with Derek Lyng, Hogi, JJ and Larks. Tommy too. It would have been easy for Tommy to get soft in 2014, to allow frustration to dilute the intensity and intent of his play. He was obviously disappointed to have been marginalised, to have been played in the forwards first, before being benched. But Tommy never allowed that haze of frustration to cloud the colour of the bigger picture.

Brian always set the tone. He was always so terrified of the insidious threat of complacency setting in that any time he sensed it, he ruthlessly extinguished it. The Monday night after Limerick beat Waterford in the 2007 All-Ireland semi-final, Brian blew the whistle before training began and called us all back into the dressing room. We had beaten Wexford in our semi-final the previous week and everybody, including ourselves, had expected Waterford to be our opponents in the final. They had played brilliant hurling that season. They had beaten us in the league final. They had taken out Cork after an All-Ireland quarter-final replay but Limerick sucker-punched them with five goals in the semi-final a week later.

I don't know if Brian sensed cockiness in the air, or if he was preventing the possibility of it happening, but he went bananas. He said that if he detected a scintilla of arrogance or over-confidence from anyone, he would do away with lads. He wasn't talking about mopping blood off the floor and scooping lads up into body bags but it was his way of knocking any giddiness out of lads. Fellas were afraid to piss crooked for the next couple of weeks.

We often were if Brian was thick. 'I don't give a shite about anyone,' he would often say. 'The county board are floating around there as if they're going to win us an All-Ireland. I'll fire them out of the dressing room too if I have to. I don't care what the media says. I couldn't care less what the Kilkenny public think. Ye will go down the town and the first thing someone will say to you is, 'Ah, ye had a great run.' Forget having a great run. Forget last year's All-Ireland. I only care about what's in front of us.'

Brian was always the only voice that ever mattered but there were times before big games when he wanted us to hear a different message. Brian often brought in guest speakers; Padraig Harrington, Nicholas Cruz, the boxing coach. The one person Brian kept returning to, though, was Gerry McEntee, the former Meath footballer.

Brian loved McEntee because nobody else had the same impact as him. As soon as McEntee walked into the room, you knew there was something about him. He is one of the top surgeons in the country. He carries that air of confidence that you'd want to see in someone if they were about to open you up with a bag of knives and scalpels.

Gerry always said that it was an honour to be asked to speak to the Kilkenny hurlers and you knew by his face how much he meant it. He always referenced stories about us, about what we have done, and how much he values our achievements.

The main reason Brian loved him so much though was because McEntee was such a hard individual himself. The Meath team of the 1990s which he played on were full of hard chaws, guys who there was no end to, fellas you'd nearly have to shoot to put them down.

On one of the first occasions he spoke to us, around 2009, Gerry emphasised the importance between being psyched up, and psyched out. He told us about his mindset for the All-Ireland football final replay in 1988, when he was sent off early in the match for clocking Niall Cahalane with a box into the head. Just as they were leaving the hotel to go to Croke Park, a woman came on to the bus and asked one of the players for an autograph. McEntee told her to get the fuck off the bus with venom splattering from his lips. He couldn't control that fury. He went onto the pitch like a crazed animal and was sitting in the dugout shortly after the match began.

Gerry emphasised the importance of channelling that fury in a colder, calculated and more deadly manner. He would paint the picture of having someone's head pushed into a barrel of water, and keeping their head pressed tightly down into the water until they had drowned. 'And you don't let up,' McEntee would say, 'until you see that last bubble.'

I used to love the way he always finished his speech with the same line. I would be waiting to hear him say it, like an anticipated punchline. 'You bring it to the absolute edge,' he would say. 'You bring it as far as you can possibly go, never backing off one single inch.'

McEntee loved Kilkenny because I'm sure he saw so much of his Meath team in us. That Meath team wasn't popular but they didn't care. McEntee knew there was a similar perception of us but he wanted us to play up on that. Despite the media or referees or the attitude in the corridors of Croke Park, McEntee or Brian never wanted us to pull back from the style which made us who we were.

We loved playing on the edge. We went overboard at times but that never bothered us. I personally got a kick out of being overly physical, of taking it as far as I possibly could. I liked being portrayed as an enforcer. It fed into my ego.

We didn't give a shite about anyone and we fed on those insecurities that teams had when they met us. We knew teams were scared of us. You would be marking lads and you could almost sense the fear off them. You would completely play on that. I marked fellas and I knew they were racked with nerves before they even came near me. I could read it in their body language. As soon as I got near those guys, I rattled into them.

That unbreakable attitude and aura represented who we were and what we stood for. I loved standing beside a corner-forward on the sideline and the opposition supporters roaring at me.

'You're a filthy bastard Tyrrell.'

'You're only a thug.'

'Ye're all a shower of filthy bastards.'

Nobody could physically live with us. We knew it. So did everyone else. They were only wasting their time trying to rough us up. When Waterford tried it on before the 2008

All-Ireland final, it only messed their own heads up. Deep down, they knew it was pointless. You could see it in their body language. We were so ready for anything anyway that it never even registered with us. You regularly got a hurley into the side of the head in training so some lad ramming his stick into your back was harmless stuff. You had got far worse off Derek Lyng or someone else the previous week.

We never really went in for that off-the-ball shit because lads were smart. We had a good hurling education. We knew we couldn't get away with the faction fighting in Croke Park that we routinely practised in Nowlan Park.

Brian never told us to rein it in but he would often mention how we were being watched. 'Ned (Quinn) told us that the referees are on our case,' he would say. 'They're out to get us above in Croke Park.'

Referees never really meant a whole lot to us. We were programmed not to hear a whistle in Nowlan Park. When we were fouled or knocked down, we were just expected to get straight back up. By that means, referees were largely irrelevant to us. We didn't play for frees. We didn't look for them. Referees that let the play flow suited us fine because nobody did the mixed martial arts stuff better than us.

A referee like Brian Gavin was ideal for the game we wanted to play but when Tommy took a chunk out of Gavin's nose during the 2011 final, we knew referees were going to be on our backs more. Psychologically, we knew we had to be more intelligent in how we calibrated the threshing machine.

It never made any difference anyway because no team could match us physically. We never worried what other teams could bring. We always knew what we had in our locker. And once we took it out, it was all over for the opposition. No team could match us.

Brian always said that if we were fully tuned in, no team in the country would match that amalgam of power and class and raw savagery. Teams rarely did. They never really had. The teams we routinely met never had that personality. Cork were a running team who found it hard to match our physicality. Waterford had some hardy boyos but they were still too hot and cold. Tipperary put it up to us but not enough of them threatened us physically. They didn't mentally have it either. Galway had big men but they were inconsistent too.

The one team Brian invariably mentioned was the Clare side of the last decade, especially if we were about to play them. 'They think they invented physicality,' he would say. 'Well, we'll show them all about physicality.'

Brian often used Colin Lynch as a reference point. 'I'm hearing stories of Colin Lynch the whole time and some of the stuff he gets up to in training,' he'd say. 'We'll show him physicality when we mix it with hurling.'

We had hit-men everywhere but I was always seen as one of the main enforcers. Any time Kilkenny's overly physical approach was mentioned, my name was at the top of the rap sheet. I actually liked that perception, and the message it transmitted. The more it was put out there, the more I loved it; the more I played up to it.

Few ever took me on. Maybe it was the position I played. Corner-forwards were not the type to go looking for aggro. Tipperary's Eoin Kelly was probably the most physical player I marked, even though I had a few inches on him. He was a serious yoke. He never backed away from anything. He even had the balls to catch me up by the neck a few times. If it was anyone else I'd have let fly but since I knew Eoin well from my time in St Kieran's, there were times when we would start laughing at each other. John Mullane was feisty but he wasn't physical. Most of the other corner-forwards were ball-players. They weren't interested in going to war with me.

I nailed plenty of them over the years but my highest profile hit was railroading Seamus Callanan early on in the 2009 All-Ireland final. I didn't consciously go out to saw him in half but when Callanan was absolutely wide open, I wasn't going to pass up the opportunity. It was a cheap shot. It would be a straight red card now but it worked at the time. It sent out an early message to Tipperary that hell was coming. From every angle.

When we played training games, Martin Fogarty would often take up position like a sentry to police me and my actions. He was always on to me about slapping and belting lads. I would just pay him lip service. 'Ah, Jeez Martin, sorry about that, I was just a fraction late.'

Martin knew I wasn't taking him seriously because I could have tried to take the head off a lad. I pulled some shocking strokes in my time. It wasn't always with the hurley either. I was laying lads out with shoulders or late hits with my body.

Eoin McGrath from Muckalee was soloing in with a ball one time and I hit him so hard that I thought I'd half-killed him.

I was belting lads up and down the county without remorse until Fogarty nailed me one time. There was this fella in

Fogarty's club, Castlecomer, who was regarded as the dirtiest hurler in Kilkenny. I never liked him. He didn't like me. We were always lacing the shit out of one another. Any time Fogarty would bring up stories about what went on between the two of us, I always had Brian in my corner. 'G'way, that fella is filthy,' he would say.

On one occasion though, myself or Brian had no defence for my actions. We were playing Castlecomer in Freshford when I got a ball and cleared it up the line. My buddy was coming in behind me and, just after I had hit the ball, I swung the hurley back like a scythe and hit your man straight into the neck.

The next night we were training, Martin came up to myself and Brian. 'You know the way yere always saying that fella is the dirtiest player in Kilkenny?' he asked. 'Well, let me show ye this.'

Martin had caught it on camera. It was Exhibit A in his prosecution against me. I had no defence. I never really had against the same fella. On another occasion, I broke his finger with a wild pull.

It wasn't just fellas in club matches who wanted to sort me out because there were plenty of lads lining me up in Kilkenny training. Willie O'Dwyer often tried it on with me. Myself and Pat Hartley once beat one another black and blue in a training game down in Wexford.

When I was coming out with a ball, I often relished lads having a go at me, to see if they could take me down. I always felt Richie Hogan wanted to take me on physically. Richie knocked me on the floor once and I was like a lunatic. I teed him up a few times where I tried to absolutely nail him but I couldn't knock him to the ground. He really enjoyed the fact that I couldn't put him down, even though I had a couple of stone weight advantage on him.

Henry and I had some good battles but I don't think he ever got the better of me. It was different with 'Taggy' Fogarty because he was so hard to hit physically. 'Taggy' would just break your heart. I went across the pitch in Nowlan Park one evening trying to clear a ball and 'Taggy' hooked me four times. It was like trying to break free from an octopus.

He had me haunted but 'Taggy' was the type of guy you wanted to mark. He had my number but that told you where you were really at. If I marked a panel member who wouldn't give you anything like the same grief, I saw it more as a missed opportunity than a chance to show dominant form. 'Look, I don't want to mark that fella again,' I'd say to Martin Fogarty afterwards. The more dogs of war you marked, the more ready for war you were. 'Give me 'Taggy',' I'd be thinking and hoping when they were calling out the teams.

It was easy to see why Brian loved 'Taggy' so much; he perfectly personified the work rate and desire that Cody always preached, that he wanted us to use as a form of torment. Brian often referenced an incident from the 2006 All-Ireland semi-final where 'Taggy' chased a Clare player from our 20-metre line to the Clare 20-metre line before eventually hooking him. That was the ultimate example of tormenting an opposition player.

Sometimes, karma can get you. Even though we are really good friends and club-mates, I used to give Eoin Larkin an awful going on during training matches. I broke his nose once in

2010. I paid for it afterwards because he snored like a train. There were plenty of occasions when we roomed together and I'd be awake at night wishing I had hit Larks somewhere else.

I'm sure the doctors and physios must often have been tearing their hair out on the sideline during those training games because there were more casualties afterwards than a war-zone. There was no way of avoiding the shrapnel.

You could be coming out with a ball but once you'd go past a player, you'd have no problem just belting him with the hurley, and just carrying on. It was vicious stuff. Physical assault with a weapon. High balls were often seen as open season.

Brian always loved being in the middle of the anarchy during training matches, roaring and shouting at lads for even more anarchy, more war. 'There are some unbelievable scores,' he would often roar. 'But this place needs to be a war-zone. There is no war here. WELL BRING IT.'

If someone went down with a really bad injury, and couldn't play on, the battle never stopped. Brian would hardly even look over. The physios and doctors would come out like stretcher bearers on a battlefield and carry the poor victim away to the field hospital in the dressing room. The next soldier stepped in. Next man up. Next ball.

It was often ill-tempered stuff but you had to be prepared to do anything to survive. If you broke a hurley, you tried to block the ball with your hand. Fuckit, those matches often represented our omnipotence, our sovereign governance of the hurling world. You'd walk off the pitch asking yourself, 'Who the hell is going to live with that on Sunday?'

You'd tell yourself, 'There's no way I'm going to face anything like that hardship and punishment on Sunday.' And you knew the lad you'd be marking was saying the same. Because everybody else was thinking the same way. 'How are we going to live with these animals?'

The Nowlan Park cauldron also acted as a mental trigger on match days. You'd often look up at the clock in Croke Park and see there were only 20 minutes gone. You'd be out on your feet, wondering how you were going to get through the next 50 minutes. Then you'd think back to what you'd experienced in Nowlan Park and realise that you were ready for anything. There was a mental steel from those internal games.

It was pure savagery but the savagery was always more voracious and ravenous on training weekends. The Mayo footballers were staying in Carton House the same weekend as us once and I'd say they got a shock when they watched one of our training matches. It was before an All-Ireland final, competition was fierce, lads were edgy and cranky and anything went. Fellas spent most of the game ramming other fellas with hurleys into the neck and chest as they were trying to break away from their marker. It was total lawlessness.

A short while afterwards, a few of us ambled up to the pitch where the Mayo lads were doing a catching drill with patches over their eyes. It was probably to improve their peripheral vision but, be the Lord Jaysus, I couldn't get over it. The only time Kilkenny lads wore patches over their eyes was when someone had tried to take it out with a loose hurley. A few of the forwards might have often needed them after the physical abuse we doled out.

I don't know, maybe footballers are more into pursuing those wacky kind of training methods than hurlers. We never went in for any of that stuff. We just wanted war.

Men of Substance

'Kilkenny... 1-21
Waterford... 0-24
Waterford played conventional 15v15 and were far better
than us in terms of intensity, work rate and just wanting
it more. We were poor. We didn't battle or fight as hard
as they did. We should have been beaten but we somehow
survived thanks to a late goal from Walter Walsh. Brian
brought us into the warm-up area and told us to park
everything for the next week. Someone is going to be in
the All-Ireland final next weekend and he said it better
be us. He talked about how Waterford bullied us. He says
he won't be naming names but, to be honest, he should,
because what we produced wasn't good enough. At least we
are still in the championship. I thought it was gone. With a
few minutes to go, I looked around and wondered to myself,
'Is this it? Is it all over now?"

– Diary entry, Sunday August 7th, 2016

The Warrior's Code

WHEN Waterford went four points ahead with 70 minutes nearly on the clock, I turned around to Mark Bergin on the bench. 'We're done here,' I said to Bergo. 'We're gone.'

Saying it railed against everything we believe in, everything Brian stands for. I knew we needed a goal but when I looked up the other end of the field, all I could see was Waterford swarming bodies around their defence likes bees around a honey jar.

We were scraping with our fingernails to get out of the shallow grave Waterford had dug for us but we were still alive because they didn't stamp enough dirt down on top of us. They had their foot on our throats but instead of choking us, Waterford backed off and allowed us to come back at them. It was nearly easier for them to win than it was for us to draw the match but we have always had the power to loom in the minds of a team that are trying to bury us.

Our mental strength, our refusal to be beaten, adds to our aura of near invincibility but how much are teams now taken, or distracted by, that aura? It has certainly added to our mystique, our air of invincibility, and by natural extension, our dominance.

Waterford should have beaten us but, like a host of other teams over the years, they got spooked. And blew it.

It reminded me a little of Galway after half-time in the 2015 All-Ireland final. They had us by the balls. We were on the ropes. On the run.

You'd think that a team that hadn't won an All-Ireland in nearly 30 years would have gone through a wall to get the job done but, once we got inside their heads, they cracked. I knew by Galway's body language five minutes into that second half that they were gone.

I always felt we were good to read body language, to sense vulnerability, to smell fear. You can see fellas on the other team starting to think. 'Are we really good enough to beat this crowd? Are Kilkenny going to storm back like they usually do?' And when you start thinking too deeply, you make poor decisions. That's exactly what happened to Waterford.

I often felt teams became obsessed with us. We didn't really change the game. Other teams changed to try and beat us. We just adapted and beat them anyway.

The media can play a part in creating this mystique around a team too. We saw that with Cork in 2006 when it was nearly portrayed that eating fields of pasta and forests of fruit and going to bed early was going to win you an All-Ireland.

We never got caught up with all of that stuff but if you are not mentally strong enough, it can get in on you and make you think that the other crowd are better than they really are.

After the drawn game, do Waterford really, really believe now that they can beat us?

The graveyard is heaving with teams who nearly drove the stake through our hearts at the first opportunity but who we buried in the replay.

Do these boys really have the balls now to take us down in six days' time?

The current Waterford team are young. We don't have much truck with them because we don't really know them. We had much more history with the old Waterford team but we really respected that group of players.

They had some great players, great characters; Ken McGrath, Tony Browne, John Mullane, Dan Shanahan, Paul Flynn, Seamus Prendergast, Eoin Kelly. They deserved to win an All-Ireland. They probably would have won a couple if we weren't around.

They were artists, purists, beautiful hurlers, but great lads too. We were on a few trips with those Waterford fellas and they were some craic. Good fun, good to be around, gas men. Their mannerisms were different but that difference made them into the characters, and unique team, they were. They could be kissing babies' heads after matches. When we saw them kissing their jerseys, we recognised that as just being them.

They were showbizzy but they were colourful. They were men of substance.

I marked Mullane in the first half of the 2008 All-Ireland final. When he came onto me, there was the usual jostling and messing. I could see all these red marks and welts down the back of his legs. I thought one of our lads must have been leathering him until I heard the sound of ash on flesh. I looked around and saw Mullane hitting his hurley off his calves and hamstrings to get himself going. 'This lad is for the birds,' I said to myself.

Even though the ball didn't come near us much, we kept nudging and pushing. At one stage, Mullane squared up to me. 'What are you going to do about it Tyrrell, boy?'

I told him to shut the fuck up. I was wearing a helmet. Mullane wasn't wearing any but he leaned back and stuck me with a head-butt. It caught me off guard because he drove into me with full force. Mullane stood there for a second and said nothing. When I looked at Mullane, I could see the imprint of the bars on the faceguard on his face. Then Mullane just ran off. 'These guys are nuts,' I said to myself.

They had that craziness about them but we loved that about that group. They were one of the few teams we feared at certain times over the years. They always brought it. They didn't show up for that 2008 All-Ireland final but there weren't too many occasions when they didn't bring the fight to the battle.

We always felt they respected us too, something other teams like Cork and Tipperary were sometimes slow to grant us. I remember playing Waterford in a league game in 2009 in Walsh Park and Tommy Walsh and Eoin Kelly going at it. Seamus Prendergast came out of nowhere and started wearing into Tommy. I started wading into Prendergast. The four of us got yellow cards. During that league, a yellow card effectively meant a sending off, where you could be replaced by someone else. As we were all walking off, we were jawing at each other, fucking each other out of it. Yet we were still all calling each other by our first names. To me, that underlined the respect between those two groups of players.

There was never really any nastiness between us. There was no historical spite or toxic spleen like there was with Tipperary. We never got agitated talking about Waterford. We had beaten them a lot of times but you still felt they just loved going out to take us on with total hurling. They never held back against us. They loved the game. And they clearly loved hurling for Waterford.

They couldn't crack us but that never stopped them from trying. For Tony Browne, Ken McGrath and Mullane to keep coming back looking for that elusive All-Ireland medal in the face of such harrowing disappointment, it said a lot to us about the men they are. They were men of real substance.

With Kilkenny, I always believed you had to be a man first, and a hurler second. Kilkenny always had hurlers but they didn't always have men. 'Kilkenny for the hurlers, Tipperary for the men,' was the old refrain that used to drive Kilkenny people wild. Kilkenny always had men but our modern history proved that you had to be more than just a man – you had to be an animal too.

That was the blend Brian wanted – men of steel with the instincts and savagery of animals. Brian always knew his main men. Noel Hickey was a brilliant leader, the best I ever heard to speak in a Kilkenny dressing room. There was such an intensity when Hickey spoke that you'd almost be entranced by his words, and the meaning behind them. He had an edge to him. He was so hyped up when he was talking that you'd be half afraid that he'd turn around and take the head off someone.

I used to love his favourite saying: 'On Sunday, it's you or him. It's me or my man.' You just knew that this lad was going to go to war on Sunday. And you knew too that there would be only one winner in his battle. He knew that. We all knew it too. In his own way, Hickey was setting the standard for the rest of us.

Noel had his own way. If training was at 7pm, the majority of us would be in Nowlan Park from 6. Hickey would arrive in at 6.40, probably after slaving on the farm all day. The sweat would still be on his brow but he could turn it on like a switch. As soon as he'd arrive onto the pitch, he was ready for war.

Henry was vocal enough but he always backed up his words with serious action on the pitch. He was supremely gifted but Henry was the ultimate team player. Brian often referenced his work rate. His off-the-ball running was something else. It was one of his greatest traits. We used to play possession games where Brian would eat the heads off us if fellas were loose. Marking Henry in those matches was a total nightmare, like trying to keep mercury from slipping between your fingers.

Henry led on and off the field, in everything he did. He was always trying to get better, faster, fitter, stronger. He was a brilliant free-taker because he practised with obsessive devotion to his craft. When you see that level of commitment, you're going to try and raise your own standard as well. We all did.

Tommy Walsh was another huge leader. He never spoke that much in the dressing room but he'd always talk in the huddle, or just before training on the pitch. He'd roar lads out of it but the way Tommy spoke, he was almost psyching himself up first, and bringing everyone else along with him. You'd often say to yourself after listening to him, 'Jeez, that lad is fit for fucking anything now.'

We had some great players and characters but Brian loved Tommy more than anyone else. Tommy had that bit of devilment in him that nobody else had, or who dared to show in front of Brian, but it was something Brian secretly cherished.

Brian often referenced Willie O'Connor's quote before the 2000 All-Ireland final against Offaly. 'I'm not willing to die but I'm prepared to kill.' Willie was a God for Cody but Willie had a cut at us one year and I'd say it hurt him. We were on the beer on the way home on the bus after a win in Dublin. Tommy was merry enough after a few bottles. He was going to the toilet on the bus and he shouted up the front: 'Hey, Cody, Cody, what the fuck would Willie O'Connor know about it anyway?'

Brian half-pretended that he didn't hear Tommy. He wouldn't have wanted to show the rest of us that he had but you could see his head rolling with laughter in the front seat. He loved that stuff but he loved how Tommy always backed it up on the pitch. He loved it even more the way he was so humble and grounded.

Brian often referenced Tommy. The first time I heard him do so was after the 2004 All-Ireland quarter-final replay against Clare. Tommy had been sent off in the drawn game but he was the best player on the pitch in the replay. 'They were writing him off last week,' roared Cody. 'Now they're giving him man-of-the-match.'

Brian regularly mentioned Tommy's desire and spirit as the baseline standard for all of us. 'We need more lads like Tommy Walsh,' the boss would say. 'He's insulted if he loses one ball. He'll go through a fella to make sure he wins the next one. If he loses one ball, it's like he's lost an All-Ireland. If we all have that spirit, we will be fine.'

Brian knew too how to play Tommy. 'Go out and take over that field today,' he would regularly tell him. Tommy would do it anyway but when Brian had said it, Tommy would almost feel that he had to prove to Brian that he could, and that he would. It didn't matter which game he played because Tommy would be as pumped up for a Walsh Cup game against UCD in January as he would for an All-Ireland final. The man would have played 365 days a year. He was never injured. And even when he was, he let on that he wasn't.

I never once saw Tommy on a physio bench. If his leg was hanging on by a tendon, he'd tell you it was grand. A month before the 2010 All-Ireland final, Tommy damaged his shoulder in a club game against James Stephens. We had Tullaroan beaten out the gap and Tommy was clearly frustrated. I was coming out with a ball near the sideline and Tommy tried to drive me into the fence. He just bounced off me and ripped ligaments in his shoulder in the process.

Two weeks out from that 2010 final, his shoulder was still in bits. Tommy went into training one evening and the doctor and physios were trying to drag some feedback out of him about the injury. When they asked Tommy if he had any pain, he said he hadn't. He clearly had. When they pushed him, he said he felt a little soreness when he hit the ball off his right side. 'But sure that's still grand,' he said. 'I'll just hit everything off my left side when the match starts.'

Dr Tadhg Crowley asked Tommy to lift his arm over his head. Tommy shot his arm straight up into the air, like an excited school kid wanting to tell the teacher the answer to the question just asked.

'Your injured arm, Tommy,' Tadhg said.

He made some attempt but it was like trying to lift a steel beam with his index finger. His arm was nearly hanging off with the pain. That was Tommy in a nutshell. He would just do anything to get out on the pitch and go hurling. He was an amazing man. Wired to the moon.

Tommy had a glorious career. He won nine All-Ireland medals and secured the status as one of the most cherished Kilkenny hurlers ever. And yet Tommy's ending wasn't as satisfying as the way he would have wanted, as what he probably deserved.

It was obvious that Tommy was struggling during the 2014 league. Danny Sutcliffe gave him a hard time in the first half of the league meeting with Dublin in Parnell Park that March. Tommy was taken off at half-time and Brian clearly made up his mind on him afterwards.

When he moved Tommy up to the forwards early in that year's championship, we all knew the end was near. After being taken off in that year's Leinster semi-final replay against Galway, Tommy never played for Kilkenny again.

We would have almost seen Tommy as invincible but the end comes for everyone. It was such a massive decline for him in such a short time but it was more that the game was at such a high level that it had just passed him by. Tommy might have got away with that slippage in the previous decade but the modern game ruthlessly exposes everything.

Psychologically, when Tommy was moved into the forwards, I think he just retired in his own mind. He knew Brian had his decision made. It was obvious. It was even more apparent with Henry during that 2014 championship. Brian went from consistently communicating with Henry to barely even talking to him.

I'm sure Henry struggled with that lack of communication, especially when he had been a sounding board for Brian for so long. I'm sure Henry wasn't happy either. How could he be after going from the most decorated player in the game's history to only playing a handful of minutes, and barely even being acknowledged to boot? Henry just had to suck it up, which he manfully did.

When the end is near, the communication lines are almost non-existent. I've seen that myself now first hand. Maybe Brian feels that if he is closer to lads that he will find it harder to cut guys. It's not easy for him, or for the guys he has lost faith in, but everything is geared towards the only goal Brian has – to win the All-Ireland every year.

It may seem cold but in Brian Cody's world, hard truth has no temperature.

A couple of years ago, we were doing a fitness test in IT Carlow in January. A handful of new fellas had been brought in for the Walsh Cup and as we were all lining up behind certain stations – press-ups, pull-ups, squats – Mick Fagan from Dicksboro decided to shoot the breeze with Mick Dempsey.

'Well Mick, what's the craic?'

Dempsey looked at him stone-faced. 'There is no craic here, Michael.'

Dempsey would be very intense. It's all business with him. Guys who have been on the panel for ten years wouldn't even try and knock a laugh out of him. We were all sniggering away in the background at how much Mick Fagan had to learn. He had talent. Mick had serious pace but the Kilkenny thing just wasn't for him. He really struggled during that fitness test. He was gone off the squad before the start of that year's league.

There were always great characters on the Kilkenny panel. Brian wanted those guys around but, as the game progressed, and it became more demanding and professional, the characters who were liable to take liberties were gradually weeded out.

That process had even begun before the game changed during the last decade. I first saw it with Philly Larkin. Philly was an All-Star in 2002 but Brian seemed to lose faith in him after Setanta Ó hAilpín gave Philly a scutching in a league game down in Cork in 2003. James Ryall came in and filled that number four spot that year and Philly eventually walked away frustrated in the middle of the 2004 season. He had given ten years' service by then. Along with his father, Fan, and grandfather, Paddy, Philly was a third-generation All-Ireland winner but sentiment is irrelevant to Brian.

It was still a different time back then in my early years on the squad. We would have a few pints after the meal at the hotel after a game in Croke Park. Lads would be buzzing. We would want to stop for a few more pints down the road but nobody had the balls to ask Brian for permission. When we'd be coming up near the Ratchcoole exit for the pub and restaurant 'An Poitín Stil' on the M7 on the outskirts of Dublin, we'd start up this chant down the back. 'Poitín Stil, Poitín Stil, Poitín Stil, Poitín Stil.' When the bus would steam past the place, we'd all collectively change the tone. 'Booooooooooooooooo.'

Unless it was after an All-Ireland final, Brian always had his game-face on. He would use Jim, the bus driver, as an excuse for not stopping, when Jim didn't give a shite. Brian knew we would be going on the piss anyway but the only time I heard him giving us a direct pass was after we beat Waterford in the 2004 All-Ireland semi-final.

For the first time ever, Kilkenny introduced recovery sessions that summer. We had gone through the back door that year, where we played four huge games in the space of five weeks. The Waterford match was our third successive weekend in action because the All-Ireland quarter-final with Clare had gone to a replay.

John Hoyne knew that Brian was in good form so 'Dougal' chanced his arm. 'Dougal was just enquiring if there was any recovery session tomorrow,' said Brian, trying to conceal the smile. 'Because he wants to go to the cinema Monday evening.'

There was a big cheer. 'Dougal' was a bould hoor. I'd say he was never in the cinema in his life. He just wanted to go on the beer all day Monday, and probably Tuesday too.

Brian loved 'Dougal'. He loved James Ryall too, who was an even bigger chancer. When we first started using weights with Kilkenny, we were all given membership of the gym in 'Hotel Kilkenny'. This big baldy Australian fella was our point of contact but he didn't know what to make of 'Dougal' and Ryall. 'Dougal' would clock in and walk straight out the door.

A group of us were in the gym one day when we got talking to the big Aussie. 'There's this red-headed guy there, James Royle,' says yer man in his Australian accent. 'Every time he comes in, he walks around for a few minutes and then fucks off.' We were all pissing ourselves laughing. You could just picture Ryall, 'Come on, we'll go in for an auld sauna and then be gone out the gap.' I never saw Ryall lift a weight in my life.

The boys had their own rules. If we were training on a Friday evening, and there was a wedding on in Langton's where the car park was full, the boys wouldn't bother heading in for food. They'd head up town for a pizza and wash it down with a few cans of Coca-Cola.

They got away with those stunts because they were hard men who always showed up on match-days. They were huge characters within the squad but 'Dougal' and Ryall wouldn't get away with that lifestyle now. They would just be squeezed out.

That is eventually what happened to 'Cha' Fitzpatrick. He was another huge character like 'Dougal' and Ryall, fit and up for anything. 'Cha' loved the comedian and actor Pat Shortt. He was always dressing up as him, like the Shortt auld farmer character from the TV series 'Killinascully'. After the All-Stars one year, myself, Tommy Walsh and 'Cha' travelled on to Galway on the Saturday for Peter Cleere's stag party. 'Cha' made us stop in a hardware shop in Loughrea. He went in and spent the guts of €100 on wellington boots, an auld jacket and shirt, and straw hat.

'Cha' got dressed up in the car. Before we went into the pub to meet 'Chap' Cleere and the boys, 'Cha' told me to tell 'Chap' that he couldn't make it. A few minutes later, 'Chap' told me to look over at the head-banger in the corner, with a blade of straw hanging out of his mouth. Then he looked again. 'CHAAAAAAAA.'

'Cha' was some character. He wasn't your average Kilkenny hurler. He was a free spirit who just wanted to enjoy life. When he won Young Hurler of the Year in 2006, Ballyhale also won their first county for 15 years that October. The All-Stars that season was on the Friday night before a big club game for Ballyhale. Henry was Hurler of the Year too that season but he was in bed early.

Before he left the hotel on the Saturday morning, Henry had to sign some memorabilia. Some guy told him that 'Cha' had just been down to perform the same duty. Henry was taken aback that 'Cha' had been up before him until your man told him that 'Cha' was still wearing his tuxedo. And yet 'Cha' went out and hurled up a storm the following day.

'Cha' was such a brilliant player that his talents looked eternal but time and Brian Cody wait for no man. Injury claimed other careers early too. John Tennyson was another huge character who quit the panel before the 2013 championship. The last championship game he started was the 2010 All-Ireland final. Tenno played with a torn cruciate ligament in that final but Brian reached a conclusion about his form afterwards that Tenno could no longer dispute.

Tenno was missed because he was some craic. When we went down to Monart Hotel and Spa on a training weekend before the 2006 All-Ireland final, I robbed his phone on the bus and changed my name and number in his contacts to a girl 'Cha' told me Tennyson had been texting. I started bombarding him with texts, talking all sorts of shite. Tennyson was mad about this girl so he was completely taken by the stream of conversation, and how a budding relationship was suddenly developing. I made it out that the girl was down in Wexford for the weekend and that she might call into Monart for a cup of tea. Tennyson was nearly beside himself with excitement. He put on his good treads, splashed on the aftershave, and went down to the lobby ready to meet this young wan. I told all the lads and we were hiding as we watched Tennyson nervously waiting for his date to arrive.

Bigger names have gone since but the irreplaceable ones are always replaced with little fuss because Brian has never remained obedient to the normal patterns of GAA inter-county life.

As the years and the game progressed, I think Brian became more serious too, more austere even. Even though we are clubmates, I'd say I have had about five conversations with Brian in the last five years, nearly all of which were in the Kilkenny squad environment, some of which involved other members of the backroom team.

Unless Brian needed to speak to you, about an injury or an

upcoming exam or something, he didn't. Unless you had to speak to him about requesting permission to do some promotional gig, or you were caught with work, you didn't. That was just how the relationship worked. Nothing personal. Just business.

Brian was always far more relaxed when you met him around James Stephens when he was just a supporter, and especially when we won something. The Monday night after the 2004 county win, we were all in Matt the Millers when the big man arrived in. A group of us got a lift home from Liam 'Chuck' O'Connor and myself and Brian were nearly sitting up on top of each other in the back seat, chewing the fat and having the craic.

When we defeated Ballyhale in the 2005 county final, Shane Egan came on that day and hit three crucial points in a tight game. Shane was a solid club player who was never going to play with Kilkenny but he went up to Brian and tried to knock some fun out of him. 'Do you want my number, Brian?' he asked.

Cody shot back straight away, in front of everyone. 'No need to ring Shane. I'll call you.'

After the 2011 county final replay, Brian and Larks were pulling the piss out of me back in the clubhouse for getting sent off. 'What do you think of that feckin' eejit?' Larks asked him.

'I don't know what planet he was on,' said Brian.

While the three of us were chatting away, Niall Rigney, our manager that year, ambled up beside us. 'Well Brian, which one is your favourite?'

Brian always loved Larks. We used to call him Cody's pet. 'That lad,' said Brian, looking at Larks, 'Lookit the size of the arse on him.'

Brian always liked a good laugh but he never showed it with Kilkenny, especially to the players. After the 2014 league final against Tipperary in Thurles, we went back to the Anner Hotel in the town. We had a few pints. We were all buzzing after beating Tipp after extra-time. We got even more revved up after sinking a few shorts before boarding the bus.

Lads were up for anything. One of the lads rifled Richie Hogan's phone. When he got his back turned, he texted Brian, who was sitting at the front of the bus. We were all watching like hawks as soon as the text dropped. We could see Brian reaching in his pocket for his phone. 'Hi Brian,' the text read, 'I think I should be put on the frees. Richie H.'

The same day, TJ Reid scored 2-9 from placed balls. As soon as Brian read the text, his head started rolling with laughter. As he showed the screen of the phone to Mick Dempsey and James McGarry, the whole bus erupted in laughter. Richie knew then that something was up.

Brian knew that we all got a great kick out of the stunt but he still tried to keep his reaction concealed from us. It was almost as if he wanted to share in the collective joke, but wouldn't allow himself to engage with us in that manner. The shield had to stay up, even after such a brilliant win, even when we were all as giddy as wild goats.

In late 2013, a group of peripheral players were brought in for fitness training in IT Carlow. Most of them were shy and reserved, as you'd expect from young fellas walking into such a successful setup. They were all in great shape. The sole exception was Paul 'Spud' Rockett, who looked like he'd landed in from a rave. 'Spud' was wearing a Jack Daniels T-shirt, with the arms cut off. He had a belly on him.

When Mick was breaking up the groups, he approached 'Spud'. 'What are your fitness levels like, Paul?'

'To be honest Mick, they're cat.'

Everyone else was trying to impress but 'Spud' didn't give a damn. He was a breath of fresh air. He was gone shortly afterwards but we were all wishing he had been kept on. It would have been some craic to have a character like him around. It would have been like having 'Dougal' or Ryall back again.

'Brother D puts it up to me today about what leadership I provided on Sunday, and what leadership I have shown since. He spoke about me living in the now and standing up like never before. I got a feeling from Damien that this is more than a game. There is a real intensity in him. 'JT, just pull these lads over the line,' he said to me. 'You have a huge influence in the group.' Damien is 100% right. When I reflected on his comments as I drove into training, I was completely honest with myself; not playing had diluted my desire. It wasn't good enough so I arrived into training with a completely different mindset. Afterwards, we watched a video with different highlights of our play from the drawn game. 'Good, bad and indifferent' it was called. It was too much. Too long. McGarry and Dempsey spoke about what we didn't do; lack of support play, not tracking Waterford runners, not showing enough desire. Brian speaks about everything. Derek Lyng is the only one who really hits the paint, telling us how we allowed them to dictate to us. Then I spoke. I talked about the difference in our mentality and theirs; they hate us; they had a killer instinct about them; we were casual, which is why we made all those mistakes

and errors we had just been shown. I challenged us all in the room to live in the now, to all back each other up, and to do whatever it takes to get us over the line on Saturday. I felt good afterwards. I realise now that it's not about playing; it's about getting that 10th All-Ireland medal. I have as much influence as any fella playing. What matters from now until Saturday is our attitude, and my role in getting all the lads buying into this, of just going at this with all I have. And I will. This is a huge challenge. I am in great physical shape. But I am actually in better mental shape.'

– Diary entry, Tuesday August 9th, 2016

It has always been about the group, the collective responsibility, and the ultimate goal of winning the All-Ireland every year. I, and loads of other fellas, have been fortunate to have won lots of All-Ireland medals but there were plenty of players on the panel over the years who had just as much ambition and desire as us and they never tasted the same glory; truck-loads of anonymous fellas whose dream flared and died.

Reams of those squad players never made the breakthrough but they were as important to what we had created in Kilkenny as Henry Shefflin, Noel Hickey, Brian Hogan, Larks, JJ and Tommy Walsh. Brian always spoke about equality of opportunity. Convincing peripheral players that they had a chance was one of Brian's greatest triumphs because the training ground dynamic in Nowlan Park depended so much on that pledge. Most of those peripheral squad members got two, maybe three, years before being moved on again. Some lads only got one year at it. Most of them got at least one All-Ireland medal.

A handful may have been pissed off that they didn't get more of a chance but they still all accepted the terms and conditions. Even some of our most gifted talents were made to wait it out for their opportunity; Richie Hogan made three championship starts in his first three seasons; TJ Reid made none in his first two years and started three All-Ireland finals on the bench.

Guys were often fed up but nobody ever really walked away because the magnetism of what Brian created in Nowlan Park was extraordinary. Peripheral players got All-Ireland medals but they knew they were getting more too than just that golden opportunity. They didn't all become better hurlers but the environment in Nowlan Park was such character-building stuff that it often made them better people. It made them mentally stronger. It turned them into men of real substance.

Nobody has shown those traits more than Conor Fogarty. Fog was on the panel for years before ever getting a sniff of action. When he finally did, in 2013, he had a difficult day on 'Dotsie' O'Callaghan in the Leinster semi-final replay in Portlaoise. Fog didn't appear again for the rest of that championship. His days with Kilkenny looked done but the experience only made him stronger. A year later, he was massive for us at midfield. Now, he is one of our most trusted warriors. In the 2016 drawn All-Ireland semi-final against Waterford, it was Fog's late point which secured us the replay we are now facing.

Fog could have given up but he didn't. When he was nowhere near a starting jersey, he was still one of the key ingredients in the mix which made us the force we were. Fog, and plenty of others like him, got me over the line in plenty of other seasons. And it's my duty to try and get Fog and everyone else over the line now.

The Oldest Enemy

'We increased our intensity levels and work rate big time to produce one of our best displays. The changes to the team worked. Larks was good. Feno at number 11 was brilliant, before going off injured. Blanch (Liam Blanchfield) got three points and made another crucial score. The defence did well so I never looked like coming on but I gave it my all and was emotionally wrecked afterwards. It was a great team performance. Padraig (Walsh) was excellent. Scruffy (Eoin Murphy) won the game for us by catching a free a foot over the bar in injury-time. Cillian (Buckley) was excellent too. Cody was elated after the game. He spoke about what we were capable of. Leaving Thurles, I decided I was taking on a bigger leadership role before the All-Ireland final.'

– Diary entry, Saturday August 13th, 2016

The Warrior's Code

THE night of the replay against Waterford, we hit the town big time. It was daylight before I saw bed. I was hung over when I woke the next morning but I headed out to Brother Damien at 1pm. We chatted about the game. We spoke in detail about how I felt. We focussed on the next three weeks and settled on two goals; fighting with everything I had to be involved in the All-Ireland final; providing the most leadership I have ever shown in my Kilkenny career.

'That's the plan now,' said Damien as I headed out the door. 'Enjoy the rest of your day now. You deserve it.'

I intended to. I headed straight into Christy Morrison's pub on Patrick Street to meet the lads. When I arrived, most of them were already there, drinking away, basking in the warm afterglow of a big win, luxuriating in the security of having an even bigger day ahead to look forward to.

The other All-Ireland semi-final between Galway and Tipperary had just begun. Most of the lads weren't even watching it on the TV. They were out in the back bar playing pool. I went into the front bar to watch the match alongside Paul Murphy, 'Scruffy' and Richie Hogan. I wouldn't say we were completely tuned into the game. We were gulping beer and having the craic among ourselves.

With about ten minutes to go, the conversation died. The game was clearly going to the wire. I was hoping Galway would win. I just felt we would have their number in the final, like we had in 2015. I also remembered what Brother Damien had forecast to me earlier on in the year. 'If Kilkenny meet Tipperary in the final they will be very hard to beat this time.'

Brother Damien is never too far wrong. He is mostly on the money but as the clock ticked down, and the game continued to oscillate wildly, I wanted Tipperary to win. There is nothing like a Kilkenny-Tipp All-Ireland final but I was also being more selfish in my train of thought. 'Brian knows I always play well against Tipperary,' I said to myself. 'He knows they bring out the best in me. If it is Tipperary, Brian is going to need men in the trenches, especially against that Tipp full-forward line. And he knows I would die rather than allow those boys to get a score off me.'

Tipperary won a classic by one point. Hallelujah. Another Kilkenny-Tipperary final. Bring it on.

My first experience of an All-Ireland final was in 1991 when my father brought me to the Kilkenny-Tipperary final. We were on Hill 16, right behind where Michael Cleary got the decisive goal in the second half. I cried afterwards when Kilkenny were beaten.

I could see the devastation on my father's face. I could see how much it hurt all Kilkenny people. I knew that Kilkenny people didn't like Tipperary. I struggled to understand that at the time but as I got older, I was reared through a culture of hating Tipperary.

I got it from my dad. He never said it but I just knew by him that Tipperary were the enemy. My aunt's husband, John 'Spud' Murphy couldn't stand Tipp. I used to spend a lot of time at Eardly's because Micky was one of my best friends. Micky's father, Johnny, couldn't abide Tipp. He detested them.

Johnny worked with cars and machinery. If he was fixing a car or a tractor, the first thing he'd do was look at the registration.

If it had a TN or TS reg, Johnny wouldn't entertain it. The car might be owned and driven by someone from Kilkenny but Johnny wanted nothing to do with anything associated with Tipperary.

Johnny sent myself and Micky into town one day to get sandwiches, soft drinks and water for him and the lads who worked in his business. We never looked at the labels but we picked up a couple of bottles of 'Tipperary Spring Water'. Johnny went nuts when we handed the bottles to him. 'What did ye bring that shite here for? Pour it down the drain.'

My uncle 'Spud' was just as militant. He was chairman of the Kilkenny Supporters Club for a few years. When I was in third year in Kieran's, Kilkenny unveiled a new jersey. To launch it, the supporters club organised a draw for a jersey. 'Spud' more or less rigged the draw so I would win it. I was the first person in the college to have the new jersey. Willie Maher, who captained the Tipperary minors to an All-Ireland title in 1996, was a sixth year boarder in the school at that time. He spotted the jersey on me one evening after school and asked another boarder to see if I would swap it with one of Maher's Tipp minor jerseys. I was delighted with the offer. I went home and told my mother. 'Spud' soon got wind of it. 'Don't you dare swap that jersey,' he said. 'If you do, you won't get any more match tickets off me again.'

They were extremists when it came to Tipp. They would verbally abuse Tipp lads at matches but those men grew up in the 1960s, when Tipperary were the top dogs. Tipp always took great pride and satisfaction in walking down on top of Kilkenny but they trampled on them in that period, kicking dirt into Kilkenny's faces at every opportunity. No matter how many All-Irelands we won, my father and his generation never let go of that spite and bitterness instilled in them from that Tipperary purge.

When our fathers and forefathers carried that hurt in their hearts, you had to hate Tipperary. If you hurled for Kilkenny and you didn't hate Tipperary, there was nearly something wrong with you.

That feeling was even more acute up around the Kilkenny-Tipperary border. After we beat Tipp in the 2009 All-Ireland final, we ended up in Urlingford on the Wednesday. The celebrations had died down everywhere else around Kilkenny by then but they seemed to be only getting started in Urlingford. It was like Mardi Gras. There were still some Tipp lads in the pub, still wearing their jerseys, still reeling from the defeat. They must have been twisted drunk. It made no sense for them to even be there because they were being showered with torrents of verbal abuse.

It nearly meant more to those people on the border than it did to the players. 'I'm married to a Tipperary 'wan',' this fella said to me that day. 'And if Tipp had won, she'd have broken my heart over the winter. I couldn't be listening to that shite. I'd be gone.'

I often wondered if he left his wife the following year when Tipp did beat us.

Apart from Tipperary's historical dominance of the relationship, and how they rammed that dominance down Kilkenny people's throats, the Kilkenny people around the border still always had a cause. It was never mentioned in our squad but you knew that the PJ Delaney incident was always very hurtful for the Johnstown boys. PJ had been nearly beaten to death by a couple of Tipp fellas outside a nightclub in Thurles in 1999. JJ Delaney and PJ Ryan would always say very little in the group but coming up to a big game against Tipperary, they were far more vocal.

JJ is related to PJ. 'Taggy' Fogarty's girlfriend is another cousin of PJ's. Their attitude towards Tipperary didn't hinge on the violent actions of a couple of mindless thugs but it certainly sharpened the edge to their outlook. Coming up to those Kilkenny-Tipperary games, you always knew that it was more than just a hurling match for those lads.

Playing Tipperary always brought pressure but we loved playing them. We loved beating them even more. We couldn't beat them enough. We'd be so juiced up on adrenaline and emotion afterwards that we'd want to play them again the following day, and give them another hiding. So would the supporters. Even when we were completely on top of Tipp, the Kilkenny people were always singing the same tune. 'You couldn't beat that crowd enough. The more we beat them, the sweeter it gets.'

That was encrypted into my DNA but it took me a long time to fully experience, or express, that feeling. We never met Tipperary at minor or U-21 level. In my first six years on the senior panel, we never ran into Tipperary. We won a bag of league titles in that period but we never played Tipp in any of those finals. We beat them in the 2003 final in Croke Park but I was only called into the panel after that game.

Tipp spent most of the rest of that decade in the doldrums. They went seven years without a Munster title. They finally ended that drought in 2008 but we didn't meet them that year because Waterford took them out in an All-Ireland semi-final, and we annihilated Waterford in the final. Tipp were much stronger in 2009 but we still didn't rate them. At that time, we didn't rate anyone because we didn't think anyone could beat us.

What had we to rate? Tipp had won successive Munster championships but that meant nothing to us because we were the acid test and Tipperary had yet to prove they could pass it. Kilkenny people are always on edge when Tipperary arrive with a new team but we were going for four in a row and we didn't believe that Tipp, or anyone else, could stop us. We were at our peak. Tipperary were just another team. They didn't register with us because we felt indestructible.

We annihilated Tipperary in the 2009 league in Nowlan Park. It was just another one of the many punishment beatings we dished out that spring but they had a chance to respond when we clashed again in that year's league final in Thurles. And that day, I finally grasped what my father and uncle and Johnny Eardly had always spoken about.

The atmosphere was partisan and electric. We won an epic after extra-time but there was still a bitter aftertaste in our mouths because Tipperary physically bullied us. They physically nailed us. From the first minute. They didn't even wait for the first minute. Tipp walked up to us beforehand, took off their gloves, slapped them across our pus, and kept swinging bare-knuckled for the rest of the afternoon.

Brian Hogan had his collarbone broken early on. 'Gorta' Comerford came on in the second half, was only on a handful of seconds when Declan Fanning got stuck into him. 'Gorta' responded and was sent straight back off again. In that year's league, players were replaced on a yellow card. Henry also walked, finally snapping after being hassled and hounded like a dog all afternoon.

You could see Tipp grow as the game progressed. Their young players were cocky but classy. Kilkenny was a proving ground and they proved they could take our best shots and remain standing. Tipperary had enviously watched our relentless crusade but the way they stood up to us that afternoon was a kind of reclamation of their heritage.

We hated that. But deep down, too, we loved it. This was a fresh challenge but it was even juicier because it was Tipperary. Although we won that league final, we felt we psychologically lost it. We prided ourselves on bullying teams but they bullied us that day. They made a big statement. After the hammering we gave them five weeks earlier, Tipp looked into the whites of our eyes and didn't see anything supernatural. They felt they had nothing to be afraid of any more.

I knew they were talented. I went to school with Eoin Kelly, who I always thought was a genius. I went to college with Shane McGrath and Conor O'Mahony. I knew they were good players too. Tipp had some serious underage talent, which was maturing now into serious senior potential. And that fusion was a serious threat to our authority.

In fairness to Brian, he never dialled up the Kilkenny-Tipperary history and rivalry. He could have pressed that vein but he didn't have to because it was everywhere else. You knew the county board didn't like Tipperary. Most Kilkenny hurling supporters hated them. It was the ultimate satisfaction for Kilkenny to win the four-in-a-row against Tipperary in 2009. Conversely, it was the ultimate for Tipperary to deny us the five-in-a-row in 2010.

Tipperary deserved to win that match but the way they celebrated it drove me nuts. They were well entitled to celebrate wildly after a nine-year hiatus but the manner and tone of the language applied to that win suggested that Tipperary had more than just arrived; the underlying implication was that they were going to take over.

Six days later, Tipperary won the All-Ireland U-21 final against Galway by 25 points, the greatest winning margin in nearly 50 years of U-21 finals. Eight of those Tipp players had won senior medals the previous week, five of them as starters. Foresight was easy: the future belonged to Tipperary.

We suddenly seemed to be past tense. Losing an All-Ireland final was hard to take. Losing the chance of five-in-a-row immortality deepened the cut. But being disregarded the way we were was like a slash down the middle of our face. Our four-in-a-row seemed to almost count for nothing. Some of the greatest players of our generation – Henry, Tommy, JJ – were suddenly being written off.

We were driven wild that winter. Any time I turned on the TV, there seemed to be a documentary on Tipperary, or some Tipp player staring back at me on the screen.

I could understand why the general public were keen to embrace that Tipperary team. They were new, fresh, energetic. They were sick to death of us and our perceived colourless personality. Tipp were right to surf that wave of new appeal but we felt they had lost the run of themselves.

By the start of 2011, they had been pissing us off for well over a year, having repeatedly raked over an old wound before ripping it apart in the 2010 final. For a full 12 months, we had to listen with silent fury about the shit from the 2009 final, the assertion that Tipp should have won, that they hurled us off the pitch, that Kilkenny got away with murder. There were other random proclamations of injustice too – the sending off of Benny Dunne, the penalty Henry scored, which they felt was dubious. Maybe it was, but our attitude was, 'Shut the fuck up and take your beating.'

Familiarity never fathered harmony in the Kilkenny-Tipperary relationship. Familiarity between the teams at the turn of the decade didn't breed anything like the same contempt and poison which strained relations between the players in the 1960s. The modern rivalry was less raw between us but we had a real dislike for Tipperary heading into the 2011 season.

In a way, it was exactly what we wanted. It fed into everything we were about because we had a completely new cause, which we were hell-bent on seeing through. When we met in the opening round of the league in 2011 in Thurles, we had to form a guard of honour and clap Tipperary onto the pitch. I didn't clap. I should have but I couldn't bring myself to do it.

Having to form that guard of honour was a horrible feeling, but in a weird way, I really wanted to experience it. I wanted to soak up that pain, to store it like rocket fuel to drive myself forward for the rest of the year.

We were agitated. We were completely pissed off. A lot of that frustration may have had nothing to do with Tipperary but we dialled it up to ensure that we always believed it had. We blamed them for everything; a winter of misery, the persecution of our people with their arrogance, their silent goading of us with their perceived new self-worth as All-Ireland champions. I was nearly so paranoid that winter that I'd have blamed Tipperary for starting the Great Famine.

Part of that was fear. We were desperate for a crack at them but we knew they had the potential to beat us again, which would have been doomsday scenario stuff. They had the capacity to take over. If they did, we believed it would have detracted from what we had achieved as a team, that it would have completely diluted our achievements.

Kilkenny had never lost to Tipperary in successive championship seasons. We didn't want that to happen in 2011 but we felt we were playing for more than just that All-Ireland. Our heritage, our modern legacy, was all on the line.

We knew we would meet them at some stage but one of the biggest challenges for us that year was to stay focussed on what was ahead of us before Tipperary even loomed into view. We went into that championship under a serious cloud of doubt. Dublin had hammered us in the league final. Everyone had written us off. Everyone said Tipp were about to take over.

We had to take care of business first before we could even contemplate taking them on but that 2011 championship was about one thing only – beating Tipperary.

When we both qualified for the All-Ireland final, Brian didn't have to say a word to us. He knew we were demented to get at Tipp. He was ready too because he closed the gates to our training sessions for the first time before that All-Ireland final. People were giving out hell but Brian didn't care. The one night that he let the public in, on the first Friday night after we beat Waterford in the semi-final, Brian played a match where he threw curveballs everywhere. I was playing wing-back. Other fellas were completely out of position. It was a sign that this time it was different, that they were looking at match-ups, that we were really going to nail Tipp big time.

We were entering a game as underdogs for the first time since the 2006 All-Ireland final but we were never as ready to wage war on anyone. That whole winter of 2010-11, the image of Eoin Kelly pointing his finger to his temple after Noel McGrath's goal drove me wrong. That, and Shane McGrath's fist-pumping, drove us all wild.

John Mullane was always at that craic but it never bothered us. Mullane is a passionate boyo but he did the business nearly every day he played. We respected him, which granted him a dispensation from the fist-pumping antics. We just believed Mullane almost couldn't help himself from engaging in the histrionics.

It was different with Tipperary. We didn't respect them as much as we did Waterford. We liked 'Bonner' Maher. We respected Eoin Kelly. I like Eoin. I like Lar Corbett and Conor O'Mahony. Some of the other Tipp lads are nice fellas. They were decent company on nights out and All-Stars trips. But when they went into their own environment, it was as if they couldn't help themselves from exercising their birthright to piss off Kilkenny. When they were showboating, we felt it was purely just to piss us off.

We also believed it was a front, that it was them trying to convince themselves that they were better than us. We didn't think they ever fully believed it. We felt it was the same with them lining up together in a line before a big game, in this show of unbreakable brotherhood. To us, it was more bullshit they were hiding behind.

We'd find a cause anywhere. The long-serving Tipperary kit man, John 'Hotpoint' Hayes seems like a grand fella but I was always stuck in him. He would come in with water to Eoin or whoever I was marking, and start telling them what to do to me. I'd tell him to fuck off. He'd tell me to fuck off back. I'd often stand in his way as he'd try and hand over the water. It was just more needless bullshit that you'd only get with Tipperary.

After the 2010 All-Ireland final, Pat Kerwick grabbed the microphone on the Hogan Stand and belted out 'Galtee Mountain Boy'. I couldn't believe it. The only time a song was sung after a Kilkenny All-Ireland final win was when Larks thought he was Michael Bublé after the 2012 final replay. The previous week, Michael Murphy had sung 'Jimmy's Winning Matches', Donegal's theme tune that summer, after they won the All-Ireland. Larks inserted the word 'Cody' for 'Jimmy' and 'Liam' (MacCarthy) for 'Sam' (Maguire). Larks sounded like a hoarse frog. It was hilarious but it was only a bit of craic. If Larks, or anyone else, started into 'The Rose of Mooncoin' we'd have all told him to shut the fuck up.

It was just typical Tipperary. They win one All-Ireland and they think they have it made. You almost felt that they couldn't help themselves, that they were teeing themselves up to allow us to eat them alive. And we routinely did. We could beat them ten times in a row but we felt it still never instilled any humility in the hearts and minds of Tipperary people. If they beat us once, they'd act as if they had been thrashing us for a decade. Tipperary just have this unbelievable ability to gall the hell out of us. And I think they know that too. What they didn't realise though, was how much that attitude and arrogance fuelled us, and our drive to keep them down. No matter what they did, no matter how much talent they had, we always felt we had more men. We just felt that if a Kilkenny player and a Tipperary player went into a room to sort out their differences, the Kilkenny fella would always walk out after having put the Tipp fella on the floor.

We didn't need to showboat or prance around to convince ourselves that we could beat Tipperary. All we had to do was be ourselves, to trust in ourselves and what we were about. I always felt coming up to an All-Ireland final against Tipperary that I never needed anyone, or anything. I didn't need a trainer. I didn't need a dietician or video analyst. I didn't even need Brian Cody. The only person I needed was Brother Damien. I could nearly tell Brian that I'd show up in Croke Park at 2.30pm on the day of the match, just give me the jersey and cut me loose.

We were all the same. Tommy Walsh could have moved to Australia the month before an All-Ireland final against Tipperary, flew in the Thursday of the game, get the jet-lag out of his system, and let him off on the Sunday. He would have been right because nothing ever mattered when we played Tipperary. If anything, the only thing Brian probably could have used was a giant harness – to hold us back from getting at them.

On the Wednesday after the 2011 All-Ireland final, Paddy Hogan rang a few of us and asked if we wanted to join the Kilkenny lads based in Dublin on a night out up there. Most of those lads were teachers and were back to work on the Thursday so a gang of us jumped into a taxi to join them.

At around 7pm, we were in Quinn's in Drumcondra, just over the road from Croke Park. We were all hammered. There was nobody else in the place so one of the barmen put on a recording of the match. At that stage of the evening, I was really beery, in that state between merry and drunk. I was nearly ready to fall asleep when I clasped eyes on the screen. It jolted my senses. It transfixed all of us.

We sat down to watch the match but it felt surreal. It was like the game had been played months ago. It almost felt time to refocus and go again, to get ready for 2012. Maybe that was just me and the river of alcohol flooding my bloodstream but I often felt my mindset that day reflected the difference between us and Tipperary. They were still thinking, and talking, about 2010 well into the 2011 season. Three days after we won that 2011 All-Ireland, I was already thinking about 2012.

When you win the All-Ireland, there is nothing else left in the inter-county season. There is no next game but you are so conditioned into thinking a particular way that your thought process just refocuses you on the next task, which is to win the All-Ireland again. Brian is always there to bring you back down to earth so that even when you get to the top, you're soon transported back to the bottom, where the climb starts again.

It's hard to describe the feeling of winning an All-Ireland. It's an inner happiness and contentment that lasts for months but the main hit for me was in those couple of minutes immediately after the final whistle. It was euphoric, like the ultimate high from a narcotic. That feeling just sucks you back in, where you want it again. And again. And again. Motivation or hunger were never an issue for any of us. For most guys, those feelings were 95% of the reason why they kept coming back for more. For me, it was always 100%. It consumed me. That feeling was addictive. And I was completely addicted to it.

Beating Tipperary in 2011 didn't sate us. It didn't scratch an irritable itch from 2010. It just made us even more pumped to keep Tipperary down. It should have made them more motivated to knock us back down but, in typical Tipperary fashion, they lost the run of themselves again.

Galway had hammered us in the 2012 Leinster final. Tipperary had beaten Waterford comprehensively in the Munster final. They were favourites going into the All-Ireland semi-final. They were the form team but, instead of believing that we were on the ropes and stumbling, they saw us in the other corner and shit themselves.

Instead of taking us on, they ran from us. Their main tactic was to get their most dangerous forward – Lar Corbett – to man-mark Tommy Walsh. It was a complete circus, with Lar following Tommy around like the circus clown.

Early in the second half, Henry was standing over a free 35 metres from the Tipp goal. Lar should have been making a run and looking for the puckout from Brendan Cummins. Instead, he was at the other end of the field where he, myself, Tommy and Pa Bourke were following one another around near the corner-flag. Everyone in Croke Park had their eyes trained on the sideshow. The match almost seemed irrelevant.

I didn't know what the hell was going on. The tactic worked, to a point. Tommy wasn't in the game. He needlessly reacted at one point and got a yellow card. It looked like they were getting inside his head. I kept telling him to focus on the ball, not to mind Lar. Any time Pa Bourke weighed in with his tuppence worth, I just told him to shut up. 'Don't worry, Pa,' I would say. 'You'll be gone off by half-time.' He was.

Tommy only touched the ball three times in the first half. He didn't have a single possession in the third quarter. The longer this went on, the more I wondered if there was a method to Tipp's madness. It was so crazy that I was wondering if it was just a gimmick, where Lar was just trying to confuse us before cutting loose in the final quarter.

It was mentally exhausting but there was no need for any of us to worry. Once we got a run on Tipp, we mowed them down. It was the same old Tipp again – shaping and hiding behind their bullshit. They hadn't the balls to come out and take us on man for man.

We never believed they did. I just felt that no matter what they did, we had their number. The only time they got the better of us was when they got their match-ups right. Their forwards were slick and beautiful ball players but, apart from 'Bonner' Maher, I always felt if we were close to them, that we'd physically swallow them up.

We also believed that we could intimidate some of their forwards. You wouldn't manage it with 'Bonner'. Or Eoin. Or Noel McGrath. You could get at 'Bubbles'. They had other flaky lads too over the years. Lar? I don't think you could intimidate Lar. What would you say to him? I tried it in 2011 but sure, I didn't know what planet he was on that day. He could turn around and say anything to you. He was liable to do anything.

We were on an All-Stars trip to Argentina one year. We were all on the beer in Buenos Aries when Lar performed this party trick. He put a one euro coin into his mouth and swallowed it. Everyone was saying, 'What the hell just happened there?'

That was Lar for you. He was a magician with the ball. He was excellent in the 2009 All-Ireland final. Lar destroyed us in 2010 but when we put it up to him on the pitch in other years,

Lar never pulled too many rabbits out of the hat against us again. 'Bubbles' was another genius who could nearly make the ball talk but he was as flaky as any of them.

In the 2014 All-Ireland final replay, 'Bubbles' did a little shimmy and got away from me. He had a couple of yards on me when the ball dropped but instead of catching it, 'Bubbles' tried to pull on it. I knew there and then that I had him. I probably had him after I blocked him down in the opening minute of that 2014 replay. My mental battle with him was 80% won there and then. I knew I had him.

In fairness to Tipp, they had some fair warriors, guys we did respect. Paul Curran was at the top of that list. Conor O'Mahony was a hardy boyo. Padraic Maher was a real leader for them, someone we always felt we had to stop to take Tipp's energy away from them. Padraic Maher would always stand up to you physically. So would 'Bonner' and Eoin Kelly but few others would. Their fluid attacking game was designed so they didn't have to physically engage us up front but we contrived a different picture of it in our minds. We viewed all this moving and switching as a means of disguising that they couldn't take us on, that they hadn't the balls to really go at us. It almost felt like they were scared to beat us.

If that Tipperary team were any good, they would have beaten us in 2013. We were on the floor at the time. Dublin had beaten us the previous week. We were strung together and were barely hanging on with injuries. My quad muscle was in bits. Michael Fennelly could only do the warm-up. TJ Reid's hamstring was only around 60% right. Paul Murphy had wrecked his ankle in the drawn Dublin game. Henry hadn't pucked a ball in nearly 12 months and they had rushed him back to shore up the bench.

That game in 2013 was only a qualifier but it is one of my best memories in a Kilkenny jersey. It was visceral and tribal, raw and atmospheric and beautiful. The Kilkenny players and hurling public were so drugged up on emotion that it was better than winning an All-Ireland. I would rate that win higher than the 2007, 2008 and 2012 All-Irelands. It was probably better than 2006 too, when I was captain. The only drawback was that we couldn't celebrate it. I nearly wanted to go on the beer for a week but we had another qualifier game seven days later.

That game meant so much because everything was on the line. In my eyes, defeat to Tipp that day would have devalued everything we had achieved. It would have completely tainted our All-Ireland final wins against them in 2009 and 2011.

I was hardly able to walk a few days beforehand but I simply had to play that game. I wouldn't allow myself not to. I don't know where it came from. I just went for everything. I almost felt my leg was going to go at some stage but I just said, 'Fuck it, I'm going for it anyway.' I was never the best in the air but I caught four high balls that evening. I never caught four balls in a match in my life but something just came out in me, a fusion of pride and fear that demanded something special from me, from all of us. It was probably inspired by how I was raised as a Kilkenny hurler because that day, I was playing for my father, for 'Spud' Murphy and Johnny Eardly, and for the honour and pride of all Kilkenny supporters. They were baying for Tipperary blood that night. We all were.

We had no form going into that game. We never hurled with any real rhythm or fluency that evening but the prize at stake stripped us down to our essential and most primal nature: absolute defiance. We absolutely resented the notion of falling to Tipperary. We simply refused to fall at their sword on our own land.

There was a photograph taken afterwards of Tommy which completely encapsulated just how much that win meant. Tommy is looking up to the heavens. His eyes are closed but the relief and joy on Tommy's face expressed how the final whistle felt like the end of time for all of us.

Throughout that 2013 summer, we couldn't impose our iron will or our game on that championship but we still summoned something special to beat Tipperary. We defeated them too the following year. Our team isn't the same animal now but Tipp still have to prove that they can beat us.

Brother Damien believes that Tipperary will be very hard to beat in the final this time around. For once, I don't think he is right. But what worries me more than anything now is I'm not sure if our defence can hold this Tipperary attack, especially Seamus Callanan.

When you think back to the 2014 drawn and replayed finals, JJ played well in both games but Callanan still took him for five points from play the first day, and for two goals in the replay. JJ isn't there any more. So what could Callanan do now?

I feel I will be needed. I still believe I will play in Croke Park again.

The Final
Countdown

Saturday August 27th, 2016

I awake at 9.30am and straight away, training springs to my mind, as if I am already late. My brain immediately recalculates; breakfast at 10am; lunch at 12.30; training at 3pm. I relax for five minutes before rising. Clare has been up and has gone to get her hair done. The house is quiet but the morning flies by as my friend Brian Dowling calls for match tickets with his baby, Tadhg.

As I pucked around before training, Brian Cody approaches. 'How's the body?' he asked.

'Good,' I replied.

'You're going well. There is huge competition for places for the 26, never mind the first 15, so just keep it going.'

I am used to the lack of communication from management

by now but Brian's comments throw me slightly off guard. I can feel myself over-thinking things and applying pressure on myself to perform in training. I try and compose myself before the heat gets turned up.

Derek Lyng approaches me five minutes later. 'I know it's hard not playing but your attitude and approach is excellent,' he said. 'And it hasn't gone unnoticed.'

I am happy to hear Derek's feedback as I return to pucking the ball across the pitch with Lester Ryan. I know Derek has been in my shoes. I respect him as a man and his words mean a lot to me.

We play two 15-minute games and I perform very well. I am happy afterwards. I feel good about myself and the last two weeks' work.

After Langton's, I head out to Damien. We chat about the session, and how I felt after my brief conversations with Brian and Derek. Out of nowhere, Damien says 'Are you ready to make a decision?' I say yes but I'm not sure what that decision actually is. Is it about next year? Will I still be around in 2017? I know deep down what I want but I am very nervous. I knew this day was coming. But now it seems to have suddenly arrived.

I ask Damien to ask me questions, to tease out my thoughts. Have I more to win/lose? How much more is really in me? How strong is my desire and attitude? I speak about not wanting to go back without a realistic chance of playing. Damien tells me that is something I don't have full control over.

Damien talks for five minutes. I listen. He tells me that I didn't deal well with the challenges I was presented with between May and a lot of August but that my mind is good now. I am in a win-win situation. It feels surreal to be talking about this stuff a week out from the biggest day of the year but I am very comfortable with the conversation. I would like to know if this really is my last time involved in an All-Ireland final. The possibility immediately comes to mind. I feel slightly excited about the huge decision but I know deep down that I want to retire.

My desire and focus has waned this year (2016) more times than before. I have become content in my mind. I love it but I know for sure now that I don't want to go back if I am not 100% into it. I am right now but I know my priorities will change even more in 2017. I have my mind made up to hurl with my club until I am 37. I believe that will happen.

So just like that, I tell Damien: 'I want to retire.'

There is silence for a few seconds. Then Damien says, 'Great.'

We chat about the next eight days and going after that 10th All-Ireland medal. I have a giddiness about myself. I am going to soak up everything this week; the build-up, the atmosphere, the anticipation, just getting ready for the game. I am even going to enjoy packing my bag. I'm already looking forward to the bus journey and the match itself.

I leave and head home happy.

Sunday August 28th, 2016

I sleep great. When I wake up, the words 'I'm retiring' come to mind. I head to mass. Every thought in my head is framed around the same series of questions. Will this be the last time…?

I head to a Village junior match. The club is more on my radar than normal this week because the end with Kilkenny is near. I head to Brother D to work on a dead leg, but mainly to chat about my decision from the previous day. I leave with two strong thoughts in my head for the week. 'Working hard' and 'Leadership'. I know I will do one, and provide the other.

I feel very clear-minded. It's as if I'm already beginning to look at things differently now.

As I reflect more during what will be my last week as part of the Kilkenny senior panel, I am even more aware that I have never regretted a day in my hurling life. Great days give happiness. Bad days give experience. And the worst days give lessons.

My ultimate goal in life is to become my best self. My time with Kilkenny allowed me to begin that journey. And I intend to stay on that path that will lead me there.

I know what I want to achieve this week, and afterwards. Above all, I know what I stand for, and what I am committed to. My sole preoccupation is doing what I do as well as I possibly can. What others or opponents are thinking or doing doesn't matter to me. I don't imitate.

Wednesday August 31st, 2016

I am a creature of habit. I want to get all my work done early. It's just another part of my mental preparation. I head to Carlow and Athy with my brain sifting through work duties and logistics for the All-Ireland final; sorting all tickets out by Thursday, gear to wear, bag, tunes, dinner in Mam's on Saturday.

My brain is in overdrive. I stop for a coffee and get some work done. I get in a 50-minute nap. I am not even tired but I want to build up as many hours of rest as possible.

I head to training at 5.30pm. We have a 30-minute skill session that I really enjoy. Afterwards, we watched the Kilkenny-Waterford replay. Brian stressed how well we played and how hard we worked but the message he delivers is simple – we need to bring more on Sunday.

On the journey home from training, my mind drifts back on my career. Embracing my power as well as my vulnerabilities and my fragility has been my path to wholeness. I believe that I achieved and won because I refused to be defeated by the many challenges and obstacles that I encountered along the journey. I have never settled for anything other than my best. And I won't settle for anything less this week.

I will continue to take risks and push boundaries in order to do myself justice. After all, what is the point in being alive if I don't at least try and do something remarkable?

All my progress has taken place when I am comfortable with myself and am willing to work outside my comfort zone. I have learned that success and achieving fulfilment and enjoyment is liking myself, liking what I do and how I do it. The more I succeed, the more I want to succeed, and the more I find ways to succeed.

I know that nobody can make me feel inferior without my consent. The fact that I have the freedom to be myself with the person whom I trust provides me with a special opportunity to achieve things which I didn't think were possible.

This week may seem like the coming of an end. But what makes it even more special for me is that it's just another step on my journey as I open a new door to the future with my head held high, knowing I did my best to finish the contest.

I can remember moments of the past. I can look forward to, and relish, the promise of that future. But most of all, I can enjoy the present because it is real and precious. I will not be denied by anyone. I will not be stopped as I fan the tiny, inner sparks of possibility into flames of more achievement. The time is now. Cogito Ergo Sum.

Thursday, September 1st, 2016

I make it a rule of life never to regret, or never to look back with regret. Damien tells me that I was born to achieve my greatest self, to live out my purpose, and to do it fearlessly. Working really hard and providing leadership, so that Kilkenny win on Sunday, is important. But there is something else that matters even more – believing in myself to make a real difference.

I never forget this is still my dream. I don't give up on achieving it because I know that nothing that is realistic is impossible. I keep moving in the right direction. I trust myself and my abilities. Just because things don't always work out as planned does not mean they won't work out. There is always a way. I can't lose unless I decide to, or, give up.

I have never felt this way on the week of an All-Ireland final before. It almost feels like I'm floating, drifting, but in a good sort of way. A certain amount of pressure is removed from your mind when you're not playing but you can carry that burden in other ways too when you don't have a starting jersey.

When I was guaranteed that sacred garment, I was always so tunnel visioned that I nearly turned into somebody else, someone most people didn't want to be around on weeks like this. There was only one thing which mattered. It was almost like the rest of the world, and all that was in it, was just a distraction from that ultimate goal of an All-Ireland medal.

This week is different. I feel a weight has been lifted from my shoulders. I feel an inner contentment. It feels so strange that I almost don't recognise myself, and how I am approaching the 2016 All-Ireland final. I almost feel giddy. I have this huge news to tell everybody but I don't want to tell anyone. I'm just happy that the decision has been made.

I just want some me time with that decision to become fully comfortable with it. I am excited by it. I wanted to enjoy everything about the week. Damien said it should almost be a precious time of recollection, like a kind of celebration of my career. I'm still asking myself as to why Brother Damien has triggered this decision this week, of all weeks. I just think that he wants me to soak up as much as I possibly can from this week, to completely enjoy this one, last, great experience.

Whatever he said, it worked. My mind was constantly drifting. Memories were flooding back into my head. I am excited about the possibilities of the future. I always looked ahead to the future but my future now is pregnant with more than just promise of Kilkenny hurling and the relentless pursuit of more All-Ireland medals.

I know it is right. It just feels right. I wanted to be even conscious of that realisation, and what it means for me. I am more realistic now, more accepting in where I am inevitably going. Injuries and the frustration contaminated my mind throughout 2016. I tried to fight reality but I never fully faced up to it. I'll admit now that part of me collapsed. Those were signs that, while I wouldn't acknowledge them earlier in the summer, I have now accepted.

I have that inner peace now that I never had before. Yet until I am officially retired from Kilkenny, every cell in my body will carry the same warrior's code DNA. I will continue to fight on my back for Kilkenny. That will be my dominant mentality as the game edges closer. Despite the injuries and lack of faith management may have shown in me, I still firmly believe that I am going to play a part in the 2016 All-Ireland final.

There is something different about this Tipperary team. They are a different animal this year. I'm not sure if we can just bully them any more. Their full-forward line, especially Seamus Callanan and John McGrath, have been awesome throughout 2016. Brother Damien said to me the other night that I will be needed to help pull Kilkenny over the line, if I am on or off the field. And I really believe that I will be.

Friday, September 2nd, 2016

The ritual is well established by now before an All-Ireland final. After our final training session on the Friday night, we always go upstairs to a meeting room to hear the team announcement. 'Rackard' Cody is either there to greet us, or else some of us are sitting down, before he starts handing out holy medals. 'Rackard' gets them from a priest he is friendly with. I already have a holy medal in my bag, one I got from 'Rackard' before, so I just put it into my pocket and waited for Brian to arrive.

I made a point of sitting beside fellas I really like – Lester Ryan and Padraig Walsh. At the top of the room was the flipchart which is always positioned in the same spot.

The normal ritual is followed. Brian flips back the cover page. Just like that, the starting line-up stares back at us in black and white, the ink on the letters often dripping with agony and ecstasy.

Brian's limited close conversation with us always adds to

the intrigue and heightened sense of anticipation before an All-Ireland final. Surprise is expected. Every training session is a new opportunity. No player is safe. Brian keeps us all guessing right up until the last second, until that page is flipped over before us.

After the drumroll goes off in all our heads, dreams are realised for some fellas, especially rookies in their first season. For others, their world collapses when they don't see their name on that page.

I remember Aidan Fogarty's face after that page was flipped before the 2012 All-Ireland final replay. 'Taggy' had been outstanding all season. Man of the match in the All-Ireland semi-final against Tipperary, 'Taggy' was fourth favourite for Player of the Year before the drawn All-Ireland final, priced at 5-1. The best price available on the three players ahead of him was 4-1.

'Taggy' played the full match in the drawn game. He fully expected to start the replay too but his devastation was instantly visible when his name wasn't on the page.

Colin Fennelly was also dropped for that replay. Form dictates everything but a handful of players are always on edge. After the drawn 2014 All-Ireland final, Brian gutted his half-back line, dropping Brian Hogan and Joey Holden. Walter Walsh was also demoted.

Padraig Walsh and Kieran Joyce were introduced into a revamped defence. It was Kilkenny's fifth different half-back line of the summer. Padraig hadn't started a game there since the Leinster quarter-final against Offaly in June. Joyce hadn't played since the drawn Leinster semi-final against Galway. Similar to Walter Walsh from two years earlier, Joyce got man of the match in that replay. Padraig was among Kilkenny's top five performers.

Brian has had a history of making big calls for All-Ireland finals since promoting John Hoyne for the 2000 final against Offaly. Hoyne had only played 13 minutes of championship hurling up to that point but he replaced Stephen Grehan, who had started in all of Kilkenny's championship matches that season.

The story is still shrouded in mystery and innuendo. The Sunday before the game, Grehan came off the bench to score the winner for Spa United against River Rangers in the Maher Shield. Brian denied that the soccer match had anything to do with Grehan being dropped. Hoyne had been going well in training but the answer was obvious.

Grehan came on as a substitute in Kilkenny's two Leinster championship matches in 2001. He started the All-Ireland semi-final against Galway that August but after Kilkenny were beaten, a more ruthless Cody reappeared in 2002. Grehan never featured again. And the big and hard calls became far more frequent.

DJ Carey wasn't part of the squad throughout the 2002 league and Leinster championship but Brian brought Carey back for that year's All-Ireland semi-final against Tipperary. Cody dropped his club-mate, Brian McEvoy, for the All-Ireland final against Clare, replacing him with Jimmy Coogan, a bolter who scored the game-changing goal in the semi-final against Tipperary.

Richie Power was dropped for the 2007 final against Limerick. Michael Rice and Martin Comerford lost their places for the 2009 decider against Tipp. In 2010, Brian took a massive chance starting Henry Shefflin and John Tennyson when both were carrying serious knee injuries. It was one of the few big calls Brian got wrong.

Brian Hogan was dropped for that 2010 decider. TJ Reid was benched for the 2011 final. Before the 2014 drawn final, Brian changed his goalkeeper, dropping David Herity and selecting Eoin Murphy. Herity was one of the few players over the years who Brian informed of his decision an hour before the team was announced. Martin Comerford was also afforded that respect before the 2009 final. I was told before the 2015 final that I hadn't made the cut but few others were ever given that heads-up. Or will be.

In his 16 All-Ireland finals (including replays) as manager, Brian has named an unchanged team from the semi-final, or drawn final, on just five occasions. That won't change now. Michael Fennelly is injured but a host of places are up for grabs after the huge reshuffle from the Waterford replay. Liam Blanchfield and Mark Bergin came out of nowhere. Kieran Joyce, Lester Ryan, John Joe Farrell, Kevin Kelly, Rob Lennon and John Power didn't start in that game but they'll all hope that their number might come up now.

I had a silent, romantic notion that my name might be there but I knew full well it wouldn't be. I didn't have that normal sense of anticipation. I wasn't squinting my eye or trying to find the right reflection from the lighting that sometimes allows you to spot the names behind the cover page. It was Lester and 'Taggy' who once copped that possibility.

The mood changed as soon as Brian entered the room. He flipped back the cover-page on the flipchart to reveal all. Kieran Joyce comes in at centre-back with Conor Fogarty partnering

TJ Reid at midfield. Kevin Kelly was named at corner forward, making his first start in the championship. Mark Bergin was dropped. Kelly, along with Liam Blanchfield, will play in their first All-Ireland final.

Brian immediately spoke about the magnitude of the game. He talked about what individuals in the room had done in the past. He mentioned me. Maybe I was being over-sensitive but it sounded like Brian was saying that I can't do it any more.

His words didn't stay with me long. I didn't allow them to float around in my mind and trigger any anxiety or concern. One of my main goals all week has been to provide leadership, and to do everything I can to help Kilkenny win this All-Ireland.

Before he wrapped up the meeting, Brian asked Michael Fennelly to talk. Feno just wasn't comfortable speaking. He talked too generically. I thought Brian was going to say something at the end, almost to refocus the lads again, but he didn't.

It doesn't matter anyway. Kilkenny have always done their talking on the pitch. Especially against Tipperary. And particularly in All-Ireland finals against Tipperary.

The Start Of
The Beginning

*'Fear is not real. It only exists in my thoughts. It is a
product of my imagination. Fear is a choice. Only those
who take great risks can possibly find out how far they can
go. I still have fears, but...'*

– Diary entry, Monday October 17th, 2016

BROTHER Damien told me today about the Latin
phrase, 'Esse Quam Videri', which means 'To be rather
than to seem'. The words were first found in Cicero's
essay on 'Friendship'. It has since often been used as a motto by
numerous different groups but I like the phrase, especially how
I want to apply it to my own journey from thinking that I was
something to actually being something.

That journey has been built on honesty, trust, taking risks,
hard work and the desire to be the best I can be. I have always

tried to be the absolute best version of myself with Kilkenny but is that journey finally over now?

For the last month, since the 2016 All-Ireland final, my mind has been constantly racing. I haven't been able to switch off. I'm mentally tired. In my head, I feel I cannot go through another season. I can't keep pushing my body to extremes at that level any more either because my body is even more likely to keep breaking down next year when I am a year older.

Deep down, I think it is finally all over. And yet, there are other days when my train of thought is at the opposite end of the spectrum. 'The Kilkenny full-back line was destroyed in the All-Ireland final. I believe I'm still as good as any of them. There isn't a whole lot of quality young defenders looking for a jersey. If I get another chance next year, I'll definitely take it.'

I still find it hard to let go of that Kilkenny jersey. I desperately want to play in Croke Park again, just one more time. I think I can but even the smallest little detail is enough to trigger the mental wrestle all over again. 'Am I just codding myself? Should I just silently walk away now with my dignity intact? What more have I really left to prove?'

The whole issue of retirement is consuming me even more because the lingering question is coming at me everywhere I turn. I routinely give a generic reply but every time the question is posed, the same thoughts keep resurfacing. 'Maybe I should go. Most people seem to think I should go. But those people don't know me, they don't know what my motivations are, why should they more or less tell me I should retire?'

My head is even more scrambled because we lost to O'Loughlin Gaels in the Kilkenny county quarter-final recently. It was a game that got away from us. A sickening defeat. When

I went out for a drink with my best friend 'Bobs' the following evening, I was already hung over from the night before. We had a good laugh but there was an emptiness and falseness to the experience.

You try and forget about the pain but every joke and laugh is only a brief interlude to the deep hurt of having lost to our arch rivals. Alcohol does very little to numb the pain.

Getting to a county final, possibly winning a county title, going on a run in Leinster were all potential platforms for me with Kilkenny but all those stages have collapsed and crumpled now like my mood. And no matter how hard I try, I cannot get the same recurring question out of my head. 'Have I got the absolute maximum from my body and mind?'

The uncertainty, the unknown about my future is only feeding my anxiety to come to the correct decision. My attitude towards Brian Cody has changed in the last few weeks. I have let go of the disappointment I had towards Brian after the All-Ireland final. I have stopped feeling sorry for myself. But I still need to find answers to questions I have myself. I need to bring an end to this uncertainty about my future with Kilkenny. Brother Damien and I decided today that I will have met Brian and have a decision made by November 8th.

That gives me three weeks.

'Why would I go back?
Keep myself on edge.
Keep providing leadership.
Keep making statements.
Keep challenging myself.

Unfinished business.
Fear of not being able to walk away.
Why would I retire?
I've just had enough.
Dropping levels of desire.
Staying just for the sake of it.
Dealing with not playing.
Less pressure on myself.
Fear of not being good enough any more.'

– Diary entry, Thursday October 20th, 2016

'Today, I let the reasons to 'Go back v Retire' float around in my head. At times, I feel that I will go back. Then other times, I decide that I have had enough. If I am being fully honest, there are more times when I say to myself that I will retire than I will go back. This isn't easy. The more I think about not retiring, there are no major thoughts that suck me in and say, 'Yeah, I'd love to keep going, I am willing to really go after that, to really work hard for it.' They still appeal to me but those reasons still don't fill me with a great sense of really wanting to do them. Playing in Croke Park again would be great but I really don't think I want it so badly that I will drive myself to my absolute limits.'

– Diary entry, Saturday October 22nd, 2016

'I meet Cillian Buckley today down town at the Savour Food Festival. We chat briefly in the street about his knee. Cillian wonders about when we will be back training with Kilkenny and, for five seconds, I answered as if I was going back. When I checked myself, and thought that I might not be back with Kilkenny, my heart sank. Deep down, I think I would love to go back but the reasons have to be right. The experience made my decision more relevant and real. It's *almost at my doorstep now. I'm still not sure what I will do but I am working through both scenarios.*

PS. I did 5km Castle Park Run today in 19 minutes and 42 seconds.'

– Diary entry, Saturday October 29th, 2016

'I meet with Damien this evening and we discuss about meeting Brian with an 'open mind' and the 'freedom to decide'. We talk about types of questions I would like to ask him; a potential role for me in 2017; what that role might be. I have no bitterness towards Brian. That is mostly down to Brother Damien, who has always challenged me positively and constructively. He helped me to see that Brian Cody was still the same Brian Cody who gave me my opportunity in 2003 and who nurtured me.

I feel very comfortable about the upcoming conversation. On the way home, I ring Brian and agree to meet him tomorrow in the Springhill hotel at 5pm. I am excited, but nervous too.'

– Diary entry, Monday November 7th, 2016

When I met Brian for a chat in November 2015, it was in the opulent surroundings of the Lyrath Estate Hotel on the Dublin road. This time around, Brian suggested the Springhill. Was that a sign of something different? I rinsed the thought from my mind immediately. I have enough flotsam and jetsam already floating around my head.

My only concern was to be there before Brian, to be relaxed and well settled before any discussion began. I pulled into the hotel car park around 4.45pm. I was almost psyching myself up in the car before I walked into the hotel at 4.53pm. Brian arrived through the doors at 5.01pm.

We sat down in the little coffee dock in the lobby. There was some small talk about the club before I inhaled deeply and said what I had come to say.

'Look Brian, I'm considering my future and I wanted to touch base with you before I made any decision. What would your thoughts be if I decided to go back?'

Brian was sitting back in his chair. He shuffled up, into a more upright position. 'You've had an unbelievable career up to this point,' he said. 'But the team is taking a different shape now. There will be a lot of changes.'

Brian sat back in his chair. I sat up. 'I appreciate your honesty,' I said. 'I just wanted to have that conversation with you before I made any decision. Whatever I'm doing, I'll keep you in the loop.'

And that was it. Like a click of the great man's fingers, the show appeared to finally all be over.

A waitress just came over and asked us if we would like to order tea or coffee, or anything from the evening dinner menu. We politely declined as we both got to our feet.

The discussion was over. I had yet to fully process the information but the conversation took a different direction as we walked out the door together. Brian's tone was very complimentary. 'You had a great career,' he said. 'You set the standard in terms of work, application and leadership. When we spoke to young fellas about leadership, we always used you as an example.'

His words made me feel warm and humble. I thanked Brian

for giving me my chance. We shook hands and went our separate ways.

When I sat back into the car, the clock on the dashboard was flashing at 5.08pm. Everything I had agonised about over the previous two months had been distilled down into seven minutes. In reality, it was probably closer to seven seconds.

I was in a good place but I still didn't know what to really feel. I wasn't completely happy. But I wasn't sad either. I was still slightly confused. I hadn't told Brian that I was retiring. I didn't definitely say I was retiring. What would happen if I rang Brian in a couple of days and told him that I had decided to go back?

I knew that conversation wasn't going to take place. So I instantly decided to retire.

And it felt good. I could feel the relief coursing through my body in waves. Immediately, it felt like the right decision. I'd had enough. The pressure was gone. I didn't have to worry about putting my body through the ringer again over the next few weeks to get ready for pre-season training.

I rang Clare. 'I'm retiring,' I said.

'Well done,' she replied. 'I'm delighted for you.'

Then I rang Brother Damien. 'Brilliant,' he said.

I had a sense Damien knew I would retire but in no way was he going to influence my decision. He probably felt it was the right thing to do, that it was the best move for me. He just wanted me to be fully happy with the decision, and to have explored all the options so that I would be fully comfortable with it.

Over the following couple of days, Brother Damien helped me with my retirement statement. He didn't want his name mentioned but I insisted that it would be on the page. I decided to release it a couple of days later.

I rang Brian to tell him I was retiring. Very little was said. I called to my parents to tell them of my decision. My mam immediately broke down crying. It was sad and emotional but Mam and Dad were delighted that I was happy and content.

The following morning, I got up at 7am. I headed to the gym to try and declutter my racing mind. When I got home, Clare was just heading out the door to work. She gave me a big hug and wished me the best of luck. I sat at my desk. I took out my phone and removed myself from the team WhatsApp Group, which I found very difficult. I opened up my laptop and cut and pasted my statement onto an email which I decided to send to all media outlets. I re-read the statement again, which reaffirmed the finality of it all. I stayed looking at the screen for a couple of minutes, clearly stalling on the inevitable. 'Come on JT,' I said to myself, 'You can do this.'

I pressed send.

After careful consideration and reflection I have decided that now is the right time for me to announce my retirement from inter-county hurling with the Kilkenny senior hurling team. I am making this decision comfortable in the knowledge that I never settled for anything less than giving it my very best. I fought to the end and I never gave up until the contest was over.

Being part of the Kilkenny senior hurling panel for the past 14 years has been an unbelievable journey that has given me endless fulfilment, satisfaction, enjoyment and happiness. I have had the privilege of playing with and against some of the greatest sportsmen of our time. I cherish the friendships I have made all over the country. There were many challenges along the way but these became my opportunities and motivation to strive even harder to achieve my very best.

My parents, my sisters and brother and my girlfriend, Clare, have been my greatest inspiration and encouragement on my journey and no words can express my gratitude to them.

I consider myself lucky to have played under the greatest GAA manager of all time, Brian Cody. I thank him and his management teams for their confidence in me right up to the present time. I wish them and the Kilkenny panel the very best in the future.

I also wish to thank Ned Quinn and the Kilkenny County Board, the Kilkenny Supporters Club, the GPA and the countless Kilkenny fans, each who in their own way encouraged me every step of the way during my inter-county career.

My employer, Glanbia, have accommodated me in every way possible over the years and for that I am very grateful.

I also wish to acknowledge and thank Br. Damien Brennan for his role in my development as a player and as a person. He challenged me to embrace my talents in order to bring my best to every situation and achieve things I would have never thought possible.

I now intend to dedicate myself and the rest of my playing career to my beloved James Stephens. It was there that my desire to play the game that I love at the highest level was nurtured and developed.

Today is not the end but the continuation of a journey, a new beginning, which I intend to fully embrace knowing now that any realistic dream can become a reality.

I made a few phone calls. I texted my brother and two sisters as I didn't want them to hear about the news before I informed them. I rang my two best friends, Niall 'Bobs' Tyrrell and Micky Eardly. We arranged to meet in Syd Harkins pub on Rose Inn street that evening, where we went on an unmerciful bender. Brian Dowling came in to join us. So did my cousin, Tommy Tyrrell. My dad arrived in too.

The following day, Clare and I travelled to Dublin to see Walking on Cars in concert in the 3 Arena. We had arranged it with a group of former Kilkenny team-mates and their wives and partners; JJ, Tommy, Brian Hogan, Larks, 'Taggy', David Herity.

I hadn't planned it to work out like it did but it felt like the ideal time to have a retirement party, especially with so many people who were with me for so long throughout my career.

We met in Milano's on Clarion Quay before walking down to the 3 Arena. On the way, Tommy told a great story to myself and Hogie, about retirement and the difference that can sometimes exist between club and inter-county, especially in terms of preparation.

Before one of Tommy's first matches back with Tullaroan in 2015, solely as a club player, he was completely hung over. He was about to throw up in the warm-up. Tommy told the manager that his groin was playing up and that he was going into the dressing room to rub on some Deep Heat. The aroma from the pain relief cream would act as a cover from the smell of drink off him but Tommy was still so loaded that he rubbed the Deep Heat so high up his groin that he nearly burned the testicles off himself. He spent most of the match waddling around like John Wayne.

The concert was brilliant. When it was over, there was only one place to go to – Copper Face Jacks on Harcourt Street.

When we were in the queue, Herro spotted the owner Cathal Jackson at the door. 'Jackie retired yesterday,' he said. 'And he decided to have his retirement party in Coppers.'

Jackson waved us all through. He brought us inside to the VIP section and told the barman to give us free drink all evening. Herro never heard him. He spent the rest of the night paying for rounds of double vodkas.

I spent the last day of 2016 in San Diego. Clare and I were with the squad on the Kilkenny team holiday, my last trip, my last time with all the lads. Before we headed downstairs to a New Year's Eve party in the Sheraton Hotel, a group of us had gathered in Conor Fogarty's room for a few drinks; Fog, Paul Murphy, Kieran Joyce, and their girlfriends, Richie Hogan, Clare and myself.

At one stage, I went to the toilet. When I came back out, a laptop and projector was sitting on a chair. There was a picture of me on a screen on the wall, a video clip with a circle around a white arrow, clearly waiting to be played. 'Sit down here,' said Murph.

I did. Fog pressed play. It was a six-and-a-half-minute montage of my career, photos and footage ranging from my minor and U-21 days right through my senior career with Kilkenny. About 50 seconds of the video was of select short clips of me mowing lads down but they had piss-pulling footage too from 'The Toughest Trade' show and the TV ad 'This is Major'.

The backing track was the Kodaline song 'High Hopes'. The boys clearly put a lot of thought into the show because the lyrics were a metaphor for where I was, how much Kilkenny meant to me, and where I now aim to go in life after Kilkenny.

'I remember it now, it takes me back to where it all first started/ but I've only got myself to blame for it and I accept that now/ it's time to let it go, go out and start again/ it's not that easy but I've got high hopes/ It takes me back to when we started/ high hopes, when you let it go, go out and start again/high hopes, when it all comes to an end/ but the world keeps spinning, around.'

When the music stopped and the video was over, I got really emotional. I was fighting back the tears. I could see the pride in Clare's eyes. I felt I should say something but I wasn't able to speak.

Murph spoke instead. 'When I first came into the panel, I clicked with you straight away,' he said. 'You were always very good to me but you always showed great leadership to all of us. And we just wanted to say thanks, Jackie.'

It was so humbling that I was overcome with emotion. The fact that the showing was so private too, meant even more to me. It was almost a greater display of affection and respect. I appreciated the gesture so much that I was almost floating.

We went downstairs and rang in 2017. We had a brilliant night. When I woke up the following morning, the first thing I did was text Fog. 'Thanks so much for last night bud. I know you and Murph did most of that and it means so much to Clare and me. I really appreciated it, and was overwhelmed by it. Thank you. Absolutely dying today!'

He texted back immediately. 'No hassles bud. It was the least we could do, hope you enjoyed it. I'm in absolute bits too.'

I sent more or less the same text to Murph. We had a great time during the rest of that trip. The craic and fun was deadly, just like it always was on those team holidays. We always got on so well, and lived in one another's company so much during those trips, that it helped build and strengthen the unique spirit we already had. We saw the world but the memories of the times we had together are the real picture postcards imprinted on our memories.

We just had an unbreakable bond, wherever we went. We were on the beer one night in San Francisco when Eoin McCormack organised a North v South soccer match. The game was supposed to take place in a park the following evening but lads were dying and only six of us turned up. We ended up playing this group of Argentinians who were training in the park.

They looked like a real serious outfit but one of them thought he was Diego Maradona, all flicks and tricks and fancy shit. We were all hung over, tired and ratty, when PJ Ryan got fed up with this lad trying to make eejits out of us. PJ used to play for Spa United out in Johnstown, who were always raw and ready, so he made a tackle straight out of the Spa playbook. Vinny Jones and Chopper Harris would have been proud of it. PJ halved your man with what looked like a karate kick with the studs up. When your man eventually scraped himself up off the ground, with his leg half hanging off, he made a go for PJ. He was wasting his time. PJ would have clobbered him with his index finger but it wouldn't have mattered if the whole Argentinian community in San Francisco had come after us — we'd have stood together and took them on.

We just loved each other's company. We were up for anything. Fit for anything. We went to Singapore another year. We arrived on New Year's Eve. We had no plans made for that evening but one of the lads copped that there was a local function on in the hotel. For 50 Singapore dollars, you could get free drink for the night.

A handful of us arrived in and it was like a free-for-all. The waitresses would ask you if you would like a glass or a jug of beer. Does a cat drink milk? We started knocking back jugs of beer like they were shorts. It didn't take long for the word to filter around. An hour later, the whole Kilkenny squad arrived in to the function room. The hotel staff were horrified. Most of the locals were only drinking a glass or two of beer but they clearly weren't aware of the Irish culture.

After training so hard all year, those holidays were naturally an opportunity for lads to let the hair down. We were in Thailand once when a group of us went golfing on this real fancy course. Richie Power was the best golfer on the squad; really tasty around the green, with a drive like John Daly.

Richie was big into the golf. He looked the part too; a fancy short sleeved shirt buttoned up to the top; a neat pair of golf shorts; a Nike hat; a pencil behind his ear; a glove on his left hand. Early on, Richie was absolutely tearing the course apart. He was -1 after the first five holes but Richie soon got distracted. There was a bar at every third hole and Heineken is always a tastier option than water on holidays, especially in crazy heat.

Richie was still going well by the ninth hole but his scores were dropping and the wheels were gradually coming off. When we passed him on the 15th, he was swaying like a bush in the breeze. The hat was turned backwards like a rapper; the shirt was almost off; a cigarette was hanging out of his mouth; a bottle of Budweiser was perched in the middle of the green. He looked like something from Straight Outta Compton.

Power had a two-foot putt for a nine and he drove it about

six feet past the hole. He could barely even see the green, never mind the hole. By the 18th, Richie didn't even tee off. He was slumped asleep across a golf buggy.

I always loved to cut loose on trips away, even when it wasn't just with Kilkenny. In 2009, the GAA staged the Interprovincial final in Abu Dhabi. Leinster qualified to meet Connacht in mid-March, bang in the middle of the League. I was talking to Henry on the plane on the way over and he suggested that we take it easy, that there was no need to go nuts, especially with important league games coming up. That advice went straight over my head anyway.

All the Leinster boys went on a right tear. The day we arrived, we headed straight for the bar and drank the place dry. The Connacht boys were on a different flight the same day and they did a training session not long after they landed. By the time a handful of the Galway boys arrived into the bar after their session, we had all gone off the reservation. When we were thrown out of the bar, we got a load of drink and started sinking that by the pool.

We all stripped off down to our boxers and briefs and started jumping into the pool. Henry wouldn't get in so I pushed him in while he still had all his clothes on. He had his phone in his pocket. We were causing so much rack that this sheikh appeared waving his arms in the air. He was dressed in his long white gandora robe and keffiyeh headscarf. I didn't give a shite what he was wearing; I sneaked up behind him and fired him straight into the pool.

All hell broke loose afterwards. The sheikh went buck-ape. He was the owner, who was nearly drowned in his own five-star swimming pool. He wanted us kicked out of the hotel immediately. I didn't hang around for the fallout. As soon as I sent the sheikh for the dip, I legged it. I went straight back to the room, which I was sharing with Brian Carroll from Offaly, and collapsed into a coma.

The following morning, there was a rap on the door from an irate Leinster official. We had all been summoned to a meeting downstairs. Everyone was dying. Alan McCrabbe had these marks and welts all over his arm, like he'd been lashed with a horsewhip. There were these palm trees all around the pool, which we had torn apart and used as weapons to leather each other. We had been chasing lads around like cowboys and indians from the Wild West.

John Conran from Wexford was the manager and he read us the riot act. He told us that Christy Cooney, then GAA president, had arrived that morning and his first act was to talk the sheikh out of throwing us out of the hotel and getting us all deported. 'We'd want to buck up,' said Conran. 'Connacht arrived here yesterday and trained straight away. They trained again this morning and here we are going around like lunatics.'

We were all trying to keep a straight face. Brian Whelehan, part of the management, had been stuck right in the middle of the chaos. Cooney had managed to talk the sheikh around. We presented him with a signed hurley and signed Leinster jersey as an apology. Two days later, we played Connacht in the perfectly manicured Ghantoot Racing Polo club and hammered them.

Clare flew home early from San Diego for work so I spent the last few days of that trip on my own with the group. It was nice to have that time with the lads but it did feel weird. For the first time, I felt detached from the Kilkenny senior panel. I knew that the boys would be going back training hard as soon as they returned but I was veering off that road and heading in a completely different direction.

After I retired, the lads added me back into the WhatsApp group but when I got home from San Diego, I pulled myself out of it for good.

I have to keep some form of distance from the boys now. John Joe Farrell said to me one day on the holiday, 'Sure you'll probably be giving out about me on the TV next year.' Maybe I will be. I'd like to be an analyst, either in TV or print, or both.

I love analysing and talking about hurling, especially with how much of a thinking game hurling really has become. I almost have an urge to relay how challenging a defender's life can be in the modern game, of the many different roles a defender has now compared to even five years ago.

Life is just moving on, but in a good way. High hopes. I am proud to say that I work for Glanbia. I work with great people. Now that my Kilkenny career is over, I may have more opportunities to climb up the ladder in the company.

Other outside opportunities have already come up since I walked away from Kilkenny. In November 2016, I was asked to be a style ambassador for Littlewoods Ireland, who signed a three-year deal as a sponsor of the All-Ireland Senior Hurling Championship and National Camogie League. I really enjoy that work.

I am really looking forward to giving everything I have to James Stephens now but the most exciting part of 2017 for me is getting married to Clare at the end of the year. I can't wait for that day, and to spend the rest of my life with the girl I love so much.

The title of Andrea Pirlo's autobiography, 'I think, therefore I Play' is a clever restatement of 'Cogito ergo sum,' which means 'I think, therefore I am'. The phrase was coined by Rene Descartes, the renowned French philosopher.

I always liked Pirlo, especially the style and grace and class he showed on the pitch. Italian footballers are more renowned for their pragmatism and catenaccio, for effectiveness more than creativity. Pirlo was different. And I like different.

In November 2014, I got a tattoo on my right bicep with the words 'Cogito ergo sum'. I just felt those words neatly encapsulated my journey. Adversity shaped that journey. Overcoming it defined me. It hasn't always been easy but, for someone who thinks very deeply, especially about his sport, I am very comfortable with who I now am.

You shape your own destiny but you are moulded by the journey and, by the people who make that journey alongside you. I was lucky to have soldiered beside some great men. Savage men. Some of those guys would trample down on your throat to get where they wanted to go but they were the guys you always wanted beside you in a war.

A lot of them were average hurlers like myself but hurling was often irrelevant. They were the guys I often gravitated towards; Peter Barry, Noel Hickey, Derek Lyng. JJ Delaney once said that the first thing Peter said to him when they began playing in the half-back line together in 2002 was that no matter what happens, no matter where JJ was on the pitch, Peter would be there for him. And he was. Peter was a man. An animal. A beast. And we were lucky to have always had so many of those guys on our squads.

Our greatest leaders never had to say much. Their actions said everything. You just knew by their body language alone that they were ready for anything, that they would face down anything. In the 2008 All-Ireland final, Eoin McGrath absolutely nailed Hickey with a hit. I thought the man was finished but Noel got up like he had just slipped on a carpet. I could see the fire blazing in his eyes.

Waterford got scorched alive that day but they were fighting a raging inferno before the game even began.

The harder and more physical the battle was, the more we liked it, the more we craved the challenge. Hard men respected us the most because they knew how hard it was to break us. Ronan Curran said after the 2006 All-Ireland final that everywhere he turned, it was like being met with a pack of ravenous animals. In his last match with Cork in the 2008 All-Ireland semi-final, Diarmuid O'Sullivan turned to one of our lads. 'Ye are some team,' he said. 'We can't beat ye. Nobody can.'

'The Rock' was in tears but it was like a final declaration of admiration, a silent admission that this was a war which he and Cork had fought for so long but could no longer win.

Curran and 'The Rock' were hardy boyos. If they thought that highly of us, and of how hard it was to break us, what did mentally weaker opponents think when they faced us?

We won our medals but we earned our respect, which is really the most important legacy any team can leave. We honoured the jersey. We filled it with pride, dignity and respect. And we all handed on that jersey in as good, if not a better, condition than when we first put on that sacred cloth.

It would have been nice to have won that tenth All-Ireland medal but it would have been even more satisfying to have experienced that feeling immediately afterwards just one more time. In the end, the memories will last when the colour of the medal will fade. A hurling life is framed anyway from a million little pixels that create the grand picture.

The journey continues, just in a different form. The picture will change. My life will change but there is no perfect life. Just perfect moments. I've been lucky to have had so many during my career. I will have even more perfect moments now as I get older, and as I begin to build a whole new life with Clare.

High hopes.

Always.